Overland Explorations
of the Trans–Mississippi West

ALSO BY HUNT JANIN
AND FROM McFARLAND

The University in Medieval Life, 1179–1499 (2008)

Claiming the American Wilderness: International Rivalry in the Trans–Mississippi West, 1528–1803 (2006)

The Pursuit of Learning in the Islamic World, 610–2003 (2005; paperback 2006)

Medieval Justice: Cases and Laws in France, England and Germany, 500–1500 (2004; paperback 2009)

Four Paths to Jerusalem: Jewish, Christian, Muslim, and Secular Pilgrimages, 1000 BCE to 2001 CE (2002; paperback 2006)

Fort Bridger, Wyoming: Trading Post for Indians, Mountain Men and Westward Migrants (2001; paperback 2006)

The India-China Opium Trade in the Nineteenth Century (1999; paperback 2014)

ALSO BY HUNT JANIN AND URSULA CARLSON
AND FROM McFARLAND

Historic Nevada Waters: Four Rivers, Three Lakes, Past and Present (2019)

The Californios: A History, 1769–1890 (2017)

The California Campaigns of the U.S.–Mexican War, 1846–1848 (2015)

Trails of Historic New Mexico: Routes Used by Indian, Spanish and American Travelers through 1886 (2010)

ALSO BY HUNT JANIN WITH URSULA CARLSON
AND FROM McFARLAND

Mercenaries in Medieval and Renaissance Europe (2013)

ALSO BY HUNT JANIN AND SCOTT A. MANDIA
AND FROM McFARLAND

Rising Sea Levels: An Introduction to Cause and Impact (2012)

ALSO BY HUNT JANIN AND ANDRÉ KAHLMEYER
AND FROM McFARLAND

Islamic Law: The Sharia from Muhammad's Time to the Present (2007)

Overland Explorations of the Trans–Mississippi West

Expeditions and Writers of the American Frontier

HUNT JANIN *and* URSULA CARLSON

McFarland & Company, Inc., Publishers
Jefferson, North Carolina

LIBRARY OF CONGRESS CATALOGUING-IN-PUBLICATION DATA

Names: Janin, Hunt, 1940– author. | Carlson, Ursula, 1943– author.
Title: Overland explorations of the trans–Mississippi west : expeditions and writers of the American frontier / Hunt Janin and Ursula Carlson.
Description: Jefferson, North Carolina : McFarland & Company, Inc., Publishers, 2020. | Includes bibliographical references and index.
Identifiers: LCCN 2020008484 | ISBN 9781476678672 (paperback : acid free paper) ∞
ISBN 9781476640150 (ebook)
Subjects: LCSH: West (U.S.)—Surveys. | West (U.S.)—Discovery and exploration. | Overland journeys to the Pacific.
Classification: LCC F591 .J39 2020 | DDC 978/.02—dc23
LC record available at https://lccn.loc.gov/2020008484

BRITISH LIBRARY CATALOGUING DATA ARE AVAILABLE

**ISBN (print) 978-1-4766-7867-2
ISBN (ebook) 978-1-4766-4015-0**

© 2020 Hunt Janin and Ursula Carlson. All rights reserved

No part of this book may be reproduced or transmitted in any form or by any means, electronic or mechanical, including photocopying or recording, or by any information storage and retrieval system, without permission in writing from the publisher.

Front cover image: "Bourgeois" W---r, and His Squaw, Alfred Jacob Miller, watercolor on paper, 23.7 × 29.7 cm, 1858–1860 (The Walters Art Museum)

Printed in the United States of America

*McFarland & Company, Inc., Publishers
Box 611, Jefferson, North Carolina 28640
www.mcfarlandpub.com*

Table of Contents

Preface   1

1. Overview of the North American Frontiers   3
2. Goals of the International Rivals   17
3. Maritime Explorations   22
4. Beginnings of Overland Exploration of the Frontiers   28
5. Pathfinding and Exploration-Settlement Expeditions   34
6. Life on the Trails   41
7. "Runners of the woods" and Other Travelers   48
8. To Wait Patiently by Hudson Bay   54
9. Taking Great Pains to Get Along with the Indians   61
10. Descended from Five Generations of "waryers" [warriors]   68
11. A Famous Explorer Follows a "grease trail" to the Pacific Ocean   74
12. The Great Lewis and Clark Expedition   80
13. "An atlas of the West"   86
14. Creating a "fur desert"   94
15. How to Hunt Buffalo   100
16. Wanting to Become President of the United States   107
17. Mountain Man Slang   114
18. "Chastise them well"   120
19. A Nevada Outlaw Named Slade   126
20. The Great Surveys   131

Table of Contents

21. A Famous Book: *The Big Bonanza*	137
22. Conclusions: Why the Explorations of the North American Frontiers Are So Important	141
Annotated Chronology, 1492–1879	145
Appendix 1: The Fur Trade in New France	155
Appendix 2: Exploration by Canoe: The Coureurs de Bois *and the* Voyageurs	157
Appendix 3: The Railroad Surveys	160
Appendix 4: Early Explorations of the Yellowstone Region, 1797–1871	163
Chapter Notes	167
Bibliography	177
Index	183

The Far West: the country whose fascinations spread a charm over the mind almost dangerous to civilized pursuits. Few people even know the true definition of the term "West"; and where is its location?–Phantom-like it flies before us as we travel, and our way is continuously gilded, before us, as we approach the setting sun.
    —George Catlin (1796–1872), American artist. *Letters and Notes, 62*; quoted by John Allen Logan in *North American Exploration: A Continent Comprehended,* "The Invention of the American West," p. 189.

Preface

This work is a concise chronicle of the activities of many explorers and writers in the western frontiers of North America, ranging from the first Spanish *conquistadors* in the early 16th century to the creation of the U.S. Geological Survey in the late 19th century. It has been written chiefly to fill a gap in the literature: to the best of our knowledge, no similar account of these frontiers has been written in recent years, if ever.

A chronicle is a sequential historical account of facts and events that follow one another in approximate chronological order. It is fundamentally different from an analytical history that tries to interpret the significance of different events by placing them into a "meaningful" context chosen by the writer.

The net result is that it is up to the reader of this chronicle to decide what the events described there mean in a broader sense. In this book, the coauthors' views on why the explorations of the western North American frontiers are so important are given in the last chapter.

This chronicle is quite far-ranging in both geographical and cultural terms because it introduces to the reader approximately 80 explorers and 17 writers. Most of these men and women will be better known to specialists in the history of the frontiers than to the general reader, but all of them are worth meeting here.

The text is divided into chapters of varying lengths; to make them very easy to follow, most of them are relatively short. The title of a given chapter is always drawn from a noteworthy event discussed somewhere within the chapter, but other events are discussed, too.

Because so many different people figure in this book and over such a long period of time, the flow of the text is not, figuratively speaking, like the placid flow of a river over a broad floodplain. Instead, it more like a turbulent mountain stream, with a good share of literary rapids, eddies, and whirlpools.

Moreover, for clarity and coherence, whenever it has not been feasible to link one chronological subject directly with its predecessor, three bullets have been inserted into the text to signal that a change of topic or of focus is now at hand.

In addition to the explorers examined in this book, the work of some contemporary writers is discussed here, too. In most cases, these writers were men and women who arrived on the frontiers long after the explorers themselves had come and gone, but whose personal experiences, coupled with their own abilities to add the human interest and local color often missing from the explorers' dry laconic accounts, qualify them to offer well-informed opinions on life and labor on the frontiers.

The most valuable parts of this book are the direct and often extensive "I was there" quotations highlighting contemporary people, places, and events. It would have been easy enough to paraphrase them, but they are at their best in their original if sometimes translated form. They have often been lightly edited for ease of reading by breaking up dense blocks of text into shorter paragraphs. Any misspellings or other errors in them are as they appear in the reference works cited in the bibliography.

Many of the historical events covered in this book have also been discussed by the present authors in their other publications. For this reason, in the interest of brevity, the endnotes in this book, which have been used extensively both for attribution and to explain selected points in the text, often cite these earlier publications, rather than the primary or secondary sources on which they are ultimately based.

In the text there are numerous references to "the Passage." This refers to the entirely mythical navigable waterway that was believed to flow across North America and to join the Pacific Ocean near Puget Sound or San Francisco. More information on the Passage will be found in the following pages.

The Annotated Chronology at the end of the book is so extensive (it covers the 387-year-long period between 1492 and 1879) that it is in effect a "stand-alone" chronology that can be read by itself, without any reference to the text. All of the entries in the chronology are explained more fully in the main text.

1

Overview of the North American Frontiers

As defined here, the concept of "frontiers" does not refer to any static or widely-recognized international, national, regional, or tribal boundaries. In fact, the frontiers of what are now the United States and Canada were inherently shape-shifting; poorly-defined; and subject to frequent military, political, economic, cultural or environmental changes.

They can also be very confusing. The notion of a single "Canadian frontier," for example, runs headlong into the facts, that in Canada, both the terms used to define the West and the mental maps of the region changed radically between 1759 and 1870.

Moreover, these terms and their meanings varied from one region to another and from one person to another. In the same period, too, English-speaking and French-speaking traders and mapmakers would often refer to a particular locality only by naming the Indian groups that held sway there at that time, e.g., "the Blackfeet Country," "the Country of the Crees," "Sioux Territory," etc.[1]

In any case, the frontiers were the lands near or beyond various recognized borders. They witnessed a complicated series of international maritime and overland explorations of lands variously inhabited by the Indians, Spanish, French-Canadians, British, and Americans. Both this chapter and the next chapter offer essential background information that is relevant to all the explorations discussed in subsequent pages.

The era covered in this book stretches over 351 years, namely, from 1528 when, looking for help, the shipwrecked Spanish explorer Álvar Nuñez Cabeza de Vaca and his three companions began an eight-year trek through the deserts of the American Southwest, to 1879, when the four "Great Surveys" in the United States were consolidated into the U.S. Geological Survey.

Consequently, the word "discover" is used here to mean "the first non-native to witness," not "the first human being ever to see." In this limited sense, then, Christopher Columbus discovered the West Indies in 1492, while trying to find a mythical trans–North America waterway, known as the Passage, to the riches of Asia. This important concept will be discussed repeatedly in later pages. After 1492, imperial competition between Spain and Portugal for control of the newly-found lands of the non–Christian world accelerated sharply.[2]

The Spanish, for example, quickly claimed the entirety of North America under the terms of the papal bull (a papal document) *Inter Caetera* (1493) and its successors. To divide the unexplored world as fairly as feasible between Spain and Portugal, the two most powerful Catholic countries of that time, the Spanish-born Pope Alexander VI drew an imaginary north-south line, pole-to-pole, running near the mid–Atlantic islands of the Azores and Cape Verde.

The pope gave the Spaniards all the lands to the west of that line, and the Portuguese all the lands to the east. To quote some of *Inter Caetera*'s sonorous phrases:

> We [the Pope] have indeed learned that you [Ferdinand and Isabella, the king and queen of Spain]…have chosen our beloved son, Christopher Columbus… to make diligent quest for these remote and unknown mainlands and islands through the sea which hitherto no one had sailed… wherein dwell many peoples living in peace and, as reported, going unclothed and not eating flesh…
>
> …by the authority of Almighty God conferred upon us… [we] give, grant, and assign… all islands and mainlands found to be discovered toward the west and south by drawing and establishing a line from the Arctic pole, namely the north, and to the Antarctic pole, namely the south… said line to be distant one hundred leagues [318 miles] toward the west and south of any of the islands commonly known as the Azores and the Cape Verde.[3]

However, Portugal protested strenuously because this bull meant that Portugal would not be able to claim Brazil. The next year, to clarify their respective boundaries for exploration and colonization, the Spanish and Portuguese drew up the Treaty of Tordesillas (1494). This new agreement defined the boundary as a straight line, pole-to-pole, located 370 leagues (1,185 miles) west of the Cape Verde islands.

The English, however, did not accept such papal grants; Queen Elizabeth pointedly refused to recognize the Pope's authority to give the New World to the Spanish as their own fief.

Imperial competition aside, the saga of frontier exploration can be said to have three interrelated and usually sequential stages. The first of these was the actual *discovery* of a new land or a new people. The second was the continued *exploration* of what had been found. The third, and usually the last to be achieved, was the *scientific understanding* of this land or people.[4]

Columbus "found" the New World in 1492 but, for almost 300 years thereafter, most of western North America was never settled permanently by

1. Overview of the North American Frontiers 5

foreign powers. They explored some of it and made some territorial claims on it, but not until the gradual liberation of European intellectual thought during and after the Enlightenment did the era of the scientific understanding of this "brave New World" really begin.

Most European and American explorers, whether they were the initial trail-breakers or the later colonizers, treated this region simply as one vast frontier. In their eyes, its untold mineral, natural, and human resources could be had simply for the taking—and at the explorers' own leisure. This was possible only because most frontier regions were, by European standards, inhabited only very lightly by small numbers of Indians, whose military, economic, and political capabilities fell far short of Western norms.

Our introduction presents some key facts about the geography traversed by the explorers, Indians, and writers of the frontiers; about their varied goals; and about how well, or how poorly, they fared in pursuing them.

What European and American explorers saw as one vast contiguous frontier can better be understood today as consisting of three of the four great geographical regions of North America. These are:

- the mountainous west, including the Rocky Mountains, the Great Basin, and California
- the Great Plains, which extend from the Gulf of Mexico to the Canadian Arctic
- the elevated but generally flat northeastern plateau known as the Canadian Shield.

The fourth great region contains the Appalachian Mountains, the coastal plains of the Atlantic seaboard, and the Florida peninsula. It will not be discussed in this book because it lies too far to the east.

There were two closely-related eras of considerable historical interest. During the first era, beginning in 1540, a relatively straightforward process of exploration and discovery, often under military auspices, was launched to find—and then, where possible, to exploit—the "new" peoples and "new" places previously unknown or little known to Europeans.

During the second era, which got underway in 1820s, a number of scientifically-oriented expeditions were undertaken to learn more about the peoples, geology, weather, topography, natural resources, and flora and fauna of the most lightly settled parts of the North American frontiers, which will be defined in this book to refer to the lands that lie in what are now the western United States, northern Mexico, and southwestern Canada.

Such a long series of explorations had so many different and sometimes contradictory objectives that the best way to present them is simply to offer them up in rough chronological order. This approach mirrors very accurately the historical reality on the ground and is more life-like than the alternative of first discussing all the *Spanish* activities, then all the *French* activities, etc. As a result, the text that follows is one that, like human life itself, moves ahead chiefly by fits and starts.

Periodically, different explorations happened at the same time in different parts of the frontier. In 1769, for example, the British explorer Samuel Hearne was traveling in Canada, while at the same time the Spanish explorer Gaspar de Portolá was ranging through Alta (Upper) California. When such "simultaneous events" do occur, the text will try to set them in their proper contexts.

Initially, one must understand that many of the men and women discussed in this book had very different goals, and that as a result they embarked on many different quests. There was no such thing, for this reason, as "a typical explorer." Because exploration was usually quite expensive and was often very dangerous, it was never undertaken lightly.

There must have been, over the decades, some explorations that were undertaken purely for the sake of adventure. Their spirit is best caught by the British novelist and playwright James Elroy Flecker (1884–1915), who wrote in his fictional *The Golden Journey, to Samarkand*:

> We are the Pilgrims, master; we shall go
> Always a little further; it may be
> Beyond the last blue mountain barred with snow,
> Across that angry or that glimmering sea.

Virtually all the explorations discussed in this book, however, were undertaken for self-serving reasons, that is to say, in pursuit of various national, military, commercial, religious, or personal goals. A few examples may help to make this clear:

- To justify legally all their extensive explorations in the New World, the Spanish often cited *Inter Caetera* (the papal bull, i.e., papal document) of 1493, which because of its complexity needs to be discussed later.
- Expanding the *frontera septentrional* (the "northernmost frontier") of New Spain and profiting from it, was thus a major goal of the Viceroyalty of New Spain, beginning in 1535. Northern New Spain did not have any well-defined boundaries but, considered from west to east, it did include a gigantic amount of real estate. An incomplete listing of these holdings would include part of Southern California; Arizona; New Mexico; western Texas; and parts of Oklahoma and Kansas.[5]
- In 1540, the Spanish *conquistador* Francisco Vásquez de Coronado (1510?–1554) set out on a military expedition far to the north of the settled portion of Mexico in order to find the mythical "Seven Cities of Gold" that were believed to be located somewhere in the deserts of the North American Southwest. During a two-year exploration, he ranged through

1. Overview of the North American Frontiers 7

northern New Spain as far north as Kansas. His party was the first one to document the geography and the Indians of a significant part of the American West.

• Between 1581 and 1598, five other Spanish expeditions, with the mutually-reinforcing goals of pathfinding, exploration, and settlement, made their way into New Mexico and the Great Plains. Their efforts ultimately resulted in the permanent Spanish occupation of New Mexico by the explorer-colonizer Juan de Oñate in 1598.

• What can be called three "human corridors" gradually funneled soldiers, missionaries, and settler families northward from New Spain. The earliest was a central corridor that led up through Nueva Galicia and Nueva Vizcaya to New Mexico, and then west on to the Hopi Indian mesas of today's north-central Arizona. A second corridor ascended through Nuevo León and Coahuila, terminating in eastern Texas. The third corridor heading northwest along the Pacific coast, divided in Sinaloa: one branch of the corridor followed the western coast of Mexico, while another branch went by sea to central California.[6]

• The fur trade became one of the most important economic enterprises of western North America, eventually tugging Canadian, French, Indian, American, Dutch, Spanish, and Russian participants into its orbit. (See Appendix 1 for a summary of the fur trade in its most important area— New France, namely, colonial Canada.) The years 1660–1763, for example, witnessed a fierce rivalry between France and Great Britain as each nation worked hard to expand its own access to the most lucrative fur-trading territories of the frontier.

• In their travels of 1659–1660, the French brothers-in-law and traders Pierre-Esprit Radisson (1636?–1710) and Médard Chouart des Groseilliers (1618?–1696?) explored and opened up for Europeans a lucrative fur trade in the unexploited lands of the Cree, who lived in remote villages lying north and west of Lake Superior.

• By 1659, these two explorers had reached the westernmost end of Lake Superior. French settlements in the *Pays d'en Haut* (that vast inland territory that embraced the Great Lakes and the Upper Mississippi River Valley) would eventually include Detroit, La Baye, Sault Sainte-Marie, Saint Ignace, and Vincennes. These settlements would be protected by four French forts: Fort Presque Isle (1753), Fort La Boeuf (1753), Fort Duquesne (1754), and Fort Machault (1754).

• France was a great colonial power in North America for nearly 300 years (1524–1803).[7] In 1660, France began a policy of expanding its influence from what is now eastern Canada into the interior of North America. During the 17th century, major French goals were to lay claim to any "undiscovered" territory before any other European power did so;

to locate and explore the mythical Passage presumed to exist in frontier North America; to convert the "heathen," i.e., the Indians, to Christianity; and, last but by no means least, to exploit to the maximum extent possible the fur, mineral, and other natural resources of the region.

- In pursuit of all these aims, the French—totally unlike the Spanish and the British—devoted a great deal of their time and money to establishing and maintaining friendly relations with the local Indians. Indeed, much like modern historians today, they tried to understand these peoples as essential and independent actors in the processes that developed the Americas, not simply as colorful "extras" on the historic stages always dominated by Europeans.
- President Thomas Jefferson very much wanted his fellow Americans to explore the trans-Mississippi West, both to prevent it from falling into foreign hands and, ultimately, to make it possible for the fledging United States to expand all the way to the Pacific Ocean. He therefore sent out the famous Lewis and Clark expedition of 1804–1806. It initially included about 48 men, and made contact with more than 70 Indian tribes; produced 140 maps; documented more than 200 new plant and animal species; and lost only one of its men (due to illness).
- Motivated by his own soaring political ambitions (he wanted very much to become President), between 1838 and 1845 the U.S. Army officer and explorer John C. Frémont led explorations into the Great Plains, the Great Basin, the Oregon Territory, and Mexico's Alta California.
- By the later 1800s, the capital of Washington, D.C. became the center of American scientific inquiry because experts needed funding to arrange exploring expeditions that would give them a better understanding of frontier peoples and conditions. Four "Great Surveys" of the West were therefore organized, drawing to a close just before the founding of the U.S. Geological Survey in 1879.

It would be a fundamental mistake, however, to focus only on the explorers and not have anything of substance to say about the Indians, even at times when they do not figure prominently in Western records. For example, although the great smallpox epidemic of 1779–1784 killed tens of thousands of Indians in the West, its impact was recorded chiefly in French, Spanish, British, and Indian sources, and only very rarely in American accounts. As a result, this disastrous epidemic did not make much of an impact on American historical thinking until relatively recently.[8]

Many of the explorers' travels described in the following pages would have been quite impossible without the Indians—that is to say, without their often-undocumented or poorly-documented roles as guides; interpreters; experts on intertribal relations and ceremonies; and, finally, as invaluable sources of information on how best to arrange transportation, food, and shelter under frontier conditions.[9]

Another example of overlooking history relevant to Indians is evident in the classic Bering Strait account of Indian migration patterns, when falling water levels during the Ice Age laid bare a huge expanse of dry land across what is now the Bering Strait. As the continental glaciers melted, the people we now know as "the Indians" (see below) are thought to have migrated, very slowly and in phases, down the ice-free Alaskan corridors and then gradually to have spread out into the remainder of western North America.

Today, however, some Indians reject this account. The story of Indian population movements cannot be told here due to limitations of time and space, but what is clear is that they had more than enough room to roam, both in the western United States and in western Canada.

By 1830, for example, a good part of the frontiers of the United States consisted of three huge blocks of land. These were (1) the Unorganized Territory, i.e., the enormous sweep of the Great Plains before they were cut up into smaller parcels; (2) the Oregon Country,[10] which was simultaneously claimed by the United States, Russia, Great Britain, and Spain; and (3) the extensive but ill-defined lands of New Spain, which were claimed by Mexico after it became independent of Spain in 1821.

At about the same time in western Canada, most of the four major geographic regions lying west of Hudson Bay and north of the Great Lakes were entirely open to human uses. These areas included (1) the narrow coastal plain in the southeastern corner of Hudson Bay, where the chief Hudson's Bay Company trading posts were located; (2) the lake-strewn Canadian Shield; (3) the extensive grasslands and woods of the Great Plains; and, finally, (4) the Rocky Mountains themselves.[11]

Each of these enormous blocks of land was home to numerous Indian tribes (and later, of course, to many non–Indians). Much like feudal Europe with its many tiny principalities, each block was a patchwork of tribes with different languages and different customs. Each tribe saw itself as being virtually autonomous, and as having unique members and a superior culture.

As the reader will have noticed, the generic term "Indians" is consistently used in this book. Technically speaking, of course, there were never, in the New World, any such people as "Indians." Instead, there were hundreds of different tribes or other ethnic gatherings of indigenous peoples *who were called Indians by people other than themselves.*

No one will ever know for sure how many Indians were living in what are now the United States and Canada in 1513, when the Europeans first reached North America (via the expedition of Ponce de León from Puerto Rico to Florida), but there may have been between five to ten million of them, consisting of at least 600 different groups.[12] They and their descendants defined themselves in terms that were carefully chosen to *exclude* all other tribes: for example, the Cheyennes called themselves "our people"; the Apaches, "the people"; and the Kiowas, "the principal people."[13]

Today, because there is no demonstrably better term to use, they will continue to be referred to in this book either as "Indians" or, where possible, by the names of their tribes. Ironically, these are not indigenous names at all, but were simply bestowed on them by other tribes, Europeans, other foreigners, or by American frontiersmen.

It must be added, too, that since Indian culture was primarily an oral culture, much of what was written about them historically has come from non-Indian sources, whose opinions had greatly varying degrees of reliability.

From the Spanish point of view, a major problem in the exploration and settlement of the American Southwest was "the Indian menace." There were in fact many threats and small-scale Indian attacks in the Southwest, but in retrospect what is most noteworthy today is that the total damage inflicted on the Spanish by the Indians, e.g., in New Mexico, was quite modest when compared to the casualties of a real war.

The underlying problem faced by the Spanish in dealing with hostile Indians was not so much military as it was financial and cultural. Spanish leaders were hopelessly bogged down by lack of money; by red tape; by long delays in formulating, sending, and receiving orders: and by pervasive military and political incompetence, e.g., fatal shortages in accountability, manpower, equipment, and training. All these shortcomings were compounded, of course, by the very low priority given by successive Spanish and Mexican governments to any of the Southwest's problems.

A point that must be made here, moreover, is that the Indians were never simply the passive tools of explorers. In 1731, for example, a French governor-general in Canada informed his superiors in Paris:

> I grant you [that] these nations [i.e., the Indian tribes] would have become far more useful to the colony [the colony of New France] had we been able to subdue them little by little. If this has not been done, it is because we have found the task to be an impossible one; nor are there any signs that it will become less so. Kindly apprise me of any means you should conceive of for securing such obedience.[14]

In the same vein, the French fur trader Nicholas Perrot, who lived with the Indians of the Great Lakes in the late 17th century, explained that the Indians always followed their own agendas, not the agendas of others. He wrote:

> He [the Indian] speaks in one way and thinks in another. If his friend's interest accord[s] with his own, he is ready to render him a service; if not, he always takes the path by which he can most easily attain his own ends.[15]

Moreover, Indians could sometimes deflect the path of European exploration simply by making up stories about the enormous wealth that allegedly lay in wait for explorers farther ahead. The Indians' purpose here might be to move the heavily-armed explorers away from their own villages and toward those of their enemies.[16]

On a more take-charge note, however, the Indians could also participate actively in many "modern" activities themselves, e.g., in the fur trade, thanks to their detailed knowledge of local geography and to their skills as pathfinders, guides, hunters, and fishermen. Maps made by the Indians for their own use, however, were not at all like maps made by the explorers for *their own use*. The modern historian Carolyn Gilman explains the reasons as follows:

> Indian maps were not intended to be naturalistic representations of the landscape. *They were visual narratives.* Native cartographers did not portray the earth as an abstract thing, a pattern to be measured on the surface of a sphere. They showed what people *did* with the land. Each map was a diagram of a human-landscape interaction—a journey or a battle or a mythic act…
>
> The most confusing difference was that Indian maps used a temporal rather than a spatial scale, showing travel time, not distance…. Space was distorted in order to show time more accurately.[17]

Indian sense of orientation differed in several fundamental ways from the European or American:

- The Indians relied not on maps themselves but on the information that was already present in the minds of other Indians travelers, much of which could readily be communicated between them simply by words, gestures, or body language.
- Unlike European and American maps, Indian maps did not rely on fixed points located within a square or some other carefully-defined geometric space, but instead used linear patterns that were clear enough to the Indians themselves but were never, or only very rarely, understood by non–Indians.
- Indian maps were never meant to be permanent documents. For example, in 1801–1802 three Blackfeet Indians and one Gros Ventre Indian visited the Hudson's Bay trading post on the South Saskatchewan River. At the request of Peter Fidler, the trader and surveyor in charge there, they drew a large map that depicted the western plains all the way south to New Mexico.
- This big map covered about 200,000 square miles of North American land, very little of which had ever been mapped before, but it did not survive because it was drawn in the snow. Fidler, however, did make a small copy of the map, on paper, which he sent off to the Hudson's Bay Company's headquarters in London.[18] For many years, this company, which was founded in 1670, would be a major player on the North American frontier. It not only maintained a monopoly over the Canadian fur trade itself but also controlled most of the exploration that took place in western

and northern Canada. It even gave its name to a simple but serviceable firearm, made in many different factories in Europe and the United States, i.e., a cheap but effective light musket traded to the Indians and technically known as the "Hudson's Bay fuke."[19] The Company's dominance lasted until the beginnings of scientific explorations in Canada in the 1850s.[20]

Despite the Hudson's Bay Company's dominance, France was a key colonial power in North America for 269 years, namely, from 1534, when Jacques Cartier first explored the Gulf of Saint Lawrence, to 1803, when Napoleon Bonaparte sold Louisiana to the United States. For this reason, a few words on "New France" (i.e., modern-day Canada) will be useful here.[21]

The total size of New France cannot be accurately calculated now, but in its heyday (1534–1803) New France theoretically embraced much of what is now southern, northern, and eastern Canada, plus all of the central United States down to the Gulf Coast.

The French presence on the ground, however, was singularly thin, with only about 150 small forts scattered throughout a vast region that was largely unknown to most Europeans. It was only on the feeble strength of these tiny trading and military outposts, which were usually based on shaky alliances with local Indian tribes, that the French could claim any "sovereignty" over the whole of New France.

Relations between the Canadian Indians and the French were usually friendly. For example, when the French explorer Jacques Cartier sailed up the Gulf of St. Lawrence, planted a cross on the Gaspé peninsula, and claimed *La Nouvelle-France* (New France) for François I, the French king, he had this to report:

> Crossing the bay we caught sight of two fleets of Indian canoes, which numbered in all some forty or fifty canoes. The Indians set up a great clamour and made frequent signs for us to come on shore, holding up furs on sticks.
>
> [Thanks to their prior contacts with European fishermen, who had sailed to the Canadian coast to catch and preserve cod for European Catholics, the Indians knew exactly what Cartier wanted. They therefore welcomed him, being very eager to begin the process of bartering their beaver pelts for metal knives and other European products.]
>
> They showed a marvelous great pleasure in obtaining iron wares and other commodities, dancing and going through many ceremonies and throwing salt water over their heads.[22]

The first official settlement of New France was the founding of Quebec, located within the New France province of "Canada," by Samuel de Champlain in 1608. He was the greatest of the French explorers and quickly realized that portaging, i.e., carrying, their canoes around Montreal's fierce Lachine rapids would give the French outdoorsmen an unrivaled access to the vast, beaver-rich interior of New France. These rapids were named Lachine—i.e., "China" in French—because they were erroneously thought to lie athwart a water route to China. Beaver fur was a very valuable commodity in that era because it was used to make the best-quality men's top hats.

Champlain wrote:

> The current [i.e., the Lachine Rapids] extends three or four leagues [a league was about 2.6 miles], so that it is vain to imagine that any [heavy European] boats can be conveyed past these rapids. But he who would pass them must provide himself with the canoes of the natives, which a man can easily carry...
>
> [With these canoes] one may travel freely and quickly throughout the country, as well as up the little rivers as up the large ones. So that directing one's course with the help of the natives and their canoes, a man may see all that there is to be seen.[23]

There would be four other early colonies within New France, too, namely, Hudson's Bay to the north, Acadia and Newfoundland to the east, and Louisiana to the south.

The *Pays d'en Haut* (the "upper country") was a huge but ill-defined territory lying north and west of Montreal. It covered all the Great Lakes and stretched westward into the North American continent as far as the French had explored. Daydreams of great wealth in the fur trade would encourage many young Canadian men to undertake the dangerous journey into this region in order to reach new trading partners. This frontier fur trade would become a law unto itself, a dangerous space which the historian Richard White has aptly described as constituting a "middle ground" where the worlds of Indians and Europeans overlapped and where the outcome of their conflicting values was never predictable.[24]

The "Illinois Country" (sometimes referred to as "Upper Louisiana" or, in French, as the *Pays des Illinois* ["land of the Illinois people"]) consisted of what is now the Upper Mississippi Valley (Illinois, Indiana, and Missouri). It was settled primarily from the *Pays d'en Haut* under the auspices of the fur trade. "Lower Louisiana," on the other hand comprised the area we know today as the states of Louisiana, Arkansas, Mississippi, and Alabama.

Over time, French fur traders would follow the broad Missouri River valley upstream toward the river's beginnings at what is now Three Forks, Montana, located just west of Bozeman. One of the most evocative paintings of their arduous calling on the Missouri was done in 1845 by George Caleb Bingham, who himself was raised on the Lower Missouri frontier in the 1820s and 1830s and who rose from obscurity to become one of the greatest American local-color painters.[25]

Entitled "Fur Traders Descending the Missouri" and now in the Metropolitan Museum of Art in New York, this famous work depicts a grizzled fur trader paddling in the stern of his dugout canoe, while his handsome *métis* son (i.e., whose mother was a Canadian Indian) lounges amidships against a cargo of furs, and a chained bear cub looks on from the bow.

Light craft could always navigate the upper Missouri successfully but gradually, because of the deforestation and erosion that occurred from the cutting down so many trees to provide fuel for the big steamboats, the Mississippi River itself became broader and shallower.

One result was that many architectural and archaeological assets were lost, both due to flooding and to the destruction of early French colonial villages built near the river, such as Kaskaskia, St. Philippe, Cahokia, and St. Genevieve.

Unlike some British explorers, the French were far more interested in trade and other matters than in simple military dominance. In 1665–1672, for example, Jean Talon, the Intendant (i.e., the chief provincial administrator of New France), argued that the French should explore this new (to them) region very carefully in order to create a vast inland-waterway-based empire there. He hoped that in the process they would discover the Passage, and urged them to claim possession of all the fur-rich lands of North America well before the British (the arch-rivals of the French) could do so themselves.

Toward these ends and acting under Talon's orders, the French explorer Simon François D'Aumont, Sieur (an honorific title) de St. Lusson, made his way to the Great Lakes and finally reached Sault Sainte Marie, the long "Rapids of St. Mary," where the waters of Lake Superior flow into Lake Huron and Lake Michigan.[26]

It was there, in 1671, D'Aumont took formal possession for New France of "all the territories from Montreal as far as the South Sea [i.e., broadly, 'the South Sea' refers to the Pacific Ocean; more narrowly, it can refer instead to the Gulf of California], covering the utmost extent and range possible." In so doing, he was claiming for France the entire interior of the North American continent. Needless to say, the local Indians were neither consulted nor told about this remarkable claim, but the French would later work out *de facto* trade and military alliances with some of them.[27]

By the late 17th century, Frenchmen from Louisiana had begun to push out onto the Great Plains and up the Missouri River. Indeed, as early as 1688, the Indians living along the Rio Grande had warned the Spanish governor that "some [unnamed] foreign people are in that territory … and are trying to thrust themselves upon the natives."[28] Other Indian sources added what to the Spaniards must have been most unwelcome news.

These new arrivals, said the sources, were decked out much like the Spaniards themselves:

> [They were] clothed and with harquebuses [heavy but portable matchlock muskets]… they [wore] coats or breastplates of steel, and helmets on their heads…. They visited these Indians many times and gave them axes, knives, beads, copper kettles, and sometimes clothing, and made gifts to women of ribbons and other little things, and for this reason they had warm friendship with them.[29]

In 1700, the Spaniards heard that Frenchmen had destroyed an Indian village on the eastern plains. By 1708, French traders were said to have ex-

1. Overview of the North American Frontiers 15

plored 300 to 400 leagues up the Missouri and even to have reached the foothills of the Rocky Mountains. The Spaniards strongly suspected from these events that France was plotting to shoulder Spain aside and thus become the dominant power in the trans–Mississippi West.

One important characteristic of French exploration and expansion in frontier North America, however, was that it was in effect very limited in scope and effectiveness. The consistent policy of the French government had always been to confine French settlement entirely to the St. Lawrence Valley, rather than permitting it to expand into the frontier West. As a result, the French presence in the West was not based on French military dominance but rather on the ability of a small number of highly-motivated Frenchmen to work closely with the local Indians, who almost always had the upper hand in this relationship.

Two unrelated historical points can usefully be made now:

The first is that the French never had the same degree of influence as the British and, later, that the Americans had over the Indians, so the Canadian Indians could afford to be more independent. In the 18th century, for example, the Indian leader Tanaghrisson wanted to keep his people out of both the French orbit and the British orbit in order to maintain his tribe's independence.

This is what he said to the French, who were then fighting the British (spelling and punctuation as in the original):

> Fathers [a term of fictive kinship used by the Indians when dealing with Europeans], Both you and the English are white, we live in a Country between; therefore the Land belongs to neither one nor t'other: But the Great Being [i.e., God] above allow'd it to be a Place of Residence for us; so Fathers, I desire you to withdraw, as I have done our Brothers the English; for I will keep you at Arm's length; I lay this down as a Trial for both, to see which will have the greatest Regard to it, and that Side we will stand by and make equal Shares with us. Our Brothers the English have heard this, and I now come to tell it to you, for I am not afraid to discharge you off this Land.[30]

The second point is that earlier (in the late 17th century), warfare with the Iroquois Confederacy, coupled with a huge glut in beaver pelts (the high prices paid for them had stimulated so much trapping that the pelts simply could not be sold and thus were piled up and allowed to rot in warehouses), led the French to halt all the legal French fur-trade journeys into the west.

This fact gave rise to the colorful, independent, and rather illegal French fur trader-explorers known as *coureurs de bois* (literally, "runners of the woods"). They played a vital if never fully-documented role in the gradual spread of French influence west of the St. Laurence River. They were "illegal" only because they avoided the normal channels of the fur trade simply by going ever-deeper into the wilderness to trade with the Indians.

Many of them therefore learned Indian languages, took Indian wives, and, in effect, became an important part of native communities. Perhaps the best-known example here is the French-Canadian outdoorsman Toussaint Charbonneau, the husband of Sacagawea. Both of them took part in the Lewis and Clark expedition of 1804–1806.

Both the *coureurs de bois* and their colleagues, the legal canoemen who were technically known as *voyageurs* ("travelers"), will be discussed in Appendix 2 so that these riveting first-hand accounts will not interrupt the flow of the text itself. In practice, however, these two terms were never mutually exclusive, and a typical canoeman might well have answered to either, or to both, of them, depending on the circumstances.

2

Goals of the International Rivals

This chapter recapitulates the goals of the key ethnic or national rivals along the frontiers, and offers some judgments on how well or how poorly they actually fared in their respective quests.[1] Listed in approximate chronological order, there were six of these rivals, namely, the Indians, the Spaniards, the French, the British, the Russians, and the Americans.

The Indians were the original inhabitants and the original explorers of all these frontiers. Although no reliable statistics are available on their likely numbers, they will be mentioned frequently in this book because, from the point of view of both the explorers and their backers, the Western frontier might well have been described as remote, often inhospitable, landscapes peopled by Indians. What is certain is that Europeans and Americans alike courted the Indians as customers in trade, as partners in diplomacy, as allies in war, and—not infrequently—as partners in bed.[2]

Perhaps the most important thing to be said here about these Indians is that, more than anything else, they simply wanted to retain their independence and their traditional ways of life. Over time, however, it would prove to be quite impossible for them to do so, given the unstoppable onslaught of European and American military power and culture that would wash over them. Eventually, all of them would be forced to make their peace with the conquerors and, often, live on reservations.

This is what the Apache chieftain Cochise told General Gordon Granger in 1871:

> When I was young I walked all over this country, east and west, and saw no other people than the Apaches. After many summers I walked again and found another race of people had come to take it. How is it? Why is it that the Apaches wait to die—that they carry their lives on their fingernails. They roam over the hills and plains and want the heavens to fall on them; they are now few, and because of this they want to die and so carry their lives on their fingernails. Many have been killed in battle...
>
> I want to live in these mountains; I do not want to go to Tularosa [the site, located in northern Arizona, of a reservation for the Mescalero Apaches]. The flies on these

mountains eat out the eyes of the horses. The bad spirits live there. I have drunk of these waters and they have cooled me; I do not want to leave here.[3]

The Indians who coped the best with the post-frontier world were arguably the Pueblo Indians, who still live today where the Spaniards found them in 1539 and who managed to retain much of their original culture by making only superficial accommodations to the demands being imposed on them by governments, churches, and schools. Many other frontier Indians, however, found themselves mired in an endless cycle of unemployment, educational failures, and alcoholism.

Spain, for its part, set up four viceroyalties to govern the lands it conquered in the New World. The first, and for the purposes of this book the most important of these bureaucracies, was the Viceroyalty of New Spain. Although it constituted only a backward and relatively unimportant sector of the world, the Spanish still had impressive ambitions for it. These included:

- Enriching themselves by finding or seizing gold and silver
- Winning personal and national glory
- Using the northern frontier as a buffer zone to protect the rich silver mines of central Mexico
- Converting the Indians to Roman Catholicism
- Discovering the Passage. This mythical transcontinental waterway was known to contemporaries by many different and overlapping names, e.g., the Northwest Passage; the Western Sea or, in French, the Mer de l'Ouest; the Sea of Verrazzano; the Ourgan, or Great River of the West; the Rio San Buenaventura; the Strait of Anian; the Canal de Floridablanca; Lake Thoyago; the passage to China, Japan, or India; or, more enticingly, simply as the "Northern Mystery."[4]
- Building five presidios (i.e., rudimentary forts) and 21 missions in California, chiefly to deal with Spain's acute but unfounded fears of Russian expansion south along the Pacific Coast.

The Spaniards failed to achieve most of their objectives, thanks in no small part to two international problems far beyond their own control. The first of these was the growing power and size of the United States. The Spanish Governor of Louisiana, Baron Carondelet, who was in power there from 1791 to 1797, understood very well that the growing number of American frontiersmen in Louisiana constituted a real threat to continued Spanish control.

He wrote, for example, that they "all have as their object the navigation to the Gulf ... and the rich fur trade of the Missouri." He warned that

> A carbine [i.e., a short-barreled musket or rifle] and a little maize [dried corn] in a sack are enough for an American to wander about in the forests alone for a whole month...
> With some tree trunks crossed one above the other, in the shape of a square, he

raises a house [a log cabin], and even a fort that is impregnable to the savages by crossing a story above the ground floor...

[If the Americans] succeed in occupying the shores of the Mississippi or of the Missouri, there is, beyond doubt, nothing that can prevent them from crossing those rivers and penetrating into our provinces.[5]

The second international problem was Spain's inability to retain control of Mexico, which declared its independence from Spain in 1821. (The history of Mexico's struggle for independence is, however, too detailed to be discussed here.)

The French had four main objectives along the North American frontier. The first and foremost of these was to maximize their profits from the lucrative fur trade.

At the same time, however, they also wanted to increase their own influence to counter that of the numerically-superior, richer, and militarily-more powerful Anglo-Americans. Hoping to make New France the center of his colonial empire, Louis XIV thus took several steps to encourage population growth there. The most dramatic of these was his decision to send to New France, from 1663 and 1673, more than 700 single women between the ages of 15 and 30, who were orphans known as *les filles du roi* ("the king's daughters").

France's third objective was to convert the Indians to Roman Catholicism. At personal and social levels in the settled areas of New France, the church became the dominant institution. Jesuit and other missionaries were very active in New France. In the 1640s, for example, the Jesuits converted many Huron Indians in the Great Lakes region.

The fourth objective was to find the Passage. When the great French explorer Jacques Cartier (1491–1673) first sailed up the Gulf of St. Lawrence in 1534, he was certain that he was heading directly for China. Alas, the continent of North America blocked his way there.

In retrospect, then, the French had some wins and some losses along the western frontier. They certainly did make money from the fur trade, but New France itself would come to a permanent end in 1763 with the Treaty of Paris, which crowned Britain's victory in the Seven Years' War (1756–1763). This treaty marked the end of the French Empire in continental North America, e.g., the French lost both Canada and Louisiana.

Interestingly, in the end, the French showed almost no interest in keeping Canada, which the philosopher Voltaire is said to have dismissed as consisting simply as of "a few acres of snow." What the French valued much more were the cod-fishing bases on the eastern Atlantic and the lucrative sugar colonies of the West Indies.

In the aftermath of the British conquest, most of the 70,000 French men and women then living in Canada had been born there and had nowhere else to go, so they had to accept the fact that, suddenly, they were now British subjects.[6]

Roman Catholicism got a firm foothold in eastern Canada but today it is no longer dominant there. The Passage, of course, never existed, but French continues to be a major language in eastern Canada today, and immigrants are still being welcomed into Canada, as they were in the past.

The British, too, had wanted to find the Passage. In addition, they aimed at establishing a colonial empire that would rival and hopefully eventually surpass that of New France. Finally, they planned to profit from the prevailing economic theory known as mercantilism.

A concept coined by the Scottish philosopher Adam Smith in 1776, mercantilism had been practiced by England and other European countries for 200 years. This doctrine held that the wealth of a nation should be measured solely by the amount of gold and silver it possessed. Its mantra was that "colonies exist only for the benefit of the mother country."

What this meant, in practice, was that the mother country should import raw materials from its colonies; turn them into finished goods; and then export these goods to the colonies. Since this trade was designed to be a national monopoly, no foreign competitors would be tolerated. In theory, all the profits would therefore flow into the mother country.

The British managed to achieve two of their three objectives. The Passage was never found, but the British colonial empire in North America did indeed surpass and outlast New France. English and Scottish merchants began to replace the French trading firms of Montreal after the fall of New France. British and French trappers now went to work for Britain's Hudson's Bay Company (often known simply as the "HBC," after its famous initials), which staffed small outposts in central and western Canada and which had a fur trade monopoly on nearly 1.5 million square miles of the vast Hudson's Bay watershed. Mercantilism, for its part, paid good dividends to Britain when applied to its North American colonies.

Very little will be said about the Russians in later pages of this book because they were not overland explorers and because they focused mainly on the marine mammal trade, i.e., on sea otters. They were so successful in pursuing this primary objective, however, that before too long the sea otter population of the Pacific Coast between Alaska and San Francisco was severely depleted.

The Russians did not immediately achieve their second objective, namely, signing a trade treaty between Russia and New Spain, but they managed to do so in 1818. In its heyday, the Russian American Fur Company had a string of 24 fur trading posts extending from Alaska to San Francisco, with a trade estimated at 7 billion rubles.

That said, however, the Russians failed entirely to achieve their third objective—turning the Pacific coast into a Russian possession. It is very un-

2. Goals of the International Rivals 21

likely that the United States, Britain, or Spain would ever have tolerated such a move.

Last but by no means least, the Americans had two major goals along the frontiers and they went hand-in-hand. The first was to prevent any other nation from occupying, permanently, any part of what is now the continental United States. The second was to expand the United States all the way to the Pacific Ocean. By a combination of great good luck and great assertiveness, the Americans managed to accomplish both these objectives.

The story of just how this was done is much too long to present here, but two of its main undertakings can be summarized in two terse phrases, namely, "Lewis and Clark," and "Manifest Destiny."

The Lewis and Clark expedition of 1804–1806 followed hard on the heels of the Louisiana Purchase of 1803, in which the United States bought Louisiana from France. The precise borders of the Louisiana Territory were never entirely certain, but what is clear is approximately 827,987 square miles of nearly-virgin land changed hands for $15 million, i.e., about four cents an acre.[7] Writing in 1953, the historian Bernard DeVoto said of the Louisiana Purchase that

> No event in American history—not the Civil War, nor the Declaration of Independence, nor even the signing of the Constitution—was more important.[8]

The most immediate and, in the long run, one of the most important results of the Lewis and Clark expedition, however, was that it ushered in the era of the remarkable American beaver trappers and explorers known as "mountain men."

These men—for example, John Colter, Jim Bridger, Kit Carson, Tom Fitzpatrick, and Jedediah Smith—were among the greatest explorers of the western frontiers. Their encyclopedic knowledge of much of the region's geography, climate, and Indian cultures, coupled with their remarkable pathfinding skills, were instrumental in opening much of the trans–Mississippi West to American and European settlers.

"Manifest Destiny" was a term coined by the author John L. Sullivan, who in 1845 forecasted "the fulfillment of our manifest destiny to overspread the continent allotted by Providence."[9] Thus, in American eyes, Manifest Destiny was the unilateral and self-proclaimed "right" of the United States to expand all the way to the Pacific—even far beyond it.

3

Maritime Explorations

Most of the explorers of the western frontiers who feature in this book were land-based, not sea-based, but some of the most significant maritime expeditions can very briefly be summarized in this chapter.[1]

Spaniards were the most active foreigners in the early maritime explorations of the North American frontier. In 1539, for example, the Spanish navigator Francisco de Ulloa explored the Gulf of California and sailed roughly three quarters of the way up the western coast of Baja or Lower California, but he never got as far north as Alta or Upper California.

In 1542, the *conquistador* Juan Rodríguez Cabrillo (1499–1543) became the first European to visit the Pacific shore of the United States. He sailed northwest from La Navidad, Mexico, to investigate the coasts of the two Californias (i.e., Baja and Alta California), and then may have intended to continue further west to pioneer what would later become the Manila treasure galleon route between Acapulco, Mexico, and the Philippine islands. (A treasure galleon was a big ship, technically more like a barque than a full-rigged ship.)

His expedition spent the winter at Santa Catalina Island. There Cabrillo either broke his arm near the shoulder as the result of a fall, or splintered his shinbone while leaping ashore to save his crew from an Indian attack. In any case, while he died from this injury, his expedition continued further north under the leadership of Bartolomé Ferrer, the senior pilot.

In November 1542, Ferrer ran into very bad weather off Point Reyes north of San Francisco. He was running low on supplies and was facing mountainous seas "so high that [his men] became crazed." As a result, he was forced to return to Mexico.

In 1577, Sir Francis Drake (1540?–1596), the most renowned seaman of the Elizabethan Age, set out to find the Strait of Anian (one of the many names of the Passage) by sailing north along the Pacific Coast.

One of Drake's officers was Francis Petty, who was an able chronicler and who was with him on this voyage. Petty's book, *The Famous Voyage of Sir Francis Drake into the South Sea* [i.e., the Pacific Ocean], *and therehence about the whole Globe of the Earth, begun in the year of our Lord 1577*, is worth quoting here.

Petty wrote:

> On the fifth of June [1579], being in 43 degrees towards the pole Arctic [i.e., roughly off Cape Blanco, Oregon], we found the air so cold, that our men being grievously pinched with the same, complained of the extremity thereof; and the further [north] we went, the more the cold increased upon us. Whereupon we thought it best to seek the land, which we did...
>
> It pleased God to send us into a fair and good bay with a good wind to enter the same. [This was either Drake's Bay, which is about 30 miles northwest of San Francisco, or Bodega Bay, slightly farther north.] In this bay we anchored; and the people of the country [the Coast Miwok Indians], having their houses close by the water's side, shewed themselves unto us, and sent a present to our General [i.e., Drake].[2]

The Miwoks were very friendly and their land was attractive. When the English sailors had finished careening their ship (that is to say, mooring it in shallow water so that at low tide first one side and then the other would be out of the water and thus could be cleaned or repaired), Petty reported that

> We traveled up into the Country to their villages, where we found herdes of deer of 1000 in a companie, being most large and fat of bodie...
>
> [The chief of the Miwoks] made several rations [i.e., he gave several good reasons] or rather supplications that [Drake] would take their province & kingdom into his hand and become their King, making signs that they would resign unto him their right and title to the whole land and become his subjects.[3]

Petty added since there was no evidence the Spaniards or any other foreigners had ever landed in this bay, Drake took possession of the whole territory in the name of Queen Elizabeth I. Because the cliffs of white sand he found there reminded him of the sea cliffs of his native Sussex, he christened the land Nova (New) Albion, i.e., New England. Albion was a patriotic nickname for England. This action established England's claim to the Pacific Northwest, north of the lands occupied by Spain, i.e., California.

Another intrepid adventurer was the veteran Spanish soldier Sebastián Vizcaíno (1548–1628), who led a four-ship expedition north from Acapulco in 1602, looking for a safe harbor somewhere along the California coast.

The Spanish wanted very much to find such a harbor for their treasure-laden galleons from Manila, which usually made landfall off the northern California coast near Cape Mendocino and then turned south to head towards Mexico. Spanish navigators remembered very well that in 1587 the English freebooter Thomas Cavendish had captured the treasure galleon *Santa Ana* off the undefended coast of Baja California, when she was returning to Mexico from the Philippines.

Perhaps with this memory in mind, Vizcaíno charted the California coast with such accuracy that his maps were still being used through the

1700s. In 1603 he sent to King Felipe III of Spain a glowing report on the port of Monterey, California, which read in part:

> ...this port is all that one could hope for. It is a convenient stopping place along the coast for ships that are coming from the Philippines. The port is sheltered from all winds, and along the shore there are many pine trees that could be used for ship masts of any size desired...
>
> It is a pleasant place. The area is populated by people whom I consider to be meek, mild, quiet, and quite amenable to conversion to Catholicism and to becoming subjects of Your Majesty.[4]

Despite Vizcaíno's recommendation that Spain should develop Monterey as a haven for the Manila galleons, for two reasons this was never done.

The first was that, from a nautical point of view, Monterey was not in fact a good choice. It was only an open roadstead, not a deep bay like San Francisco or some other harbor well-sheltered from the always-variable and often-strong ocean winds.

The second reason was that Vizcaíno had been replaced by Juan de Mendoza y Luna, who argued that what Spain needed was not a port somewhere on the California coast but rather a mid-ocean station on one of two Pacific islands, Rica de Oro and Rica de Plata.

These islands were believed to be located somewhere in the northern Pacific Ocean—but, in fact, they did not exist. In the end, plans to develop Monterey were therefore delayed until 1770, but the Manila galleon trade managed to flourish without either a California or a mid-ocean base.

The explorer/colonizer Gaspar de Portolá (1723?–1784?) founded the California settlements of San Diego and Monterey, discovered San Francisco Bay, and became the first governor of Alta California. By sending him out to explore the western coast of California, the Spanish wanted to counter a perceived threat of Russian expansion. For the same reason, they also wanted, over time, to plant a long string of missions along or close to the California coast.

In 1769, accompanied by the tireless missionary Fray Junípero Serra, Portolá left Baja California, bound for San Diego, where the first of California's 21 missions was established. The expedition then continued northward, looking for what Vizcaíno had, much too-enthusiastically, described as the excellent harbor of Monterey Bay.

Despite Portolá's best efforts, however, the search for this bay was a total failure: thick fog obscured the Santa Cruz shoreline, making the choppy waters of the bay look just like the open sea itself.

Portolá decided he had not gone far enough to find the bay, so he led his expedition further north, until he reached Half Moon Bay (about 30 miles south of San Francisco) in November 1769. There he realized, from the landmarks Vizcaíno had described, that he was now too far north. But this error turned out to be a great blessing in disguise.

3. Maritime Explorations

To get his bearings, Portolá sent his sergeant and a small team of men up into the adjacent coastal mountains to see what they could find. From the top of a 1,200-foot-high ridge they became the first Europeans to see San Francisco Bay, which because of the surrounding hills and the frequent ocean fogs was usually very difficult to see from the sea.

Father Crespi, the expedition's diarist, would later record that this bay was so big that "doubtless not only all the navies of our Catholic Monarch, but those of all Europe might lie within the harbor."[5] As the finest natural harbor along the entire Pacific coast, it would later become a foothold for Spanish expansion into Alta California.

Early maritime explorers were very active along the "watery frontiers" of the Pacific Northwest, too. Some of the significant expeditions that took place there during the years 1786 to 1792 are summarized below.[6]

(1) The Pacific Northwest expeditions of John Meares (1756–1809), a former British naval officer who transferred to the merchant navy, came about thanks to Captain James Cook, whose posthumously-published journals described the exceptionally rich and—especially to Chinese buyers—the exceptionally valuable sea otter furs that the coastal Indians were eager to trade for pieces of iron or copper.

Inspired by Cook's accounts, Meares organized several voyages to the region. A fundamental problem, however, was that in this area the fur trade took place close to Nootka Sound, located on western side of Vancouver Island in British Columbia. This spot became such an important crossroads of rival Spanish-British imperial designs that it might even have become a cause for war.

To make a long and very complicated diplomatic story quite short, however, Spain's seizure of some foreign ships there ultimately led to the Nootka Convention of 1790, which opened up to all nations any territory in the Pacific Northwest that had not already been settled by Spain at that time.

(2) The Navarez expedition of 1789 confirmed the existence of the Strait of Juan de Fuca, which Captain Cook, who had been blown off the coast during a storm, had not seen and which he therefore speculated did not exist. Navarez concluded that

> From what has been said it may be inferred that up to the present time neither Spanish nor foreigners have been able to give any exact information about these straits; even most people up to now have denied their existence…
>
> It is believed that this strait has a communication with the Mississippi River.… If Captain Cook had lived to the present time there is no doubt that he would have been undeceived about the existence of these straits as all Europe will be made to see in a short time.[7]

(3) The expedition of 1790 was led by a Spanish naval officer, Manuel

Quimper (c. 1757–1844). He explored the Strait of Juan de Fuca from the entrance to the basin at the eastern end and also traded for a few sea otter pelts with the Indians along the coast.

However, when Quimper sailed out of the strait, bound for Nootka Sound, he spent six days lost in such a dense fog that he could not find the entrance to the sound. As a result, he reluctantly turned south and sailed all the way down the Pacific coast to reach the port of Monterey. From there he made his way to the naval base of San Blas in Mexico. His own journal and the notes made by his mapmaker are now valuable records of this expedition.[8]

(4) The expedition led by Francisco de Eliza (1758–1825) left Nootka in 1791 to continue the early explorations of the Strait of Juan de Fuca and inland Washington waters. He discovered and named what is now Port Angeles, Washington, as well as other places, and drew up charts covering much of the Strait of Georgia.

In addition, a letter from Francisco de Eliza to the Viceroy, Conde de Revilla Gigedo, coupled with an account by the pilot Don Juan Pantoja y Arriaga of the packetboat (i.e., a storeship) *San Carlos*, offers some good contemporary insights into the lives of the coastal Indians.[9]

(5) Dionisio Alcalá Galiano (1760–1805) and Cayetano Valdéz (1767–1835) set sail from San Blas in March 1792, on an expedition bound for the Strait of Juan de Fuca, from which they may have hoped to find the Passage.

After exploring the waters and coasts around the southern end of Vancouver Island, however, they became convinced that such a waterway could not be found, at least not by the route they were then sailing.

During their search, they encountered the Vancouver expedition (see below). Vancouver suggested that the two Spanish ships and his own two ships should work together to look for the Passage. Needless to say, the Passage was not found, but there were in fact two bits of interesting news.

The first was that it had now been proven, conclusively, that the Strait of Juan Fuca did not lead to any Passage. The second was that the report and the illustrations produced by José Cardero, a member of the Galiano and Valdéz expedition, were published by the Spanish government in 1802 and would be used by Spain to reassert its claims to the whole northwestern region of North America.[10]

(6) George Vancouver (1758–1798) had served on James Cook's second and third voyages, and the British Admiralty chose him to command the Royal Navy expedition in 1792 to explore the coast of the Pacific Northwest.[11] He would spend three years (1792–1795) exploring and charting it.

3. Maritime Explorations

The expedition had two goals: to look for the Passage, and to reestablish Britain's claims (contested by Spain) to fur-rich Nootka Sound. First sailing north, Vancouver passed but did not enter the mouth of the Columbia River because he did not see it, although he did suspect presence of a river there. (The American captain Robert Gray would enter the Columbia in May 1792).

Vancouver realized very quickly that the Pacific Northwest coastline was so deeply indented that proving or disproving the existence of a transcontinental waterway would take a long time and would be very difficult. He wrote that

> I became thoroughly convinced, that our boats alone [i.e., the ships' rowboats] could enable us to acquire any correct or satisfactory information respecting this broken country; and although the execution of such service in open boats would necessarily be extremely laborious, and expose those so employed to numberless dangers and unpleasant situations, that might occasionally produce great fatigue, and protract their return to the ships; yet that mode was the only one in our power to pursue for ascertaining the continental boundary.[12]

The net result was that through 1794 Vancouver painstakingly surveyed many of the islands from Puget Sound to the outer Aleutians, circumnavigating and charting the largest one, which is now known as Vancouver Island.

Learning from the Spanish at Nootka that Gray had entered the Columbia River, Vancouver sent an officer, William Broughton, in command of the British ship *Chatham*, to explore the river. Broughton did so successfully, going 100 miles up the Columbia.

Vancouver was one of the most noteworthy maritime explorers, and in 1798 he published a well-received account of his travels. Illustrated by his excellent charts, it was entitled *A Voyage of Discovery to the North Pacific Ocean*. His coastal charts were so good, in fact, that they were still being used by maritime fur traders into the 1830s and by other navigators in the late 1800s.

4

Beginnings of Overland Exploration of the Frontiers

What would become a long series of famous Spanish adventures in the western frontiers of North America began very inauspiciously. Between 1528 and 1536, "four ragged castaways"—namely, the explorer Álvar Núñez Cabeza de Vaca (c. 1485–1492 to 1559) and his three shipwrecked companions—spent eight years wandering through the deserts of the American Southwest, looking hard for ways to survive and trying to meet other foreigners who could help them.

Cabeza de Vaca's unusual name means "cow's head" in Spanish. Legend has it that one of his ancestors helped to win victory for Christian forces at a Spanish battle against Muslim invaders by marking an unguarded—and therefore a safe mountain pass—with the skull of a cow.

Cabeza de Vaca himself would write one of the earliest first-hand accounts—it is arguably still the most dramatic single account—of the trans–Mississippi West before the Lewis and Clark expedition of 1803. Because it is one of the greatest adventure and survival stories of North American history, it is worth summarizing here.

He and the three other "ragged castaways" (the phrase is Cabeza de Vaca's own) were shipwrecked in November 1528 near the western tip of Galveston Island, Texas. They managed to survive by becoming traders in Indian produce and artifacts and, most remarkably, by becoming faith healers to the local Indians.

Cabeza de Vaca explains how this was done. He later wrote:

> We remained with the Avavares [a Texas tribe] for eight months, according to our reckoning of the moons. During that time people came to us from far and wide and said that we were truly children of the sun.
>
> Until then Dorantes [another *conquistador*] and the Negro [the North African slave Estevánico] had not cured anyone, but we found ourselves so pressed by the Indians coming from all sides that all of us had to become medicine men...
>
> We never treated anyone that did not afterward say he was well, and they had such confidence in our skill that they believed that none of them would die as long as we were among them...

4. Beginnings of Overland Exploration of the Frontiers

> They all came to us so that we might touch and make the sign of the cross over them. They were so obtrusive that they made it difficult to endure since everyone, sick and healthy, wanted to be blessed.... They always accompanied us until we were again in the care of others [i.e., when they left one tribe, the Indians would escort them to a neighboring tribe]. Among all these people it was believed that we came from Heaven. What they do not understand or is new to them they are wont to say it comes from above.[1]

In the western desert, Cabeza de Vaca and his men eventually encountered a team of Spaniards who were trying to enslave some of the local Indians and sell them at the nearest Spanish settlement. This meeting marked the end of his long travels, and he surely must have told the slavers that, as he later wrote,

> We [Cabeza de Vaca's group] traveled more than a hundred leagues, always coming upon permanent houses and a great stock of corn and beans, and [the Indians] gave us many deer hides and cotton blankets better than those of New Spain. They also gave us plenty of beads made of the coral found in the South Sea and good turquoises, which they get from the north. In the end, they gave us everything they owned.
> They presented Dorantes with five emeralds shaped like arrow points, the arrows of which they use in their feasts and dances. Because they seemed of very good quality, I asked where they got them, and they said they came from some very high mountains toward the north, where they traded feather brushes and parrot plumes for them. They also said there were villages with many people and big houses there.[2]

Cabeza de Vaca was wrong about the "emeralds," which were probably bits of green turquois or pieces of malachite (a green carbonate of copper), but in a sense he was right about the villages. The only bad news was that these were only the mud pueblos of the upper Rio Grande, not the rich towns Cabeza de Vaca must have imagined.

Cabeza de Vaca had so many quarrels with the slavers (he wanted them to seize the throng of Indians who followed him and his men on the last leg of their travels) that when his group finally parted company with the slavers, they forgot to take the "emeralds" back to the Spanish settlements with them. Nevertheless, even without any concrete proof, many eager Spaniards were prepared to accept the rumor of "emeralds" as convincing proof that untold riches did indeed await the *conquistadors* somewhere in Mexico's unexplored northern frontier.

As a result, in 1539, Antonio de Mendoza, the viceroy of New Spain, sent out toward the Zuni pueblo of Hawikuh a reconnaissance party protected by Spanish soldiers and led by the Franciscan friar Marcos de Niza. With Fray Marcos went the well-traveled Moor Estevánico as a guide.[3] Their journey, however, would be a classic and fatal case of explorer-Indian cultural misunderstandings.

Estevánico set out first and sent back encouraging messages to Fray Marcos, who followed some considerable distance behind him, urging him to push on rapidly to the pueblo of Hawikuh. En route, however, Fray Marcos met two bloodstained Indians, who told him that Estevánico had just been murdered.

The chronicler Pedro de Castañeda of Nájera reported as follows:

> When [the Indians] were well informed [about Estevánico's travels], they held councils for three days. As the negro had told them that farther back two white men, sent by a great lord, were coming, that they were learned in the things of heaven, and that they were coming to instruct them in divine matters, the Indians thought he must have been a spy or guide of some nations that wanted to come and conquer them.
>
> They thought it was nonsense for him to say that the people in the land whence he came were white, when he was black, and that he had been sent by them. So they went to him, and because after some talk, he asked them for turquoises and women, they considered this an affront and determined to kill him. So they did, without killing any of those who came with him. [As a charismatic faith healer, he had attracted an entourage of about 60 Indians.][4]

Fray Marcos himself fled to safety, but later claimed that he had stood on a hill from which he could see the fabled golden city of Cíbola and that it was bigger than "the city of Mexico." Such news prompted Mendoza to send out another expedition, this one very heavily armed and commanded by Francisco Vásques de Coronado.

The younger son of a wealthy Spanish family, Coronado had first traveled to Mexico in 1535, with the twin ambitions of earning money and making a good name for himself in the New World. The present expedition consisted of over 300 Spanish soldiers, more than 1,000 Mexican Indians, and over 1,500 horses and other animals.

In 1540, Coronado, guided by Fray Marcos, led an advance party of 200 soldiers from Culiacan. That same year, Fray Marcos, unable to rein in his vivid imagination, elaborated on Cíbola as follows:

> When I showed the [local] natives the sample of gold I had, they said there were vessels of it among their people [i.e., their people in Cíbola]. They wore ornaments of it hanging from their noses and ears, and also they have blades of gold to scrape the sweat from their bodies. Many of the people I saw wore silk clothing down to their feet.
>
> Of the richness of that country I cannot write, because it is so great that it does not seem possible. They have temples of metal covered with precious stones—emeralds, I think. They use vessels of gold and silver for they have no other metal.[5]

In reality, however, when Coronado finally got to Cíbola, he found that it was only a typical and very unimpressive pueblo village locally known as Hawikuh. There was, however, another and much more serious problem, too.

In religious terms, Hawikuh happened at that moment to be a "sacred space" for the local Indians. Two hundred Zuni warriors therefore interposed themselves between the Spaniards and their village. They carefully sprinkled a line of sacred corn across the path, therefore symbolically closing it to all outsiders until the tribe's religious ceremonies were over.

4. Beginnings of Overland Exploration of the Frontiers

Although from the Indians' point of view this action was perfectly clear and very polite, the Spaniards did not understand it in the same way. Instead, they took it as a deliberate insult. So, shouting their battle cry of "Santiago!" (meaning "St. James!"), the Spanish cavalrymen spurred their horses over the sacred corn-line, and combat immediately erupted.

Both sides fought hard. The Indians got so close to the soldiers when firing their arrows that the Indians were almost trampled by the rear hooves of the Spanish horses. Coronado himself fell from his horse, knocked out by stones hurled down from the terraces of the pueblo. In the end, however, the outcome of the skirmish was never in doubt: the heavily-armed Spaniards soon captured Hawikuh.

After the dust settled, as it were, Coronado sent Fray Marcos home in complete humiliation and in 1540 he reported to Viceroy Mendoza:

> It now remains for me to tell you about the city and kingdom and province of which [Fray Marcos] gave your Lordship an account.
>
> In brief, I can assure you that in reality he has not told you the truth in a single thing he said, but everything is the reverse of what he said except the name of the city and the large stone houses [that are there]…The Seven Cities are seven little villages…. They are all within a radius of 5 leagues. They are all called the kingdom of Cevola, and each has its own name and no single one is called Cevola, but all together they are called Cevola…
>
> The people of the towns seem to me to be of ordinary size and intelligence, although I do not think they have the judgment and intelligence they ought to have to build these houses in the way in which they have, for most of them are entirely naked except for the covering of their privy parts.[6]

Coronado experienced yet another serious setback in 1541, when, having listened to Indian accounts about a very rich kingdom known as Quivira (located in what is now central Kansas), he hired an Indian guide who was nicknamed El Turco ("the Turk") by Coronado's soldiers because they imagined that he looked like one. This Indian was probably a Pawnee or a Wichita from the eastern plains of Kansas, and he had a marvelous story to tell about what he claimed was his native land.

According to Pedro de Castañeda of Nájera, the chronicler of Coronado's expedition, El Turco's account ran as follows:

> …the Turk claimed that in his land there was a river, flowing through the plains, which was two leagues wide, with fish as large as horses and a great number of very large canoes with sails, carrying more than twenty oarsmen on each side.
>
> The nobles traveled in the stern, seated under canopies, and at the prow there was a large golden eagle. He stated further that the lord of the land took his siesta under a large tree from which hung numerous golden jingle bells, and he was pleased as they played in the wind. He added that the common table service of all was generally wrought silver, and that the pitchers, dishes, and bowels were made of gold. He called the gold *acochis*.

> At first he was believed on account of the directness with which he told his story and also because, when they [the Spanish] showed him jewels made of tin, he smelled them and said that it was not gold, for he knew gold and silver very well, and that he cared little for other metals.[7]

However, after very long and apparently aimless wanderings over the High Plains with nothing but an endless sea of grass and countless buffalo herds in sight—and, equally important—with very little to eat, Coronado finally lost patience with El Turco and had him interrogated, i.e., tortured, to find out what he was really up to.

The bottom line was that, as Coronado put it, El Turco had carefully planned to "take us to a place where we and our horses would starve to death."[8] Coronado was furious with this deception and, as punishment, he ordered that El Turco be garroted, i.e., strangled, which was the usual Spanish death penalty for treachery.

In the meantime, Coronado had sent Captain Alvarado, one of his officers, back to a local pueblo to demand the return of some gold bracelets that El Turco claimed had been taken from him when he was captured by the Spaniards. Alvarado went there and found that the local people received him in a friendly way, but

> when he asked for the bracelets they denied in all possible ways that they had them, saying that the Turk was lying and deceiving them. When Captain Alvarado saw that there was no other resource, he managed to get [two of the Indian leaders] to come to his tent. Upon their arrival he arrested them and put them in chains. The men in the pueblo came out to fight, shooting arrows and berating [Alvarado], saying that he had broken his word and friendship.
>
> [Alvarado] took [the two captives to where Coronado was staying at the moment], where they were kept prisoners for more than six months [and were tortured, too]. This was the beginning of the distrust the Indians had from then on for the word of peace which was given to them…[9]

At last, however, in 1542, having failed in most of his endeavors, Coronado beat a sullen retreat back to Mexico. He arrived there with less than 100 men and had to report directly to Viceroy Mendoza. The viceroy, it might now be said with considerable understatement, "did not experience true pleasure" with Coronado's visit.

As a final admonition, Pedro de Castañeda reports that the unfortunate Coronado

> should have paid more attention and regard to the rank to which he had been elevated [in New Spain], or at least to the honor that he had won and was to win by having such caballeros [Spanish gentlemen of noble birth and good breeding who traveled on horseback] under his command. However, it did not turn out that way for him…. Neither did he know how to preserve his position [i.e., his personal position as a favorite of the viceroy] nor the government he held [i.e., his official position]…
>
> [He] was not well received by him [the viceroy], although he presented his excuses.

4. Beginnings of Overland Exploration of the Frontiers

From then on, [Coronado] lost reputation and retained only for a short time the government of New Galicia that had been entrusted to him, for the viceroy assumed the administration of it [himself]...And this was the end of these discoveries and of the expedition that was made to the new land.[10]

After the governorship was stripped from him, Coronado gradually faded into obscurity. The main lesson that contemporary Spaniards learned from his failures was that the deserts of the American Southwest, specifically those of New Mexico itself, were so forbidding and so dangerous that, in the future, no early Spanish colony could hope to survive there without a great deal of financial and logistical backing from Spain itself.

Both for this reason and due to other more pressing issues (e.g., a local war in Mexico; discovery of a silver bonanza there; the expansion of New Spain into other parts of Mexico; New Spain's struggles with European powers; and, finally, Spanish expansion into South and Central America), New Spain would allow 39 years to slip by before it was willing to risk sending any more exploring expeditions into the north. That said, however, local officials never forgot that settlement and colonization might somehow, and some day, be possible in the north.[11]

5

Pathfinding and Exploration-Settlement Expeditions

At last, beginning in 1581, five Spanish pathfinding and exploration-settlement expeditions were sent out into New Mexico and onto the Great Plains, culminating in the Spanish occupation of New Mexico by Oñate in 1598.[1] These five expeditions can be outlined briefly as follows.

The first of them (1581–1582) began in southern Chihuahua (Mexico) and was led by Fray Agustín Rodríguez (?–1582) and Captain Francisco Sánchez Chamuscado (?–c.1582). This low-key venture came about because Rodríguez had been advised by a local Indian that in a region somewhere to the north there were large settlements of Indians who made their clothing out of the cotton that they raised, and who also had a large supply of food. If so, reasoned the Spaniards, these people might well be ripe for conversion to Christianity and should welcome the Spaniards.

The expedition consisted of three friars, nine soldiers, and 19 Indian servants. After they reached the area near what is now Bernalillo, New Mexico, one of the friars set out alone to return to Mexico and report on their travels but he was killed en route by Indians, who probably feared that he was going to bring back more Christians and thus effectively dispossess the Indians.[2] The remaining members of the expedition continued their travels, leaving two friars to teach religion to the Pueblo Indians. However, these friars, too, would later be killed by Indians.

An underlying reason for these last two deaths may have been that the Spaniards had given the Indians to understand that they (the Spaniards) were "children of the sun" and were thus, by implication, immortal.[3] The death of the first friar must have proved conclusively that this was not in fact the case; indeed, it must have proved, too, that the unarmed Spanish friars were pitifully easy to kill.

Captain Chamuscado managed to lead the rest of the party back to Mexico but he died during the journey. The survivors finally straggled in to Santa

5. Pathfinding and Exploration-Settlement Expeditions   35

Bárbara in Chihuahua, Mexico, with exciting but highly exaggerated reports of a new kingdom, possibly ripe for religious and economic activities. The eventual outcome of this expedition would be Oñate's 1598 campaign to conquer and settle New Mexico.[4]

The second expedition was launched in 1582 as a follow-up to the above expedition and was commanded by Antonio de Espejo, a local cattle rancher-turned-explorer. Its purpose was two-fold: to rescue the two friars left in New Mexico the previous year, and to investigate rumors of mines in the area. This expedition had mixed results.

The bad news, of course, was that the two friars had already been killed. Making a bad situation even worse, Espejo extorted provisions from the Pecos Indians—by threatening to burn their pueblo to the ground if they did not provide *pinole* (a gruel made from ground corn) for his expedition. Moreover, even after they received the *pinole,* the Spaniards captured two Indians from the Pecos pueblo—to be used as guides to take them to the great buffalo herds of the eastern plains. One of these men managed to escape, but the other one was taken to Mexico so that Spanish linguists there could learn his language and teach some of it to future Spanish explorers.

The Espejo expedition also did terrible things to the Tiwa Indians of the Puaray pueblo. Most of them had fled from their pueblo as soon as Espejo and his men came into sight, fearing that the Spaniards would punish them severely in retaliation for the murder of the two friars. About 30 Tiwas, however, remained on the rooftops of the pueblo and hurled insults down on the Spaniards below. This is what a soldier named Diego Pérez de Luján, who was the principal chronicler of the expedition, says happened next.

He wrote:

> In view of this [i.e., the rain of insults], the corners of the pueblo were taken [captured] by four [Spaniard soldiers], and four others with two servants began to seize those natives who showed themselves. We put them in a kiva [an underground ceremonial chamber entered through a hole in the roof]. Because the pueblo was large and the majority had hidden themselves in it, we set fire to the great pueblo of Puala [Puaray], where some we thought were burned to death because of the cries they uttered.
>
> At once we took out the prisoners, two at a time, and lined them up against some cottonwoods close to the pueblo of Puala where they were garroted and shot many times until they were dead. Sixteen were executed, not counting those who burned to death. Some who did not seem to belong to Puala were set free. This was a remarkable deed for so few people [i.e., so few Spaniards] in the midst of so many enemies.[5]

The only good news is that Espejo's expedition had pioneered a new route in eastern New Mexico and western Texas, in addition to exploring both east and west of the Rio Grande in central New Mexico and northern Arizona. The archbishop of Mexico wrote approvingly of the lands thus discovered: "If what they tell me is true they have indeed discovered ... another new world."⁶ Such a favorable report would encourage New Spain to do more to explore; to pacify; to colonize; and, finally, to exploit the region.

Before any more official expeditions were sent out, however, two unauthorized expeditions (the third and fourth of the five mentioned earlier) set out into New Mexico, western Texas, and the Great Plains. Both of these were Spanish *entradas*—literally, "entrances" or "openings"—designed to explore unknown and potentially hostile lands without any undue use of force. They were, in short, supposed to be fact-finding missions, not punitive expeditions, but both came to grief.

Led by the lieutenant governor of Nuevo Léon, Gaspar Castaño de Sosa in 1590–1591, the first unauthorized exploring-colonizing adventure was launched in direct defiance of the viceroy's specific order that the Indians must not be enslaved.

Castaño, however, not only attacked the Pecos Pueblo Indians but killed many of them and seized others to be his guides. As a result, the viceroy had him pursued by other soldiers led by Captain Juan de Morlete, who arrested him and his men and took them in chains back to Mexico City to stand trial.

In the second unauthorized expedition, in 1593 Captain Francisco Leyva de Bonilla, who was leading a foray to punish Indians for raiding cattle ranches, decided—on his own authority—to invade New Mexico. In the process, however, he was stabbed to death with a butcher's knife by an irate member of his own party, who then assumed command himself.

However, Indians later killed the murderer, as well as all the other Spanish members of the party. Only one Indian member of the expedition survived (after being held in captivity by local Indians for a whole year,) and managed to make his way back to New Mexico to relate his sad story to Juan de Oñate (1552?–1626).

Known as "the last *conquistador*" and as the first colonial governor of "Nuevo México" (New Mexico), which was located in the region around the upper Rio Grande and was the northernmost province of New Spain, Oñate led the final major Spanish expedition into the American Southwest.⁷

The modern historian Marc Simmons has said of him:

> In a very real sense, Juan de Oñate represented the end of a tradition. He was the last conquistador, the final knight in burnished armor who sallied northward under the authority of Cross and Crown to find wealth, glory, and fame. In that sense, he was a medieval figure, confirming the old observation that the Middle Ages drew its last breath in the New World. On the other hand, some of his behavior and attitudes show him to have been, at the same time, a man of the New Era, one grappling with changes rapidly overtaking his society.⁸

Thanks to his aristocratic family background, his excellent political connections with the viceroy, and his own considerable skills as an Indian fighter, he was given official permission from Spain to take charge of exploring, con-

5. Pathfinding and Exploration-Settlement Expeditions 37

quering, and settling the poorly-defined region known as New Mexico. He said, in his 1598 Act of Possession of New Mexico:

> I also take possession of all the ... ores of gold, silver, copper, mercury, tin, iron, precious stones, salt, *morales* [i.e., "economic values" in this context], alum, and all the lodes of whatever sort, quality, or condition...[9]

He therefore set out in 1598 with a 130-man military force; 10 Franciscans; and assorted women, children, servants, and slaves. This was a total of over 500 people, strung out in a two-mile-long column that included 80 wagons and carts and 7,000 head of livestock. He also sent his nephew Vincente de Zaldívar ahead to look for a direct route through the Chihuahua Desert to the Rio Grande.

Oñate's greatest failure was his willingness to use brute force against the local Indians, rather than trying to use his head. Matters came to a boil at the end of 1598, when a fracas erupted between the Indians of the high "sky pueblo" of Ácoma, on the one hand, and a Spanish foraging party led by Vincente de Zaldívar, on the other.

There are conflicting contemporary accounts about who started the fighting, but the most interesting one for modern readers is "the affair of the turkey."[10] This is a classic example of what anthropologists see as a total failure of cross-cultural communication; less scholarly observers can be pardoned if they see it simply as great stupidity on the part of the Spaniards.

From the Spanish point of view, these Indians were formally subject to Spanish law: any unprovoked attack by them against Spanish soldiers was therefore treason and deserved the harshest possible punishment. From the Indian point of view, however, some Indians thought that some Spanish soldiers had been rightfully killed because they had demanded Indian corn, flour, and blankets. One Indian claimed that the Spanish had set off the fighting by killing an Indian; another said it was because a Spaniard had wounded an Indian. Yet a third said that fighting began when a soldier either asked for, or had seized, the turkey of an Indian woman. In any case, the Spanish would conclude that the Indians had attacked them without provocation and were thus guilty of premeditated treason.

What the Spanish did not understand was that the Indians never *ate* turkeys but cherished them only for their feathers, which were used for clothing (e.g., to make warm cloaks) and for religious purposes (to make prayer sticks and ceremonial headdresses). Thus, from the Indians' perspective, to seize a turkey was therefore not simply a minor theft but a major sacrilege.

Ignorant of this fundamental fact of Indian life, the Spanish, in their ignorance and culture-bound pride, subjected the Indian defenders to a four-day trial, and sentenced them as follows:

- All male captives over 25 years of ago were condemned to have one foot cut off and had to submit to 20 years of personal service to a Spaniard.
- Boys between the ages of 12 and 25, and women over 12, were sentenced to 20 years of personal service.
- Children under 12 were placed under Spanish supervision.

In order to terrorize the Indians and to deter any Indian rebellions, the Spaniards made a point of widely publicizing their punishments. They chopped off the feet of Ácoma men in public ceremonies in different pueblos on successive days. To frighten the remote pueblos, two innocent Hopi Indians, who happened to be visiting Ácoma when the Spanish captured it, were sent home—after their right hands had been cut off. If there was any shred of good news in this tragic story, it was only that Oñate was in fact showing some mercy by handing out these dire punishments: a Spaniard who had been convicted of treason would immediately have been put to death.

Despite his brutal treatment of some Indians, Oñate was eager to learn from others. In 1602, for example, an Indian named Miguel, who had been captured during Oñate's travels and who had been taken to Mexico City for interrogation, made a rough map for the Spanish.

It covered a vast area, probably more than 100,000 square miles of the central or southern Great Plains, and depicted the preferred routes, the rivers, and the Indian settlements. The map also gave the distances between destinations in terms of the number of days of travel required. This map was not a fluke.

Another Indian map successfully guided Oñate across the Arizona desert in 1605, and in 1718–1720 the French explorer Jean-Baptiste Bénard de la Harpe, traveling with Indian guides up the Red River, had this to say about their mapping skills:

> [The Indians] do not make any mistake when they show the part of the world where the nation dwells of which they have knowledge, and that, taking the bearing of the places with a compass, one is certain of their situation.[11]

In 1604, Oñate set off on his final expedition but it, too, came to naught. He had planned to blaze a trail west from the Zuni pueblos to the Colorado River and then south to the Gulf of California, but he never made it to the sea. Finding no gold or silver en route, he retraced his steps, pausing only long enough to carve this message among the Indian petroglyphs on Inscription Rock at El Morro National Monument, where it can still be seen:

> Pasó por aquí el Adelantado Don Juan de Oñate al descubrimiento del Mar del Sur 16 a abril de 1605.
>
> (The *Adelantado* ["one who goes before," i.e., the representative of the king of Castile] Don Juan de Oñate passed by here from the discovery of the Sea of the South, the 16th day of April 1605.)[12]

5. Pathfinding and Exploration-Settlement Expeditions 39

Despite his failures, Oñate did make some contributions to the slowly-growing body of knowledge about the American Southwest. His support for the Franciscan missionary program from Texas to California eventually led to further explorations on its behalf. He extended the Camino Real ("royal highway") 600 miles into New Mexico by marking the way from the Chihuahua mining settlements into northern New Mexico. Oñate also chose the official campsites along this new stretch of road. At a total length of 2,000 miles, El Camino Real would remain, for several centuries, North American's longest road.

While the Spanish were preoccupied in the American Southwest, in 1659–1660 the two French brothers-in-law, explorers, and traders Médard Chouart (who bore the title of Sieur de Groseilliers) and Pierre Esprit Radisson helped to open up the western Great Lakes area and its northern wilderness to the Canadian fur trade.[13] Radisson, who had been captured and adopted by the Mohawks as a boy, would also provide the first written account of the Sioux.

Among many other adventures, these two men explored Lake Superior's northern shore, where the local Indians may well have told them about what would later become the U.S. National Monument known as Grand Portage. This would prove to be the easiest and best fur-trade canoe route into the far west of Canada, i.e., along the Pigeon River and then following the United States-Canada border to Lake of the Woods. (The Treaty of 1818 would establish the 49th parallel as the boundary between the United States and British North America.)

In more general terms, this fur-rich region was part of Rupert's Land, which had been granted to Prince Rupert of the Rhine, who was a nephew of the English King Charles I and was also the first governor of the Hudson's Bay Company. The boundaries of Rupert's Land were exceptionally vague and undefined but, centered on Hudson Bay, this territory clearly included very large portions of eastern Canada, of central Canada, and much of western Canada (up to what is now the southern British Columbia border).[14] Because of the apparently-unlimited riches of the fur trade, it attracted numerous European explorers and adventurers, despite its great distances, cold, and dangers.

In the 1660s, for example, with the Canadian fur trade booming, Groseilliers and Radisson became very annoyed with the high costs of (1) sending their furs from the western wilderness all the way back to Quebec by canoe, and (2) then having to pay a stiff tax on them there. They decided to find a better way to make money in this business, and therefore made their way first to New England and thence to England itself. In London, they were able to persuade a group of merchants that great riches could be won simply by controlling the fur trade closer to its source, i.e., in the *interior of Canada*.

Consequently, in 1670, a new enterprise with the sonorous title of the "Governor and Company of Adventurers of England Trading into Hudsons

Bay" was incorporated in London. King Charles II generously granted to this new company, which was governed by his cousin,

> the sole Trade and Commerce of all those Seas Streightes Bayes Rivers Lakes Creeks and Soundes in whatsoever Latitude they shall bee that lye within the entrance of the Streightes commonly called Hudsons Streightes together with all Landes and Territoryes upon the Countryes Coastes and confines of the Seas Bays Lakes Rivers Creeks and Soundes aforesaid that are not already possessed by or granted to any of our Subjects or possessed by the Subjects of any other Christian Prince or State with the Fishing of all Sortes of Fish Whales Sturgions and all other Royal Fishes of the Seas...[15]

The Hudson's Bay Company would have four major objectives: to look for the Passage; to claim for England the entire watershed of Hudson Bay; to engage in the fur trade with the Indians; and to displace the French fur traders.[16] This final point was important because, as one of the Company's English employees explained, the French traders

> are masters of all the Indian languages & greatly have the advantage of us...[They have] adopted the very Principles and Ideas of Indians, and Differ from them only a Little in Colour.[17]

6

Life on the Trails

Spanish explorers, for their part, pushed east and west from the existing New Mexican settlements in the Rio Grande valley and greatly broadened their ambitions. In so doing, the Spanish hoped to accomplish some or all of the following goals[1]:

- To rescue Pueblo Indians who were being held captive by other tribes, e.g., the Apaches or the Comanches; to find a mythical tribe of "bearded Indians," who were allegedly the descendants of Spanish sailors shipwrecked along the California coast; and to locate the rumored (but non-existent) Indian pueblos in the north that had not yet been introduced to Christianity.
- To confirm or disprove persistent rumors that French frontiersmen and traders were trying to butt into Spanish territory by forging trade alliances and close relationships with the Indians of the Great Plains.
- To open up new trade routes that would help to encourage commerce between New Mexico, Arizona, Missouri, Texas, and California.
- Finally, to locate the mythical Passage. If ever found, the Passage would have greatly facilitated transcontinental trade and even encouraged trade with the Chinese mandarins. Experience eventually proved, of course, that this waterway never existed.

As a result of these Spanish interests, the major pathfinding expeditions of the late 18th and early 19th centuries took place in the Southwest and in parts of Colorado and Utah. Memorable travels included those of Captain Juan Bautista de Anza (c. 1736–1788); Father Francisco Atanasio Domínguez (c. 1740–c.1803–1805); Fray Silvestre Vélez de Escalante (c. 1750–1780); and Pedro Vial (c. 1746–1814) a Frenchman who was employed by Spain. All of them merit brief discussions here.

In 1773, Anza, who was then commanding officer of a small presidio in the remote outpost of Tubac (located 45 miles south of today's Tucson), received permission from his viceroy to blaze a 1,200-mile-long trail from Sonora in Mexico to northern California. He was so successful that much later (in 1990) the U.S. Congress would honor his memory by establishing the Juan Bautista de Anza National Historic Trail.[2]

Since storms and high seas often made it too dangerous to supply the Spanish missions and presidios in California by sea, Anza hoped to find a safe overland way to transport badly-needed supplies there. Moreover, he also wanted to set in motion the Spanish colonization of California, largely to guarantee Spanish control over San Francisco Bay, which he described as the greatest harbor in the world and which in his view was certain to be threatened in the future both by British and Russian encroachments.

In January 1774, Anza therefore left Tubac with almost 300 people, 140 saddle horses, 35 mules, and five mule drivers. He crossed the Colorado River at Yuma; and finally reached Mission San Gabriel Arcángel, near what is now San Gabriel, California, in March 1774. In the process, he went through deserts and crossed mountain passes never before traversed by anyone but Indians. For this successful expedition, Anza was promoted to lieutenant-colonel.

To get a feel for his travels, an excellent literary source can be consulted here. This is Walter Nordhoff's fine book, *The Journey of the Flame* (1933), a fictional but historically accurate account of a journey from the tip of Baja California to San Francisco in 1810. Nordhoff wrote:

> A small fire served our cook, while around a larger one—for our nights are chilly in winter even on deserts—those who rested lay and talked of days past and those to come. We ate chiefly meat, fresh when it was to be had, or otherwise dried bull's beef, which tests the teeth but fills the belly with substance.
>
> Fruits when we were in their vicinity, or sugar cane peeled and chewed. Afterwards on our trip, when all else failed, the cook gave us dry, hard, white cheese to be eaten with lumps of *panocha* [small round cakes of hard brown sugar, formed in molds]...
>
> Each man carried a cup slung to his belt [for coffee, when it was available], just as his own knife cut such meat as politeness demanded his teeth should not touch. [Since civilian Spaniards did not carry firearms at this time, a man's knife was his only weapon for self-defense.] Not even a savage uses his teeth to sever a string of dried meat from that other portion of which his neighbor must eat.[3]

After returning to Tubac, Anza was sent out again by the viceroy in 1775, this time with the assignment of leading a large party of settlers to California, where they were to build both a mission and a presidio. His expedition reached Monterey in March 1776 and continued on to San Francisco. Responsibility for establishing a settlement there was assigned to the colonists, under the leadership of another army officer. Anza himself left California for Mexico City, where in 1777 he was promoted to the position of governor of New Mexico.

His successes continued apace. For example, in 1779 he led a punitive expedition against the Comanches, who had been raiding Taos. In late 1779, he pioneered a new route from Santa Fe to Mexico. In 1784, he led a campaign against the Comanches and concluded a peace treaty with them in 1786. The famous Comanche chieftain Cuerno Verde was killed in combat with Anza's forces in what is now Pueblo County, Colorado.

Anza's earlier achievements in pioneering an overland route to California in 1774 and his subsequent shepherding of colonists there the following year had seemed to auger well for the future of the Spanish northern frontier. Although, in the end, this would turn out *not* to be the case, what became known as the Gila River Trail did in fact contribute modestly to the growth and development of California. A short digression on it may therefore be of interest here.[4]

The Gila River Trail was unlike northern trails, in that it was never a simple, clearly-defined passageway connecting two fixed points. Instead, its route was one of a kind, consisting of a changing and ill-defined network of roughly parallel trails and tracks which had been used over many years by Indians, Spaniards, Mexicans, and Americans alike. These trails and tracks generally followed the 649-mile-long Gila River, which rises on the western slope of the Black Range Mountains in western New Mexico and ends at Yuma, Arizona, where it joins the Colorado River.

The Gila River, including its chief tributary, the Salt River, was once one of the biggest perennial streams in the West, but in modern times its flow has been diverted considerably for agricultural and urban uses. During the 19th century, however, it was still navigable for small craft all the way from near the Arizona-New Mexico border to its mouth.

The width of the river then varied from between 150 feet to 1,200 feet. It was between 2 and 40 feet deep—enough to permit some modest commercial uses. In 1849, for example, the California-bound traveler John Hudgins built a barge out of abandoned wagon boxes; loaded it with 5,500 pounds of assorted freight; and piloted his box-shaped "boat" down the Gila to its junction with the Colorado. In that same year, too, another California-bound adventurer built a raft and used the Gila to carry supplies to the mining company he had set up.

The eastern part of the Gila River Trail consisted of a very rugged mule trail that ran from what is now Truth or Consequences, New Mexico, to the villages of the Gila River People, an Indian tribe living along the Gila near Phoenix.

During the Mexican-American War, General Kearny ordered Captain Philip St. George Cooke to lead heavy wagons full of supplies along the Gila River trail. This proved to be quite impossible, however: the going was simply too rough for wagons, so Cooke and his expedition had to head for Tucson instead. There they rested, obtained supplies, and successfully continued on to California along a less arduous route, which became known as "Cooke's wagon road."

Anza's 1786 peace treaty with the Comanches, even if not permanent, was a boon not only for the well-established traders but also for the low-income itinerant Spanish traders, known as Comancheros, who eked out a very modest living by bartering goods with the Indians.

Writing in 1844, the American merchant, explorer, naturalist, and author Josiah Gregg (1806–1850) had something to say about the Comancheros in his definitive two-volume work, *Commerce of the Prairies: Life on the Great Plains in the 1830s and 1840s*.[5] He reported that the small-scale traders were only marginally better off than their Indian clients. Gregg wrote:

> The parties of *Comancheros* are usually composed of the indigent and rude class of the frontier villages, who collect together, several times a year, and launch upon the plains with a few trinkets and trumperies of all kinds, and perhaps a bag of bread and maybe another of *pinole* [a food made from parched ground grain], which they barter away to the savages for horses and mules. The entire stock of a trader very seldom exceeds the value of twenty dollars, with which he is content to wander about for several months, and be glad to return home with a mule or two, as the proceeds of his traffic.[6]

Gregg traveled back and forth along the Santa Fe Trail four times in nine years (1831 to 1840), so he came to know this passageway intimately. He very carefully and very conscientiously wrote about a wide variety of trail-topics—e.g., buffalo hunting, Indians, gold mining, and Mexican agriculture.

In the process, however, he made so many scientific measurements that the impatient members of one of his parties joked about murdering him, throwing his body and his instruments into a river, and then pressing on themselves to their destination before they ran out of food or other supplies.

In any case, *Commerce of the Prairies* solidly established Gregg's literary reputation. Because many readers wanted a current and accurate account of the Santa Fe Trail, the book became an immediate success; went through several editions; sold very well in England; and was soon translated into French and German. Moreover, Gregg's map of the Santa Fe Trail and of the surrounding plains was the best of its time and would prove very useful to later explorers.

As a classic example of Gregg's direct, no-nonsense style of writing here is his account of what happened in 1826 to a traveler named Broadus in the valley of the Arkansas River:

> ...Mr. Broadus, in attempting to draw his rifle from a wagon muzzle foremost [i.e., the muzzle of the rifle was now pointed directly at him] discharged its contents into his arm. The bone being dreadfully shattered, the unfortunate man was advised to submit to an amputation at once; otherwise, it being the month of August, and excessively warm, mortification would soon ensue.
>
> But Broadus obstinately refused to consent to this course, till death began to stare him in the face. By this time, however, the whole arm had become gangrened, some

spots having already appeared above the place where the operation should have been performed. The invalid's case was therefore considered perfectly hopeless, and he was given up by all his comrades, who thought of little else but to consign him to the grave.

But being unwilling to resign himself to the fate which appeared frowning over him, without a last effort, he obtained the consent of two or three of the party, who undertook to amputate his arm merely to gratify the wishes of the dying man; for in such a light they viewed him.

Their only "case of [medical] instruments" consisted of a handsaw, a butcher's knife and a large iron bolt. The teeth of the saw being considered too coarse, they went to work and soon had a set of fine teeth filed on the back. The knife having been whetted keen, and the iron bolt laid upon the fire, they commenced the operation; and in less time than it takes to tell it, the arm was opened round to the bone, which was in an instant sawed off; and with the whizzing hot iron the whole stump was so effectively seared as to close the arteries completely.

Bandages were now applied, and the company proceeded on their journey as though nothing had occurred. The arm commenced healing rapidly, and in a few weeks the patient was sound and well...[7]

As for Anza himself, he served as governor of New Mexico until 1787, when he returned to Sonora, Mexico. Appointed in 1788 to be the commander of the presidio at Tucson, he died before taking office there.

The Domínguez-Escalante expedition of 1776–1777, for its part, came about because the Spanish in New Mexico wanted to find a safe way to resupply their missions and presidios in Alta California, it being too risky and too slow to rely only on supply by ships.[8]

These two men were Franciscan missionary-explorers. They did not plan to try blazing a direct southerly trail from Santa Fe to Monterey because of the hostility of the Pima Indians and other tribes along that route. Instead, they decided to pioneer a new northerly trail from Santa Fe to Monterey in order to avoid these hostile tribes. Their tiny expedition, consisting only of 11 Spaniards, two Indians, and beef on the hoof, set out from Santa Fe in July 1776.

This was the first Spanish expedition to explore southwestern Colorado and eastern Utah. As the chronicler of the trip, Escalante kept a first-rate journal, which is still worth reading today (see the Selected Bibliography).

To make a much longer story very short, however, this expedition was in many ways a failure. The two explorers could not reach their stated objective of Monterey, and therefore they failed to open the overland route they believed would be so important for Spain's diplomatic, defensive, political, economic, and missionary purposes.

It is possible that, had they succeeded and had conditions in New Mexico itself not deteriorated so sharply (making it impossible for them, as they had promised, to return to the Utah area; to send more missionaries there; and gradually to usher this region into the Spanish mission fold), Utah would have become a lightly-settled part of New Spain.[9]

On 7 October 1776, barely two months into their journey, the party encountered severe weather. Escalante recorded in his journal:

> Today we suffered greatly from the cold because the north wind did not cease blowing all day, and most acutely. Up to here we had kept our intent of reaching the garrison and new establishments of Monterey...
>
> [However,] since winter had already set in most severely, for all the sierras [mountains] we managed to see in all directions were covered with snow, the weather very unsettled, we therefore feared that long before we got there the passes would be closed to us, so that they would force us to stay two or three months in some sierra where there might not be any people or the wherewithal for our necessary sustenance. For the provisions that we had were very low by now, so we could expose ourselves to perishing from hunger if not from the cold.[10]

The Spaniards on this expedition were all highly religious people, so they agreed to invoke the will of God to learn what they should do next. The solution was to cast lots, which they did by inscribing "Monterey" on one lot and "Cosina" (the name of an Indian tribe that was living in the Grand Canyon and which the explorers wished to visit) on the other.

Escalante does not explain just what these "lots" were or how they were cast. Two reasonable guesses today are that they were either (1) two pieces of paper with the names of the destinations written on them and were drawn from a hat, or (2) a flat stick, tossed into the air, with "Monterey" on one side and "Cosina" on the other, the winning side being the one that landed upright.

A more heretical or perhaps a more "human" possibility is that neither Escalante nor Domínguez did not want to leave anything to chance because the stakes were so high, i.e., they knew that they would almost certainly die if they continued to head west at that time of year. Perhaps they therefore made very sure that only one word, namely, "Cosina," was written on both of the papers or on both sides of the stick.

In any case, this expedition made its way back toward Santa Fe, reaching it safely in January 1777. The explorers never got to California but their journey of 159 days and more than 1,700 miles did pay some good dividends. For example:

1. It increased Spain's understanding of the geography and the Indian cultures of a large part of the Southwest that had not been explored before by non-Indians.

2. One of the members of the expedition—the mapmaker Bernardo Miera y Pacheco—produced in 1777 the best map of the western interior drafted thus far, and the first to record the Great Basin on the basis of personal observation. It showed some geographical features, e.g., Great Salt Lake, that would not appear on other maps for many more years.

3. One part of the Domínguez-Escalante route would later become heavily used by traders as the eastern leg of the Old Spanish Trail. This trail has been described by the American historians Leroy and Ann Hafen as "the longest, crookedest, most arduous pack mule route in the history of America." Pioneered in the late 1700s, it reached its heyday in the 1830s and 1840s, when annual mule caravans carried woolen blankets from New Mexico to California to trade there for horses and mules. The caravans came to an end after the end of the U.S.-Mexican War in 1848.[11]

4. The difficult experiences of the Domínguez-Escalante expedition proved conclusively that it would be foolish to try to supply Spanish missions and presidios in California via a northerly route from Santa Fe.

7

"Runners of the woods" and Other Travelers

While the Spanish were exploring the western frontier, the French continued their deep involvement in eastern and central Canada.

By way of background, it must be remembered here that France was a colonial power in North America for nearly 300 years, beginning in 1524, when Giovanni Verrazano, a Florentine in the service of François I, king of France, sailed along the eastern coast of North America. France's empire in North America, known as "New France," came to an end in two different phases. The first phase ended in 1763, when the British won the Seven Years' War. The second phase lasted until 1803, when Napoleon sold Louisiana to the United States.[1]

Unlike the early Spanish explorers, whose leaders were military personnel, the early French explorers were often independent French-Canadian traders and trappers who ranged throughout New France and elsewhere in the interior of North America. They were known as the "*coureurs de bois*" (literally, "runners of the woods"). Moreover, in sharp contrast to their Spanish counterparts, who had a very low opinion of the Indians and often treated them very badly, the *coureurs de bois* were under strict instructions to develop and cherish very close personal relations with the Indians so that a mutually-beneficial trade relationship might develop and flourish.

This profession arose because, after founding a permanent settlement at Quebec City in 1608, Samuel de Champlain had decided to send some French boys to live with the local Indians. He believed—correctly, as it turned out—that when they became expert in local languages and cultures, they would not only strengthen the French role in the fur trade but would also tend to displace the Dutch traders who were then at work along the Hudson River and the northern Atlantic coast.

Thus between 1610 and 1629 dozens of French-Canadian boys spent many months living with the Indians, who welcomed them because they were seen as harbingers of a mutually-beneficial trade between the Indians and the French. This trade held out the promise not only of the European goods so

7. "Runners of the woods" and Other Travelers

highly prized by the Indians (who paid for them with furs), but also of possible French military help against their many enemies.

A partial listing of what the French traders had on offer would include, in random order[2]:

Firearms
Brandy
Iron knives, axes, and hoes
Needles and brass kettles
Colorful blankets and textile yardage to replace hide robes and to enhance the wearer's prestige
Glass beads to replace porcupine quills in Indian embroideries
Copper bangles and bells
Vermillion for face- and body-painting

Finally, as if all this was not enough, French officials and priests—unlike their Spanish counterparts—did not demand that the Indians totally abandon their own religions and accept French ways of life.

One of the boys who spent time in Indian villages was Étienne Brûlé, who would become a great traveler. He later explored the Ottawa River (a tributary of the St. Lawrence) and was the first European to see the Lachine Rapids and to visit all of the Great Lakes. During the 1820s, he may have gone as far west as the present site of Duluth, Minnesota, which is located at the westernmost edge of Lake Superior.

A very colorful French explorer was Jean Nicolet (or Jean Nicollet, Sieur de Belleborne, c. 1598?–1642), who is now remembered for exploring Lake Michigan, Mackinac Island, and Green Bay, and for being the first European to set foot in what is now Michigan.

Recruited by Champlain, he lived with a group of Algonquin Indians, first in order to learn their language, and then to serve as an interpreter when they needed to negotiate treaties with the French. He did so well, in fact, that the Algonquin tribe formally adopted him as one of its own warriors.

A key aspect of his career as a *coureur de bois* was his firm belief that China must not be too far away from Green Bay, Wisconsin. He arrived at this conclusion because he and other French explorers learned that the Indians who lived near Green Bay were locally known as the "Ho-Chunk." The French translated this name to mean "People of the Sea." In the Indians' language, however, it really meant something like "harvesting rice"—a reference to the fact that wild rice was a staple of their diet.

At that time, there was no exact knowledge about how far China was from North America. When Champlain learned from his Algonquin informants about "salt water in the westernmost Great Lakes," he judged that the Pacific was only about 1,000 miles from these lakes.[3]

Nicolet himself decided that the rice-eaters must have come from somewhere near the Pacific Ocean and that, through them, he would certainly be able to make direct contact with the Chinese. In about the late 1630s, he therefore styled himself as the French Ambassador to the Ho-Chunk. He wore brightly-colored robes of his own design which he thought would appeal to the Chinese. He also carried two big-bore pistols, slung in holsters on either side of his saddle, and fired them into the air from time to time, purely for theatrical effects.

The Indians enjoyed his antics and they agreed to take him by canoe along the Fox River and then along the Wisconsin River in search of what he and other Europeans of the times termed the "South Sea," i.e., the Pacific Ocean. Indeed, when the Wisconsin River began to widen, Nicolet became so sure that he had found the long-sought Passage to the Pacific that he ended his travels then and there, and returned to Quebec to report his great discovery. The irony here is that, had he continued along the Wisconsin River just a little while longer, he would have discovered, near what is now Prairie du Chien, Wisconsin, something almost as interesting as the Passage, namely, the upper Mississippi River.

In 1658, two French *voyageurs* (fur traders), i.e., the brothers-in-law Médard Chouart des Groseilliers and Pierre Esprit Radisson, became the first Caucasians to circumnavigate Lake Superior, by sailing south along the North Shore. When they returned to their starting-point, they found that they were being followed by a whole flotilla of Indians in canoes, who wanted to sell them fur pelts. This colorful event is said to have marked the beginning of the fur trade in the Lake Superior region.

By 1659, however, profits from the fur trade were beginning to slip, and Groseilliers and Radisson objected to the heavy expenses they were forced to incur by shipping their furs all the way back to Quebec by canoe, and then having to pay a stiff tax on them there.[4]

In 1660, for example, Groseilliers and Radisson arrived at Montreal with 60 canoes carrying 300 Indians and laden with cargoes of prime furs worth 200,000 livres (possibly the equivalent of about $800,000 today). However, these two men were immediately arrested for disobeying the orders of the government of New France. They were later fined and taxed about 40 percent of the value of the furs.[5] They therefore decided that, in the future, there must be a better way for them to make money in the fur trade.

Accordingly, they first went to New England and then to London, looking for financial backers. In London, they were able to persuade a group of merchants that great profits could be made if only they could arrange to control the fur trade nearer its source, that is, in the interior of Canada itself.

Their arguments were quite persuasive, so in 1670 a new enterprise was incorporated in London with the sonorous title of the "Governor and

Company of Adventurers of England Trading into Hudsons Bay." Known as the Hudson's Bay Company, this firm was launched to achieve the following objectives:

1. To look for the Passage. This idea was so paramount in the thinking of the Hudson's Bay Company that when Radisson reached the mouth of the Nelson River in 1670, which is located on the west coast of Hudson Bay, he was positive that it would become a commercial route as important as the elusive Passage.
2. To claim for England the entire watershed of Hudson Bay. Its real size was not known then but this watershed is now judged to total 1,490,900 square miles.
3. To engage in trade with the Indians.
4. To replace French fur traders with English or other pro–Hudson's Bay Company traders.

The travels of Groseilliers and Radisson helped to open up the Great Lakes region and Canada's northern wilderness, not only to fur traders and explorers but also to territorial claims and commercial interests by European states. Remarkably, the fur trade route to Europe that they pioneered by way of Hudson Bay was the most efficient one of their era.

Impressive as these achievements were, however, they pale in comparison with the single-handed labors of the Italian Jesuit missionary, explorer, writer, geographer, agricultural expert, cartographer, and astronomer Eusebio Kino (1645–1711).[6] He was a blur of activity, especially during the last decades of his life when he worked in Pimería Alta (northern Sonora and southern Arizona below the Gila River) with the local Indians, e.g., the Tohono O'Odham, Sobaipuri, and other Upper Piman tribes.

In terms of this book, Kino's most important discovery as an explorer of the western frontier was that *California was not in fact an island*. The first map known to have depicted California as an island dates from 1542, and this geographical error would later gain wide currency among the mapmakers of the 17th and 18th centuries.[7]

While studying in Europe, Kino himself had accepted the prevailing doctrine that California was an island, but after he reached Mexico he began to have serious doubts. He therefore undertook a series of very difficult overland expeditions from northern Sonora to places in or close to the delta of the Colorado River. In so doing, he had two goals: first, to find a practical route to link the Jesuit missions in Sonora and Baja California, and, second, to resolve the above "island question."

As a result of his far-flung travels, Kino became convinced that a land connection must in fact exist, and that therefore California was *not* an island. To set matters straight, he wrote:

But now, thanks to His Divine Majesty [God], through various expeditions.... I have discovered all details, certainly and with evidence, by means of a magnetic needle [a compass] and astrolabe in my hand, that California is not an island but a peninsula or isthmus, and that in thirty-two degrees of latitude [i.e., at the end of the Gulf of California] there is a passage by land to California.[8]

European cartographers remained divided on this issue, however, and it was not finally settled until the expeditions of Juan Bautista de Anza between Sonora and the west coast of California in 1774–1776.

The French, for their part, wanted to explore what the team of the Jesuit priest Jacques Marquette (1637–1675) and the explorer-trader Louis Jolliet (1645–1700) knew as the "Messi-Sipi." They were a unique and well-matched pair. Marquette was a 35-year-old Jesuit missionary-explorer who was such a superb linguist that he had become fluent in six Indian languages since arriving in Canada in 1666. Jolliet was a 27-year-old former philosophy student who had become a fur trader.[9]

They wondered whether this big river was indeed the long-sought Passage that flowed into the Pacific Ocean and would thus facilitate trade with China (they also wondered the same thing this about the Missouri River, which they passed en route), or whether it ended up either in the Gulf of California or in the Gulf of Mexico.

After setting out in canoes from the northern reaches of Lake Michigan in May 1673, by mid-July they had reached the junction of the Mississippi River and the Arkansas River, a location which their Quapaw Indian guides told them was still a 10-day journey from the sea (it was in fact much further, being 700 miles away from the Gulf of Mexico).

This information persuaded them to leave the Mississippi River and to head up the Arkansas River, because, as they put it correctly, "Judging from the direction of the course of the Mississippi, if it continues the same way, we think that it discharges into the Mexican gulf."

Moreover, they feared that if they continued further down the Mississippi they would at some point encounter either hostile Indians or hostile Spaniards, neither of which they would be strong enough to repel. Thus they felt they had now gone far enough: in their view, their expedition was already successful.

In the process, they experienced some real adventures. For example, Marquette noted in his journal that

> From time to time, we came upon monstrous fish, one of which struck our Canoe with such violence that I thought it was a great tree, about to break the Canoe to pieces. [This fish may well have been a blue catfish, which can weigh up 128 pounds.]
>
> On another occasion, we saw on the water a monster with the head of a tiger, a sharp nose like that of a wildcat, with whiskers and straight, erect ears; the head was grey and the neck quite black. [This animal may been a Florida panther, *Felis concolor coryi*, which was then found throughout the southeastern United States.][10]

7. "Runners of the woods" and Other Travelers 53

The two men finally returned safely to Lake Michigan. Marquette died shortly after revisiting the Kaskaskia Indians on the Illinois River, while Jolliet later led an expedition to the Hudson Bay and drew up some useful navigation maps of the St. Lawrence River.

In retrospect, then, their joint expedition was clearly a success. It pleased the Jesuit Order, which saw in these newly-discovered lands the potential for some new missions. It also pleased Jolliet in his capacity as a trader. He thought that the region might well become a colony for New France: the climate was mild, and the land had enough natural resources to support some hard-working colonists.

8

To Wait Patiently by Hudson Bay

The mouth of the Mississippi River itself was discovered by the French explorer René-Robert Cavelier, Sieur de La Salle (1643–1687), who is better known to history simply as "La Salle."[1] Authorized by France to begin trade with the Mississippi Valley, he also explored the Great Lakes region, the Gulf of Mexico, and claimed the entire Mississippi River for France. He relied on Indian maps to help his expedition make its way down the Mississippi in 1681.[2] These efforts, however, would end in a cascade of failures.

Descending the Mississippi, by mid–March 1682 he was at the Arkansas River, the southern limit of the Jolliet and Marquette expedition of 1673. He reached the Gulf of Mexico on 6 April, briefly explored the Mississippi Delta, hosted a ceremony claiming the Mississippi Valley for France, and then headed back upstream. This would not be an easy trip.

One of his men later wrote as follows:

> We were out of provisions, and [had] found only some dried meat at the mouth [of the Mississippi], which we took to appease our hunger; but soon after perceiving it to human flesh, we left the rest to the Indians. It was very good and delicate.
>
> At last, we began to remount the river, living only on potatoes and alligators. The country is so bordered with canes and so low in this part that we could not hunt without a long halt.[3]

Once home in France, La Salle wanted to get permission to found a colony in Louisiana, and for this reason he presented falsified maps that claimed incorrectly that the Mississippi River was really quite close to northern Mexico. He did this in order to buttress a plan then being put forward by one faction of the French court, i.e., that France should invade New Spain. His map of a setting up a French colony at the mouth of the Mississippi supported this idea.

Returning to the Texas coast in January 1685, La Salle arrived from the Atlantic Ocean (i.e., the opposite direction of his previous arrival) and landed at what is now Matagorda Bay, 80 miles northeast of Corpus Christi, which he mistakenly believed to be one of the mouths of the Mississippi. His serious errors now followed hard upon one another. They included the loss of French ships, supplies, and people due to accidents, desertions, disease, famine, Indian attacks, and his series of unsuccessful searches for the Mississippi. All these problems were compounded by his incompetent leadership and, indeed, by his mental instability.

The last act began in 1687, when La Salle set out with a small party for the Illinois Country, only to be assassinated later on in East Texas by some of his own men. The few remaining French colonists at Matagorda Bay were killed by the Indians.

La Salle's major legacy to history was the French territorial claim to the whole Mississippi Valley. In practice, however, the network of small forts/fur trading posts that he established along the Great Lakes and the Ohio, Illinois, and Mississippi Rivers would later come to define French possessions there until the surrender of New France to Great Britain in 1763–the result of France's losing the Seven Years' War.

In terms of exploring the Lake Superior region, in the latter half of the 17th century the French were tireless travelers. Jacques de Noyon (1668–1745), for example, was born in Trois-Rivières, Quebec, and made many trips westward. In 1688, he reached Rainy Lake and, possibly the next year, Lake of the Woods, as well, both of which lie northwest of Lake Superior in the border lakes area.[4]

During his travels he heard vague reports of the Winnipeg River and of Lake Winnipeg, which he may have thought was the entrance to the long-sought but entirely mythical Passage. At that time, Noyon may have traveled farther into the Canadian west than any other European before him. He led a traders' group west from Fort Nipigon in Lake Superior's Thunder Bay area and wintered with the Assiniboine Indians of Rainy Lake. The meager documentation about his life, however, has nothing to say about his other explorations.[5]

While the French were focusing on the Illinois Country, the unexplored reaches of western Canada attracted British attention. In about 1684, for example, the 19-year-old Englishman Henry Kelsey (1667?–1724) arrived in the New World as a young apprentice in the Hudson's Bay Company.[6]

In 1688–1689, on what was his first expedition, he proved that he was indeed made of very stern stuff. He had sailed from York Factory (located on the western shore of Hudson Bay) to explore the lands north of the Churchill River. When ice made further progress impossible by ship, however, he and an Indian guide simply went ashore and then explored, by foot, about 235 miles north of the Churchill before turning back.

They turned back only because the guide was terrified that the local Inuit (i.e., the Eskimos) might hear them and attack them. The guide told Kelsey that he (Kelsey) was a fool who "was not sensible of dangers."[7] In any case, Kelsey was always full of high spirits: his contemporaries described him as "a very active Lad, delighting much in Indian Company."[8]

On his most famous journey, Kelsey left York Factory in 1690 to establish official trade relations with the Indians living west of Hudson Bay. Instructed by the Hudson's Bay Company to look for minerals and botanic medicines en route, he carried with him a wide range of items to barter with the Indians. His stock-in-trade included English firearms, Brazilian tobacco, a brass kettle, a lace coat, blankets, hatchets, and beads.

Probably after paddling up the Hayes and Fox Rivers to Moose Lake (close to the Manitoba-Saskatchewan border), he formally took possession, for the Hudson's Bay Company, all the western lands of this vast region. He spent the winter of 1690 near the Saskatchewan River and then, in July 1691, canoed up the Saskatchewan and walked to the prairies of central Saskatchewan. There he met the local tribes; wrote the first Canadian descriptions of the grizzly bear and the American bison (i.e., the buffalo); and included detailed ethnographic notes in his journal.

Kelsey returned to York Factory by the summer of 1692. His later exploits included expeditions to begin trade with the Inuit in whalebone, oil, and walrus tusks. His epic 1690–1692 explorations into western Canada would not be equaled by other travelers until the 1750s but, remarkably, they were never officially acknowledged or rewarded by the Hudson's Bay Company: it saw no need to risk the lives of any other employees by sending them out into the distant northern wilds. Indeed, for some time after Kelsey's safe return, the Hudson's Bay Company was quite content to wait patiently by Hudson Bay and encourage the Indians to do all the hard work, i.e., by requiring them to bring their furs from the wilderness back to York Factory.

Turning once again to the French explorers, a Canadian whose father had recently been ennobled and whose own achievements were highly praised in his lifetime was Pierre Le Moyne d'Iberville (1661–1706).[9] He was, among other things, a military hero; the discoverer of the mouth of the Mississippi River; an explorer of Louisiana; and, last but by no means least, the father of the New France administrative district known as *La Louisiane* (Louisiana), which he and his family founded between 1699 and 1712.

This district originally covered a very far-flung landscape that included most of the drainage basin of the Mississippi River and that stretched from the Great Lakes to the Gulf of Mexico, on the one hand, and from the Appalachian Mountains to the Rocky Mountains, on the other.

The French government put Iberville in charge of its Louisiana expedition because he had been such a hero in King William's War (1689–1697). With a four-ship expedition, he sailed from France in 1698, and then had to ask local pirates and other sailors in Santo Domingo where, exactly, the Mississippi River was located.

8. To Wait Patiently by Hudson Bay

The reason for his uncertainty was that the topography of the lower Mississippi River is still quite complicated today. The phrase "Mouth of the Passes," for example, refers to the aggregate of the individual mouths of the passes connected to the "Head of the Passes," including the Southwest, South, North Passes, and the Pass a Loutre.

In any case, while looking for a safe refuge for his ship during a storm, he and his brother Jean-Baptiste (see below) eventually found the North Pass. These two brothers thus became the first Europeans to enter the Mississippi River from the sea. In so doing, Iberville also proved that the Mississippi Delta was a peninsula.

To summarize Iberville's meteoric career: he made a total of three expeditions to Louisiana. Since he wanted to make the Indian trade in skins a major part of Louisiana's economy, he ordered sturdy flatboats to be built in order to carry both beaver pelts and buffalo hides down the Mississippi for onward transshipment to France.[10] He also drew up plans for French expansion in the Mississippi Valley, and helped to develop France's military strategy during Queen Anne's War (1702–1713) between France and England. Now hailed as one of France's most able colonizers and most energetic explorers, Iberville died of illness in Havana, Cuba at the age of 45.

Iberville's younger brother, Jean-Baptiste Le Moyne, Sieur de Bienville, was himself a key figure in the exploration and colonization of French Louisiana.[11] In fact, he is sometimes known as the "Father of Louisiana."

On his first voyage of exploration, he went with Iberville to the Hudson Bay area and in 1699 accompanied him on the successful search for the mouth of the Mississippi. Later, while serving the Louisiana colony in a variety of exploring, military, and administrative posts (including that of governor), Bienville strongly supported a policy of French expansion and encouraged others to get out into the field and learn about the potential of the land. The French hoped that tobacco, indigo, and other commercial crops could be grown in that semi-tropical climate for export to France and to other countries.

Bienville was a very effective officer with both military and diplomatic skills. In 1716, for example, he founded Fort Rosalie (present-day Natchez), which was the first permanent European settlement on the Mississippi. Relations between the French and the Natchez Indians, however, were not peaceful and friendly at that time. In fact, Bienville had been ordered to build the fort in response to Natchez villagers having murdered some Frenchmen in 1716, and he led a war against them in 1723.

A contemporary observer noted Bienville's diplomatic skills. If a given tribe of Indians began to favor the British, who were the great colonial rivals of the French, Bienville would then

> stir up secretly some other powerful [Indian] nations to which he would furnish powder, bullets, and the greatest number of guns that he could to make war on

the one that he saw was being moved by the English and especially to bring [Bienville] many prisoners from the nation for which he would give them something [in exchange].

He would then send the prisoners back home free, sending word to their chiefs that he had done all that he had been able to do to prevent others from making war on them, but that not being able to accomplish it he had at least rescued their men whom he was sending back to them to show that the French nation was a friend of theirs, and that he himself would be glad to protect them as far as it was in his power to do so, that he hoped that henceforth their nations would pay more attention to the messages that he would send them.[12]

Despite his diplomatic efforts, however, French-Indian relations gradually soured. In 1729, the Natchez Indians attacked Fort Rosalie and killed more than 200 French settlers there. In retaliation, the French (aided by their Choctaw allies) killed most of the Natchez. In the following years, the French either dispersed or enslaved the Natchez survivors.

Never one to rest on his laurels, Bienville wanted France to explore for a route to New Mexico, perhaps via the Arkansas River. However, when Louisiana itself began to suffer from economic problems and from Indian attacks, he left New Orleans in 1743 and retired to Paris.

The first official French expedition to visit the Osage and Wichita Indians in what is now the American state of Kansas was led by the French army officer Claude Charles Du Tisne (or Dutisne or Dutisné, c. 1681–1730) in 1719.[13] His superiors instructed him to visit both the Wichita and Apache Indians as a first step toward establishing amicable trade relations between New France and the Spanish colony of Santa Fe in New Mexico.

At that time, the French had heard of these Indians but had not yet met any of them in person. Du Tisne's job was to make sure that they would not pose any threats to French traders passing over their lands. What the French and Du Tisne did not understand, however, was that, as a matter of national policy, the Spanish authorities in New Mexico were strongly opposed to any trade with the French.

With his small band of French and Indian employees, Du Tisne journeyed by canoe up the Missouri River to the village of the Missouria Indians. These Indians, however, turned out to be very unhappy with the French because French traders had been bypassing them.

They wanted to become middlemen for any French trade with the Indians living further upstream. The Missouria were especially worried that French traders would provide guns to the up-river Indians who, if newly-armed with French firearms, might well become their mortal enemies. As a result, they refused to let Du Tisne and his party continue upstream from their own village. He was thus forced to turn around and return to his starting point.

Not a man to give up easily, later that summer Du Tisne made a new attempt to get further west. After crossing the Ozarks region, he finally reached the village of the "Great Osages" tribe in Vernon County, Missouri. He was very impressed by the height of the Osage men, who were often more than six feet tall and who wore their hair in a scalp-lock, i.e., a long tuft of hair on the crown of the otherwise-shaven head of a warrior.

The bad news was that, like the Missouria, the Osage were very much opposed to letting Du Tisne cross their territory and then, they feared, to sell guns to the Pawnee Indians. After long negotiations, however, he was allowed to continue on his journey but was only allowed to bring in a total of six guns—three for himself and three for his interpreter—plus some trade goods. (Since almost all the firearms of that era were single-shot muzzleloading weapons that took a long time to reload and often failed to fire in very damp conditions, traveling with three of them was a good insurance policy.)

His next stop was with the Wichita Indians in Kansas, but he got a hostile response there, too. These Indians thought he was a slave trader, but he managed to convince them that he was not. Their real enemies were the Plains Apache, who the French called the Padoucas. Both sides fought to get slaves and horses, and are said to have practiced ritual cannibalism.

Du Tisne believed that peace between these two warring tribes could eventually be achieved, perhaps with French mediation; if so, he reasoned, this might open up trade with New Mexico. But his hopes would be cut short. After this expedition, he continued to serve on the frontier, was promoted to Captain, and was given command of Fort de Chartres in Illinois. He died there in 1730, however, of a wound received from a Fox Indian, whose tribe was opposed to French traders and settlers.

A contemporary of Du Tisne, though not a military man, was Louis Juchereau de St. Denis (1674–1744), the eleventh of twelve children of a Canadian (Quebec) couple and a colorful and resourceful French adventurer.[14] Indeed, he would become one of the most important traders, Indian experts, and explorers on Louisiana's western frontier.

Educated in France, he sailed from France to Louisiana in 1699 at the age 25, on the second expedition of his relative by marriage, Pierre Le Moyne, Sieur d'Iberville. His first assignments were to command a French fort on the Mississippi River and another fort at Biloxi Bay.

These early travels brought him into frequent contact with the Karankawa and the Caddo Indians, who taught him how to get along in wilderness areas. The French governor of Louisiana then sent St. Denis and a company of men from Mobile to explore more remote places. He visited the Natchitoches Indian villages in what is now northwestern Louisiana, made his way to the lands of the Hasinai Indians, where he left some of the trade goods he was carrying, and then pressed on to the Spanish outposts on the Rio Grande.

It was there, at San Juan Bautista (present-day Piedras Negras, Mexico), that, it is said, he fell in love with Manuela Sánchez, the young and beautiful granddaughter of Diego Ramón, the officer in charge of San Juan Bautista. Another less romantic possibility (see below) is that St. Denis decided that Manuela, over and above her physical charms, would be the ideal wife for his part-time role as a French spy.

In any case, what happened was that as soon as St. Denis arrived at San Juan Bautista, Commander Ramón had him placed under a very gentle form of house arrest, while waiting for instructions to arrive from distant Mexico City telling him what to do with this foreigner who was importing contraband goods in violation of Mexican law. During this long, slow process, St. Denis used his endless amount of free time to court Manuela and won a promise of marriage from her.

This done, he was then ordered to present himself in Mexico City to explain what he was doing in Mexico. He was so persuasive, however, that the Spanish appointed him to be the commissary officer of an expedition going out to build Spanish missions. He returned to San Juan Bautista, married Manuela, and helped to build six missions and a presidio in East Texas in 1716–1717.

By the spring of 1717 he was back in San Juan Bautista with a sizeable amount of contraband merchandise for sale. But his long run of good luck finally ran out. The Spanish may have welcomed him during his first visit, but the vagaries of the changing political relationship between France and Spain now made him very unwelcome. He insisted, however, that his marriage to Manuela proved his strong desire to become a Spanish subject—but some of the local Spaniards were still sure that he was really a spy for France.

Ordered to go to Mexico City for a second hearing, St. Denis fled to avoid being sent to Spain as a prisoner. He made his way back to Nachitoches in 1719. The Spanish allowed Manuela to join him there in 1721 but refused to let him retire in New Spain, as he wished. In the end, he died at Natchitoches in 1744.

9

Taking Great Pains to Get Along with the Indians

An even more interesting French explorer and trader was Étienne de Veniard, Sieur de Bourgmont (1679–1734), who documented his journeys on the Mississippi River and on the Platte River, and who drew up the first European maps of these regions.[1] He was so colorful and so intrepid—and, indeed, his whole life was really so kaleidoscopic—that it is difficult to summarize it briefly, but an attempt can be made here.

In an era when very few frontiersmen had any well-developed literary skills, Bourgmont was an outstanding exception. His two works—the *Exact Description of Louisiana, of its Harbors, Lands and Rivers, and Names of the Indian Tribes That Occupy It* (1713), and *The Route to Be Taken to Ascend the Missouri River* (1714)–were both well-received by his contemporaries. Indeed, he was recommended for the Cross of Saint Louis, an important French award, in 1718, and the next year the Colony of Louisiana passed a resolution praising his descriptions of the lives and cultures of the local Indians.

On the exploration front, in 1723 Bourgmont built Fort Orleans, which was located near present-day Brunswick, Missouri, and which was the first European-style fort on the Missouri River. The following year he led an expedition into the Great Plains of Kansas in order to set up trading relations with the Apache Indians there. He was very successful with them because, unlike the Spaniards, who were prevented from doing so by Spanish regulations, he was quite willing to offer them guns, powder, and lead for bullets in trade. An Apache chief was impressed to the point where, grabbing a fistful of earth, he assured Bourgmont, "Now I regard the Spaniards as I do this dirt!"[2]

In addition, Bourgmont also offered the Indians a much wider variety of non-lethal trade goods than they had ever seen before. His stock-in-trade apparently included pickaxes, axes, red cloth, blue cloth, mirrors, knives, shirts, scissors, combs, vermillion (red paint used to decorate the face and the body), awls, beads, and brass wire.

These achievements seem even more impressive in light of the checkered beginnings of his own career. He grew up in central Normandy in France and loved to hunt. In 1698, however, at the age of 19 he was found guilty of poaching on the lands of a local monastery and was fined 100 *livres*, a hefty sum for a young man. To avoid having to pay this fine, he fled to the New France settlements of North America and there, as an outlaw, supported himself for several years as a *coureur de bois*.

In 1702, thanks to his contacts with Juchereau de St. Denis, he joined the French armed forces and in 1706 assumed command of Fort Pontchartrain at present-day Detroit, Michigan. He was severely criticized by his superiors, however, for bad judgment during an Indian attack, and apparently deserted his post as a result. Nevertheless, his knowledge of the Indian tribes and their territories was of such great value to the French that he was pardoned.

He then had an affair with a married woman (the daughter of a Frenchman and an Indian woman); separated from her in about 1709; and in 1712 married the daughter of the chief of the Missouria tribe, by whom he had children. Bourgmont went to Paris in 1721, where he was honored for his explorations and his reports. He married a French woman in Normandy but did not end his relationship with his Missouria wife. Bourgmont always had a lively eye for the ladies, however, and soon had an affair, and a son, by an Apache woman.

He also maintained close contact with officials in France, and in 1725 he was authorized to invite some Indian chiefs and then accompanied them to Paris. After seeing the sights of Paris, the Indians and Bourgmont's Missouria wife all returned to North America. Bourgmont and his French wife remained in Normandy, however, where he was ennobled with the title of *écuyer* ("squire"). He died in France in 1734.

The first historian of New France was the French Jesuit priest, scholar of Japanese culture, and explorer of the Great Lakes François Xavier de Charlevoix (1682–1761).[3]

He was sent out from Quebec by the French government in 1721, with secret orders to try to locate the Passage to the Pacific. As a cover story, he was instructed to explain, if asked, that he was merely undertaking an inspection tour of the Jesuit missions on the western frontier.

Traveling by canoe, he went up the St. Lawrence River, crossed the Great Lakes, and eventually entered the Illinois River. Unable to make any progress further west by canoe, he then followed the Mississippi River down to New Orleans and Biloxi, where he ended his North American explorations in 1722.

After returning to France, he told his superiors that there were two possible routes to the Pacific. The first, he said, was via the Missouri River, whose source, he thought, must be very close to the sea. The second route required establishing a mission in Sioux territory, from which, he believed, it would be possible to contact Indian tribes living much further to the west. His superi-

9. Taking Great Pains to Get Along with the Indians 63

ors, however, showed no interest in trying to set up a mission in a region so hostile to the French, so his ideas came to naught.[4] He then returned to the quiet life of a scholar in France and never traveled again.

However, his *Journal Historique* (*Historical Journal*), published in 1744, described the North American lands he had seen; the customs of the Indian tribes there; and summarized his interviews with Indians and traders. His notes on the local geography were later used to improve regional maps. Charlevoix is thus often considered to have been the first historian of New France. He was not a long-suffering saint, however, and is said to have complained loudly and at length about the dangers, the discomforts, and the disagreeable companions that were the unavoidable realities of his protracted canoe journeys.[5]

The first European to reach present-day North Dakota and the upper Missouri River was the French-Canadian military officer, fur trader, and explorer Pierre Gaultier de Varrenes, Sieur de La Vérendrye (1685–1749).[6]

As the last of the great French explorers of North America, La Vérendrye ranged from Lake Superior to the mouth of the Saskatchewan River in Alberta, Canada. He was also the first to visit the Mandan villages near what is now Bismarck, North Dakota. His two sons (see below) made their own way to Wyoming, where they were the first Europeans to see the Rocky Mountains north of New Mexico.

La Vérendrye's own travels arose from two grave concerns of French officials. First, they worried that if France failed to undertake further explorations, the Indians living west of Lake Superior would have no choice but to begin trade with the British. Second, the French feared that these same Indians would then be motivated to help the British find an easy route across the continent to the Pacific (Europeans were always dreaming of this non-existent interior sea) that would give them access to the riches of China.[7]

In the 1740s, La Vérendrye's sons explored the region lying west of Lake Superior and established trading posts there. Largely thanks to Vérendrye and his boys, the frontiers of New France were appreciably extended: they now stretched west to North Dakota, and northwest to Fort á la Corne near the forks of the Saskatchewan River.

It should be noted here that the Treaty of Utrecht (1713) had prohibited the French from harvesting any furs around Hudson Bay itself, but they managed to bypass this annoying restriction by trading instead *northwest* of Lake Superior. La Vérendrye set up a string of eight trading posts in western Canada east of the Rockies. Undoubtedly dreaming of the Passage, he named them the "Posts of the Western Sea." They helped French fur traders to compete with the outposts of the Hudson's Bay Company.

La Vérendrye also built Fort La Reine on the north bank of the Assiniboine River, near what is now Portage La Prairie, Manitoba, to serve as his headquarters during his search for the Western Sea.

A word about his sons is in order now. In 1742, he sent his sons—Francis, known as the Chevalier, i.e., "knight," and Louis-Joseph—further west to look for the Passage. They got as far as the Black Hills in western South Dakota and may even have reached the Big Horn Range in northern Wyoming.

En route, the local Indians regaled them with stories of "very lofty mountains" further to the west, e.g., the Canadian Rockies, but since these mountains did not tally with the mental geography of the low-lying Passage that these young men had uppermost in their minds, they did not believe the Indians. What is certain, however, is that, on their way back, they did bury a lead tablet near Fort La Reine.

Quite remarkably, this tablet was unearthed in 1913 by a 14-year-old schoolgirl named Hattie May Foster. It is now on display at the South Dakota Cultural Center in Pierre and has two inscriptions on it, one in Latin and, on the reverse side, the other in French. Translated, they read as follows:

> (Latin). In the twenty-sixth year of the reign of Louis XV, the most illustrious Lord, the Lord Marquis of Beauharnois being Viceroy, Peter Gaultier de La Vérendrye placed this.
> (French). Placed by the Chevalier de la Vérendrye, witness Louis-Joseph, La Londette and A. Miotte, the 30th of March 1743.[8]

In 1743 La Vérendrye resigned and returned to France, while his sons remained as traders in the west. Reappointed to his old post in 1746, he was planning another expedition (this time up the Saskatchewan River) when he died in 1749. Shortly before his death, he was awarded the prestigious Order of St. Louis.

Exploring primarily in United States were the two French Canadian Mallet brothers—Pierre Antoine Mallet (1700–c. 1750) and Paul Mallet (?–1753)—*voyageurs* and traders who were the first Europeans known to have crossed the Great Plains from east to west, i.e., from Kaskaskia, Illinois, to Santa Fe, New Mexico.[9]

The Mallet brothers led three expeditions there in an effort to establish some trade relations with the Spaniards in Santa Fe, but they, as other French traders before them, were consistently rebuffed.

On their first expedition in 1739, together with seven companions, they made their way from Fort de Chartres in Illinois to Santa Fe. Unluckily, when crossing a river en route, they lost all the nine pack-horses carrying the goods they had planned to sell. Indeed, they hardly had enough clothing to wear themselves when they finally got to Santa Fe. The loss of their goods turned out to be a blessing for them, however.

Because Spain maintained a very strict monopoly on foreign trade, any goods on which Spanish taxes had not been paid were considered contraband and were duly seized. To make matters even worse, the Spanish of New Mexico also considered all foreign traders simply to be spies for the French or British governments or French or British businesses.

9. Taking Great Pains to Get Along with the Indians 65

For these reasons, the Mallets were immediately ordered to appear before Spanish authorities and to explain what they were doing in New Mexico. These authorities were very cautious bureaucrats, however, so rather than judging the Mallets then and there, they first sought instructions from their viceroy in the very distant Mexico City.

It took nine months for these instructions to reach Santa Fe. When they finally did arrive (in 1740), the Spanish officials there were ordered to expel the Mallets and not let any other traders into New Mexico unless they could first prove that they had the Spanish government's permission to trade there.

By this time, some of Mallet's men had married local Spanish women and did not want to leave Santa Fe. The Mallets themselves and the rest of their party, however, were free to make their way back to French territory.

By mid–June 1740, the Mallets and two Canadian companions—using only their hunting knives, since they had no other tools—built and launched two elm-bark canoes into an east-flowing tributary of the Arkansas River, now known as the Canadian River. These fragile craft carried them safely all the way downstream to New Orleans, where they promptly told others about the potential profits they believed could be made from the Santa Fe trade. (Due both to Indian attacks and Spanish hostility toward foreign traders, however, the Santa Fe trade would not actually begin until very much later, i.e., not until 1822.[10])

Nevertheless, Jean-Baptiste Le Moyne de Bienville, the governor of Louisiana, was sufficiently impressed by the prospects for trade that he sent the Mallets out again towards Santa Fe, but this time armed with documents testifying to their status as trade emissaries of the French.

French colonial officials were interested not only in trade with New Mexico but also in the more remote possibility that France might be able to seize the rich Spanish silver mines that lay somewhere south of Santa Fe. Bad luck struck again, however: the Mallets' canoe was swamped in the Red River; their documents were waterlogged and ruined; and they were forced to abort their trip.

Never one to admit defeat, ten years later, in 1750, Pierre Mallet set out yet again for Santa Fe. This time he ran into even more trouble: the Comanches stole his trade goods and his documents. The Spanish therefore immediately arrested him as an illegal trader as soon as he got to Santa Fe, charging him with selling guns to the Comanches.

From there, the last disaster was that he was sent to Spain for interrogation. At this point (about 1751), he vanishes entirely from the historical record, and a good guess is that he died while still a prisoner in Spain. His brother Paul died in Louisiana in 1753. In the end, all that was left of the Mallets were three place-names: the Canadian River, Bayou Mallet, and Bois Mallet (both of the latter in Louisiana).

• • •

The dramatic rise of the Comanches to regional power in the American Southwest is reflected very clearly in a Spanish map of 1778, which states the following:

> The Comanche nation some years ago appeared first to the Yutes [now spelled "Utes"]. They said they left the northern border, breaking through several [Indian] nations and the said Yutes took them to trade with the Spaniards, bringing a multitude of dogs loaded with their hides and tents.
> They acquired horses and weapons of iron, and they have had so much practice in the management of horses and arms, that they excel all other tribes in agility and skill, making themselves lords and masters of all the buffalo country, wresting it from the Apache Nation, who were then the most extensive known in America, destroying many Nations of them and those which remain have been pushed to the frontiers of the Provinces of Our King.[11]

Jacques Legardeur de Saint-Pierre (1701–1755) is an excellent example of the French policy of taking great pains to learn about, and get along peacefully with, the local Indians. An officer in the French colonial regular troops, he was also an explorer and an interpreter of Indian languages.[12] He is also remembered for having made a very favorable impression in 1753 on a young British Virginia major named George Washington, who met him at a frontier fort and who described Legardeur as follows: "He is an elderly Gentleman, and has much the Air of a Soldier."[13]

While Legardeur was still in his teens, he joined his father, who had spent many years in the *pays d'en haut* and who founded a trading post near what is now Ashland, Wisconsin. His later reputation as a gifted linguist of Indian languages and life was noted in several accounts from Montreal. In 1732, a French governor reported that Legardeur had been living in the west for nine years and that he "Knows the savage language better than the savages, as they themselves admit."[14] As a result, he would become one of the foremost advisers on French affairs in New France.

Legardeur was also good at maintaining friendly relations with other French explorers, who could be quick to take offense at any slights—whether real or imagined. In 1750, for example, Governor La Jonquière appointed Legardeur to be the commander in the west and thus to take charge of leading the French search for the Passage.

This project had initially been headed by Pierre Gaultier de Varennes et de la Vérendrye, who had died in 1749 while planning a new expedition to find it. Two of his sons had also been actively involved in this project, however, and they now took great offense that Legardeur Saint-Pierre should have, in effect, been promoted over their heads. They now demanded some public recognition in the search and, if the Passage was discovered, their fair share in the glory of finding it.

Legardeur diplomatically defused this tricky situation, however, by publically recognizing their past role and by apologizing to them. Although the Passage was, of course, never found, in 1771 the French did establish a western post, either at Fort La Jonquière in northeastern Saskatchewan, or less likely, perhaps even further west, i.e., within sight of the Rockies.

On balance, it can safely be said that few if any of the professional soldiers in colonial France could equal Legardeur's unique combination of bravery, intelligence, dedication, and linguistic and diplomatic skills. He was finally killed in action in 1755 near Lake George, New York, while leading a force of Canadian militiamen and hundreds of Indian warriors in a battle against the British.

10

Descended from Five Generations of "waryers" [warriors]

Anthony Henday (fl. 1750–1762), whose explorations were authorized and funded by the Hudson's Bay Company, initially worked for the company's outpost at York Factory.[1]

He was one of the first European fur traders to explore the interior of the Canadian northwest, specifically the huge and ill-defined region west of Hudson's Bay that was known as "Rupert's Land." Between about 1668 and 1808, a fair number of other British fur trading and exploring expeditions did travel through Rupert's Land, but most of them will not be discussed here because much of the region lies too far north of this book's primary east-to-west focus.

In 1754, setting out from York Factory in canoes with a party of Cree Indians, Henday reached the Saskatchewan River via the Hayes River and then, partly by canoe and partially on foot, made his way as far west as present-day Red Deer, Alberta. There he could have seen the high peaks of the Rockies.

He did in fact see the enormous buffalo herds of the Canadian prairies. These animals were so numerous, he says, that he watched Indians kill buffalo for their delectable tongues alone, leaving the rest of carcasses for the wolves.[2] This was an unusual sight, because explorers of the frontier usually report that the Indians took pains not to kill more game than they could eat or could process for future use (e.g., by drying the meat in the sun and then making pemmican of it).

Henday spent that winter with the Crees at a large encampment in the Red Deer area, returning to York Factory, now laden with prime furs, in 1755. He made another trip to Red Deer in 1759, spending much time with the Blackfeet Indians. Because he felt that the Hudson's Bay Company was not paying him enough for his efforts, he cut his ties with them and ultimately returned to England in about 1762.

10. Descended from Five Generations of "waryers" [warriors] 69

Samuel Hearne (1745–1792), also an English explorer, fur trader, writer, and naturalist, was the first European to travel overland across northern Canada, via the Coppermine River, to the Arctic Ocean.[3] He took part in three expeditions into the Canadian Arctic, trying and failing to discover the fabled Passage.

Guided by a Chipewyan chief named Matonabee in 1770–1772, Hearne traveled northwest from Hudson Bay to the Coppermine River, following a map of the route the chief drew for him.[4] Although most of Hearne's activities took place too far north to justify discussion in this book, he is significant in the history of the Hudson's Bay Company for having built its first trading post, known as Cumberland House in 1774. Located deep in the interior, it was thus also the first permanent settlement in present-day Saskatchewan.

Located on Cumberland Lake (a tributary of the Saskatchewan River) about 175 miles west of Lake Winnipeg, Cumberland House soon became the most important of the Hudson's Bay Company's western posts primarily because it competed directly with the independent French traders who had been bartering with the local Indians by going directly to their villages.

These traders had been exchanging goods with the Indians, conveniently close to where the fur-bearing animals themselves lived, and the new pattern of trade effectively choked off the traditional flow of furs that had previously gone directly to the Hudson's Bay Company.

This kind of itinerant peddling, known in the French of the day as *en dérouine* trade, required the traders to sally forth and negotiate with the Indians in their own villages, which were located far away from the traditional trading posts. The resulting sharp decrease in the flow of furs into the posts forced the Hudson's Bay Company to abandon its long-standing and relatively comfortable "wait by Bay" approach, which was now being reviled by its critics as a very ineffective "sleep by the frozen sea" policy.[5]

The bottom line was that the Hudson's Bay Company soon realized that it had to expand westward—and very vigorously, too—if it wanted to stay in business. Cumberland House, accessible from several watersheds and located close to three tribes of fur-rich Indians, quickly became a key Hudson's Bay Company trading center.

In fact, the rival Montreal-based North West Company was forced to build its own post nearby, simply to remain competitive. In 1821 the two forts were merged. Cumberland House eventually became the residence of the governor of Rupert's Land and is now preserved as part of Cumberland House National Historical Park.

Hearne himself took part in three expeditions into the Arctic, trying and failing to discover the fabled Passage. In time, he retired to England and wrote *A Journey from Prince of Wales's Fort in Hudson's Bay to the Northern Ocean*. It was published three years after his death in 1792 and was one of the most accurate early-contact descriptions of Indian life in northern Canada.

In 1769, a year before Hearne began his explorations in northern Canada, the Spanish explorer and colonizer Gaspar de Portolá (1723?–1784?) was named commander in chief of a Spanish expedition into Alta (Upper) California that had two important assignments: to look for good harbors for Spanish ships, and to set up missions in order to convert the local Indians to Christianity.[6] Working closely with the indefatigable missionary Fray Junípero Serra (1713–1784), it was Portolá who was initially responsible for the permanent settlement of today's California. In what can be called the "post-exploration era," however, Serra and his fellow Spanish Franciscan missionaries eventually built more than 20 missions in California.[7]

Spain had learned from its ambassador in Moscow that Russia was increasing its involvement along the Pacific coast of North America. In 1768, the Spanish in what is now Mexico therefore agreed that California must be kept out of Russian hands by installing Spanish presidios and missions there. This process began in 1769 and continued until 1823.

Portolá first tried to find Monterey Bay, which the earlier Spanish explorer Vizcaíno had mistakenly described in too-glowing terms as a fine and sheltered harbor. The reason for Portolá's failure was that thick fog had obscured the Santa Cruz shoreline, making the choppy waters of its bay look just like the open sea itself. In fact, there was no natural harbor there at all—only what modern sailors would call "an open roadstead," i.e., a place where, under good conditions, a ship could consider mooring.

In any case, Portolá then decided that he had not gone far enough, so he led the expedition further north. When he reached Half Moon Bay (about 25 miles south of San Francisco), however, he realized, from sketchy information he had about the coastline, that he was now much too far north. This mistake, however, turned out to be a great blessing in disguise. In November 1769, when he sent his sergeant and a small party of men up into the nearby hills to the top of 1,200-foot-high Sweeney Ridgetop, they became the first non-Indians ever to see San Francisco Bay.

As Father Juan Crespi, the explorer-diarist of the expedition, put it, this enormous bay—"a large arm of the sea"—was so big that "doubtless not only all the navies of the Catholic Monarch, but those of all Europe might lie within the harbor."[8] It was the finest natural harbor along the Pacific coast and, as such, would offer a solid foothold for further Spanish expansion in California. However, because of the thick fog that often still hides the narrow entrance to San Francisco Bay, the first Spanish ship would not actually sail into it until 1775.

Father Crespi also reported, in 1769, that local Indians told him that

> They had heard of the sailings of the packets [i.e., the ships of the expedition] to the coast and channel of Santa Barbara; they drew on the ground the shape of the channel with its islands, marking the route of the ships.[9]

10. Descended from Five Generations of "waryers" [warriors]

That same year, too, Father Crespi was the first to describe the site of what would later become the city of Los Angeles. He wrote:

> We entered a very spacious valley, well grown with cottonwoods and alders, among which ran a beautiful river. The plain where the river runs is very extensive. It has good land for planting all kinds of grain and seeds, and is the most suitable site of all we have seen for a mission, for it has all the requisites for a large settlement...
>
> After crossing the river we entered a large vineyard of wild grapes and an infinity of rose bushes in full bloom. All the soil is black and loamy, and is capable of producing every kind of grain and fruit that may be planted.[10]

On the way back to San Diego, the food supplies for the expedition ran so low that Portolá wrote:

> I ordered that at the end of each day's march, one of the weak old mules which carried our baggage and ourselves, should be killed [for food]...we shut our eyes and fell to on the scaly mule (what misery!) like hungry lions. We ate twelve in as many days.... At last we entered San Diego, smelling frightfully of mules.[11]

The Franciscan priest Fray Francisco Thomás Garcés (1741?–1781) was an early and very vigorous explorer of frontier lands in the west, especially those crossed by the Old Spanish Trail, which linked Santa Fe and Los Angeles.[12]

Because of the many intervening deserts, canyons, and hostile Indians, however, this trail did not run directly east to west between these two destinations. Instead, it formed a giant parabola, swinging from Santa Fe northwest into central Utah, where its northernmost point was near today's Castle Dale, Utah, about 115 miles southeast of Salt Lake City, and then dipping southwest to Los Angeles.

In order to find a way to get by land to the California missions, in 1774 Fray Garcés set out from the Yuma Indian villages along the Gila River in southern Arizona. He then made his way north to the Mojave Indian villages along the Colorado River, where he was given four guides who led him along Indian trails to the Mojave River near Soda Lake, California. He followed this river for several days, finally reaching Mission San Gabriel Arcángel.

Fray Garcés was the first foreigner to report on the Mojave Indians. He was quite astonished to learn how physically tough they were, being able to endure cold, hunger, and thirst remarkably well. He wrote that "the men go entirely naked, and in a country so cold as this [in the winter] this is well worthy of compassion."

Moreover, the Indians told him that they routinely crossed the desert into California, in order to bring highly-prized seashells back to their homeland, but carried nothing to eat nor any bows and arrows for hunting. They explained to Fray Garcés that they had no need for these items because they could "endure hunger and thirst for four days" during this crossing.[13]

A fellow missionary, Fray Font, explained why Fray Garcés was successful with these Indians:

Father Garcés is so well fitted to get along with the Indians and to go among them that he appears to be but an Indian himself. Like Indians he is phlegmatic in everything...

And although the foods of the Indians are nasty and dirty as those outlandish people themselves, the father eats them with great gusto and says that they are good for the stomach and very fine. In short, God has created him, as I see it, solely for the purpose of seeking out these unhappy, ignorant, and rustic people.[14]

• • •

Another explorer and fur trader whose later maps of the Canadian Athabasca region owed much to knowledge gained from the local Indians was Peter Pond (1740–1807). Although born and died in Milford Connecticut, Pond lived his life far from home as an army officer, sailor, fur trader, explorer, map maker, and writer.[15] The most memorable thing about him, however, is that he was also an exceedingly violent and eccentric man, coming from a family (according to his own account and his own spelling) well known for five generations as "all waryers [warriors] Ither by Sea or Land."[16]

From 1773 to 1775, Pond had trapped successfully in Minnesota and Wisconsin. However, the Indian wars along the upper Mississippi, coupled with reports of a great treasure trove of furs to be had for the taking in the Lake Athabasca drainage system in northern Saskatchewan and Alberta, encouraged him to try his luck there.

Therefore, in 1778 and using Grand Portage (on the western end of Lake Superior) rather than distant Montreal as his supply base, he led a party of 16 canoemen in four canoes into northern Saskatchewan and crossed a nearly 12-mile-long portage, whose sides were so steep that it took him fully eight days to get his men, food, and trade goods over them.

Finally, however, he and his team succeeded, and thus left the Hudson Bay hydrographic basin behind them. He was now well-positioned to open up the fur trade in the Athabasca region itself. It is clear that Pond did very well in the fur trade: indeed, it has been estimated that in 1779 he had 80,000 fine beaver pelts on hand, i.e., about 60 tons of furs.[17]

Pond's violent temper came to the fore, however, when he was wintering in 1781–1782 at a northern lake. He later claimed that a rival fur trader had deliberately insulted him there: the result was a duel with pistols.

Pond said later, "The abuse was too grate. We met the next morning eairly and discharged pistols, in which the pore fellow was unfortenat." The rival trader was shot dead, and this murder occurred in a region so far beyond the reach of the law that Pond claimed he had reported the killing but that "thare was none to prosecute me."[18]

In 1783, Pond explored the waterways around Lake Athabasca and learned from local Indians about the big lakes and turbulent rivers of the region. Armed with this knowledge, during the winter of 1784–185 he drew up a map that showed the major rivers and lakes stretching west from the Great

10. Descended from Five Generations of "waryers" [warriors]

Lakes and Hudson Bay to the Rocky Mountains, and those extending toward the Arctic.

His map had two features that would have been of great interest to contemporary travelers. First, it showed the Rockies (incorrectly, of course) as consisting only of a single range of low and, by implication, easily crossed mountains that might not be too far from the shores of the Pacific. Second, it also depicted a non-existent great river that sprang from a source somewhere on the western side of the Rockies and conveniently ran all the way to the ocean—i.e., the long-sought Passage.

Although Pond sent one copy of his map to Congress, and another to the Lieutenant Governor of Quebec requesting funds for an expedition by Pond to explore the remote parts of the northwest, no action was taken on it by either government, so no travelers ever saw it.

In the meantime, however, he was involved in yet another murder. During the winter of 1786–1787, Pond had become a member of the North West Company. At a meeting in the Peace River, he quarreled with John Ross, a rival fur trader. During a brawl, Ross was killed by a gunshot—said to have been fired, on Pond's orders, by a Canadian trapper.

This second murder forced the North West Company to fire Pond and to replace him with Alexander Mackenzie, who will be discussed here later. Pond himself sold his shares in the company and returned to his native Connecticut, where he died, forgotten and in poverty, in 1807. Much later, however, his maps would earn him international if posthumous attention. He was a pioneer of the last great fur-bearing region of North America, and the first to outline the general features of Canada's Mackenzie River system.

11

A Famous Explorer Follows a "grease trail" to the Pacific Ocean

Pedro Vial (c. 1746–1814), a Frenchman in the employ of Spain, explored the American Southwest at will, on foot or on horseback, for 26 years.[1] Often traveling with only one companion, he was the last of the great Spanish explorers of this region and got along exceptionally well with the Comanches and other hostile tribes. In so doing, he blazed what would later become the Santa Fe Trail.

His major pathfinding explorations linked Santa Fe to such then-distant cities as San Antonio, Texas; Natchitoches, Louisiana; and St. Louis, Missouri. Vial gave invaluable advice to his Spanish employers, who simply could not understand why, even after great efforts, they had made peace with one band of Comanches, they would then be attacked by another band.

Vial explained that the reason was the Comanches' highly decentralized life style, under which every warrior was, in effect, his own lord and master. Vial told them:

> The Comanche Nation has no fixed villages because they have many horses, because of which it is necessary to find places to pasture them, and which have buffalo and deer, for that is their food, and clothing, and with which they make the tents in which they live from buffalo hides which they make white, and very strong, useful, and durable.
>
> Their *rancherías* [small-scale Indian settlements] are organized by the captains, each endeavoring to have his own [*ranchería*], they do not have a fixed number of subjects, but only those who can adjust to the spirit of the captain.[2]

In 1788, Vial left Santa Fe for Natchitoches, journeying via the Texas Panhandle and the Red River. From Natchitoches, he pressed on to San Antonio and then made a second trip to Santa Fe, traveling an estimated 2,377 miles in fourteen months.

Subsequently, over successive summers from 1792 to 1793, he pioneered the future route of the Santa Fe Trail, making a round trip estimated at 2,279

11. A Famous Explorer Follows a "grease trail" to the Pacific Ocean 75

miles between Santa Fe and St. Louis. This feat proved to American businessmen that the distance between the Louisiana Territory and New Orleans was not in fact insurmountable. Indeed, Vial claimed that, had he not been captured en route and held by hostile Indians, he could actually have made this trip in only 25 days.

Resting on his laurels, Vial left the Spanish in 1798 and went to live with the Comanches. He returned to Santa Fe in 1803, however, and died there in 1814.

• • •

The first European trader-explorer to come to the Pacific Northwest looking for sea otter furs was James Hanna (?—1787).[3]

He sailed from the port of Macao on the China coast in 1785, bound for Nootka Sound on the western side of British Columbia's Vancouver Island. There he traded iron bars for furs and skins—so successfully that one year later he sold his peltries in Canton for the tidy profit of 20,000 Spanish dollars.

He then sailed back to Nootka to trade for more furs but discovered that, in his absence, two other ships had anchored there and had already collected nearly all the furs the local Indians then had on hand. This forced Hanna to continue sailing farther north along the coast.

In the meantime, however, he had certainly put Nootka on the map. During the rest of the 1780s, it became a very busy place as more European and American trading ships moored there. The Indians offered these sailors prime sea otter pelts; in return, they wanted such desirable foreign goods as sheets of copper, heavy blue cloth, muskets, powder, and shot. As a result of this bustling trade, prices increased: the cost of one sea otter's skin, for example, rose from one musket to five muskets during the late 19th century.[4]

Exploration of the Canadian Northwest continued with Alexander Mackenzie (1764–1820), one of Canada's greatest explorers. A Scotsman best known for achieving the first east-to-west crossing of North America north of Mexico, he traversed what is now Canada, reaching the shores of the Pacific in 1793.[5]

Earlier, in 1789, Mackenzie had led what is now known as the Mackenzie River expedition to the Arctic Ocean. The Mackenzie River—the longest river system in Canada and the second-longest in North America—is named after him.

On his subsequent and more famous 1792–1793 Peace River expedition, he managed to reach the Pacific coast in 1793 at Bella Coola, British Columbia, thereby beating the American explorers Louis and Clark (who will be discussed later) by 12 years. He used Indian guides and maps on both his Arctic and his Pacific travels.[6]

Mackenzie set out on this latter voyage from Chipewyan in the autumn of 1792 in a 25-foot canoe, together with six French *voyageurs* and two Indian interpreter-guides in other canoes. They all paddled up the Peace River to what is now Fort Fork in west-central Alberta. There they wintered until May 1793 and then pressed on to the Fraser River, which they mistook for the Columbia.

Abandoning their canoes and beginning to walk, they turned west and marched for 200 miles, finally reaching the Bella Coola River. This was not an easy trek. As Mackenzie wrote in 1801:

> We began our journey about twelve noon, the commencement of which was a steep ascent of about a mile; it lay along a well-beaten path, but the country through which it led was rugged and ridgy, and full of wood.
>
> When we were in a state of extreme heat [i.e., they were sweating profusely], from the toil of our journey, the rain came on, and continued all evening, and even when it ceased the underwood continued its dripping upon us.[7]

Friendly Indians gave Mackenzie some invaluable advice, warning him that the Fraser Canyon was unnavigable and was the home of hostile tribes. He was therefore told to follow a "grease trail" that would lead him to the Bella Coola River and thence to the sea. (A "grease trail" was an overland route used by Pacific Northwest Indians for trade, particularly for trade in processed eulachon oil, locally known as "grease," which was used as a condiment, much like butter.)

Other friendly Indians on the Bella Coola River kindly transported Mackenzie's expedition downstream in their canoes, and on July 17, 1793, he recorded in his journal that he "could perceive the termination of the river, and its discharge into a narrow arm of the sea." This was the North Bentick Arm, an inlet of the Pacific Ocean, and Mackenzie in effect left a "calling card" of his visit, reporting that

> I now mixed up some vermillion in melted grease, and inscribed, in large characters, on the South-East face of the rock on which we had slept last night, this brief memorial—"Alexander Mackenzie, from Canada, by land, the twenty-second day of July, one thousand seven hundred and ninety three."[8] [The inscription was later made permanent and can still be seen there today.]

During this expedition, by following a route based both on his own trailblazing instincts and on the advice of his Indian guides, he covered 1,200 miles in 74 days, averaging about 20 miles a day over very rough country. He ended this trip at Fort Fork in May 1794; passed an uneventful winter at Fort Chipewyan; later served as a senior North West Company partner in Montreal; and then returned to Britain in 1812.

While in Montreal, in 1801 he published the journals of his two exploring expeditions, under the fulsome title of *Voyages from Montreal on the River St. Lawrence through the Continent of North America to the Frozen and Pacific Oceans in the Years 1789 and 1793 with a Preliminary Account of the Rise, Prog-*

ress, and Present State of the Fur Trade of That Country Illustrated with Maps. Happily, this work is now cited by scholars simply as *Voyages*.

Thomas Jefferson read this book in 1802, and it helped him plan the great cross-country journey of Lewis and Clark. Moreover, in geopolitical terms, it also alerted him to the real threat to the United States posed by any British plan to dominate the frontier West by monopolizing the fur trade.

Mackenzie wrote:

> By opening this intercourse between the Atlantic and Pacific Oceans, and forming regular establishments through the interior, and at both extremes, as well as along the coasts and islands, the entire command of the fur trade of North America might be obtained, except that portion of it which the Russians have in the Pacific. To this may be added the fishing in both seas and the markets of the four quarters of the globe.[9]

As if this were not enough, Mackenzie also argued that the lands along the Columbia River, which was imagined by some to be the Passage, would be ideally suited for colonization by industrious British traders and farmers. Jefferson understood very well that if this settlement should ever come about, it would doom his own dream of a United States literally stretching from sea to sea.

Thomas Jefferson also carefully studied the expedition of 1795–1797 up the Missouri River by the Scotsman James Mackay and the Welshman John Thomas Evans. In geographical terms, it was the most significant European or American venture out onto the northern Great Plains before the coming of Lewis and Clark.[10]

This expedition consisted of 32 men shoehorned into four shallow-draft boats, i.e., barges and pirogues[11] powered by paddles and, when necessary, by poles, that were filled with goods to barter with the Indians in exchange for their furs. In 1795, Mackay established Fort Carlos IV, i.e., Fort Charles, named in honor of Charles IV of Spain, located about a mile from the Omaha Indian village near what is now Homer, Nebraska. This little trading post was set on a hill in a favorable spot.

Mackay confidently described it as follows:

> The location of the fort seems to have been prepared by nature. It is in a commanding district, which rises for a circumference of about one thousand feet. It looks on the shore of this river, as if to command the rest of the area. I have established my settlement and my fort there, although at a distance from the woods; however, the horses of the Prince [i.e., the local Indian chief] are at my service.[12]

The bad news, however, was yet to come. The bottom line was that the expedition lost a good deal of money for its sponsor, the Missouri Company, which had been set up by the Spanish after 1792 to regulate trade in the newly-opened Illinois Country. However, the Spaniards simply could not deliver enough goods both to the upriver Indians to win their support and to make an adequate profit at the same time. Thus the Missouri Company went bankrupt in 1797, leaving over $100,000 in debts. Bad management, stiff competition from British traders, and the shoddy goods it offered for sale all turned out to be insurmountable problems.

There was, however, a little good news, too. Mackay and Evens eventually returned to St. Louis with a much better knowledge of the tribes living in the upper reaches of the Missouri and had learned much more about the course of the river itself. Moreover, in 1787, drawing on information he had gathered from the Mandan Indians, Evens drew up a manuscript map that mentioned for the first time both the Yellowstone River region and the falls of the Missouri. Since the Yellowstone region is so unique (in 1872 it became the first national park in the world), some of the early explorations there are summarized in Appendix 4 of this book.

Although the Missouri Company went bankrupt in 1797, the North West Company of Montreal was doing exceptionally well, partially due to the skills of one of its most renowned explorers and cartographers, David Thompson (1770–1857). Lauded for having descended the Columbia River in 1811, thus proving that it connected to the Pacific, Thompson came to Canada from London in 1784 as a 14-year-old apprentice with the Hudson's Bay Company.[13]

Working from the settlement of Churchill on Hudson Bay, Thompson explored and trapped as far west as Lake Athabasca in present-day Alberta. By 1790 he undertook a serious study of map-mapmaking under the tutelage of the Hudson's Bay Company's chief surveyor. As a result, Thompson would be able to provide the first accurate depiction of Canada's western regions.

On May 23, 1797, setting out from his post at Reindeer Lake in the Churchill District, he quit the Hudson's Bay Company and joined the "Company of Merchants from Canada," i.e., the North West Company. By this time he had already traveled nearly 9,000 miles along the rivers and lakes of the interior. As a trained mathematician and astronomer, he made careful geographical surveys and recordings of climatic and other natural events. In so doing, he had added important information to the geographical lore being collected by the Hudson's Bay Company in its London archives.

He explored and mapped routes to North West Company's chain of posts lying east of the Rockies in 1797. The next year, while using snowshoes and dog teams to trade with the Indians of North Dakota and Manitoba, Thompson made this remarkable entry in his journal on 22 January 1798:

> A most terrible Storm with thick snow and excessively high Drift.... The Dogs are drifted over with Snow [so] that we walk on them without seeing them, such is the effects of the Storm and Drift, that it is almost as dark as Night, and we cannot actually see distinct 10 yards before us ... it is as much as we can [do] to Keep from being buried under the Snow, it is without Doubt the worse day I ever saw in my Life. We

have no Meat, fortunately yesterday I picked up a Marrow Bone of a Buffaloe which had been pretty well Knawed by a Wolf—this is my day's allowance [of food].[14]

Known for the precision of his surveys, he discovered the headwaters of the Saskatchewan River and, beginning in 1806, explored the mountain passes west of the Saskatchewan and Athabasca rivers. The result of these journeys was the founding, in 1807, of the North West Company's Kootenay House, the first fur-trading post located on the Columbia River.

In 1811, Thompson built a canoe big enough and strong enough for him and his party to risk the tumultuous descent of the Columbia River itself, beginning at Kettle Falls on today's British Columbia-Washington border. The current was very fast: he and his men were carried along so rapidly that on their first day they traveled 70 miles and could see snow-covered Mount Hood.

At The Dalles, a key trading settlement[15] located on the Columbia River in north-central Oregon state, the wide river was squeezed by the landscape into a foaming width of only 60 yards. Thompson wrote of this sight:

> Imagination can hardly form an idea of the working of this immense body of water under such compression, raging and hissing as if it were alive.[16]

Since no canoe could possibly survive such a maelstrom, Thompson and his party immediately steered for shore, and then carried the canoe and their gear safely down a mile-long portage paralleling the rapids.

They finally reached the Pacific on 15 July 1811—ironically, just a few weeks after John Jacob Astor's ship-borne party of Americans had founded Fort Astoria and had thus established an American foothold in the Pacific Northwest. Although Thompson was later criticized for failing to win the "race to the Columbia's mouth," his orders had never instructed him to get there first.

In any case, he then retired to the Montreal area; completed his master map of western Canada; and surveyed the U.S.-Canadian borderline from the St. Lawrence River to Lake of the Woods, the latter being located near the center of the continent. All told, by the end of his career he had explored an area of about 50,000 miles of western Canada and the northwestern United States. His maps were the most detailed and most precisely accurate of his time.

12

The Great Lewis and Clark Expedition

Before looking at the very successful Lewis and Clark expedition, it may first be of some interest to consider a more typical "marginal" wilderness experience—one that, in the following case, was marked by both modest successes and failures, and which has now been long forgotten except to specialists in the field.

In 1802, because of his family's relative poverty and his own immature daydreams of money and glory, a 15-year-old English boy named George Nelson (1786–1859) signed a contract near Montreal to become a clerk with a major Canadian fur trading firm known as the XY Company.[1] It operated in the remote, far-flung regions west of the Great Lakes, e.g., southwest of Grand Portage, the famous trading post located at the western end of Lake Superior.

Nelson was exceptionally well-educated for his time by his schoolmaster father but because he was a timid and very passive young man, he could not stand up for himself in the rough-and-tumble of the fur trade business. For example, he did not receive (and probably never even asked for) any hands-on professional guidance from his superiors, and as a result he was blamed for mistakes that were not his own fault.

He also let himself be pressured into marrying the daughter of a local Ojibwa Indian leader, even though he realized that his own boss, Sir Alexander Mackenzie, was very much opposed to his employees marrying Indian girls at such a tender age. The predictable net result was that Mackenzie had a very low opinion of Nelson and saw to it that promotions would never come his way.

Nelson was first posted to the Folle Avoine ("Wild Rice") district of western Wisconsin. His canoe journey there in 1802 marked the beginning of what would become for him a marginally-successful 20-year-long career as a clerk in the Canadian fur trade.

By about that time, the major fur trade routes formed an intricate interlinking network of waterways, portages, trading posts, and small forts. They

12. The Great Lewis and Clark Expedition

stretched west from Montreal to the Rocky Mountains; northwest from the Pembina, North Dakota, area to Fort Chipewyan on Lake Athabasca; and northeast from Pembina to York Factory on Hudson Bay.

The good news for the modern reader, however, is that since his most important duty was to keep accurate accounts of buying furs from and then selling manufactured items to the Indians and other customers, his extensive diaries, which cover the years from 1802 to 1836, are gold mines of information on the local fur trade itself. The quotation below is a good example.

It is set in Grand Portage, a trading post on the Pigeon River that was an important administrative center and access point for trade with the interior of south-central Canada. The portage itself was a nine-mile-long route between Lake Superior and a spot above the falls of the Pigeon River. It had 16 "pauses," i.e., well-established resting-points where canoemen could halt during the arduous process of transporting which required relying only on their own strong bodies, their heavy canoes and trade goods.

Nelson wrote:

> We were here for several days before anyone arrived either from Montreal or from the interior of the Country. I was placed in the Stores to Serve the people. At last they began to come in. All was business. Receiving Goods, corn, flour, port &c.&c. from Montreal and Mackinac [another trading post], & furs from the different wintering posts [outlying trading posts where some employees spent the winter months when snow and ice made travel too difficult].
>
> Gambling, feasting, dancing, drinking & fighting. After a couple of weeks to rest, [and] for the Winterers to give in [i.e., to submit] their returns & accounts, & to make up their outfits, they began to return again [to their remote posts], to run over the same ground, toils, labors, and dangers.
>
> But in this country, too, where every step was beset with difficulties of themselves sufficient to exert every faculty & try the nerve, even here the Demon of ambition followed us, blinded our better judgment, & sharpened our wits only to oppose, annoy & injure each other.
>
> One of our brigades [teams of canoemen], fitted out I believe for Fort de Prairies [on the Saskatchewan River], slept as usual at Portage le Perdrix [Partridge Portage, on the Pigeon River near the western end of the Grand Portage], only a few hundred yards from our Stores at the north end of the Grand Portage, where they feasted & got drunk upon the "régale" [i.e., a much-appreciated treat traditionally consisting of very strong rum], that was always given to them when they arrived from, or departed for, their winter quarters.
>
> When they arose the next morning they found thirty Kegs of High Wine [undiluted over-proof rum that would be diluted with water before being consumed or sold] containing 9 Gall[on]s ea. had all run out! Upon examination it was found that they had been bored with two gimlet holes each!
>
> The consternation & injury this occasioned may be imagined. Enquiries were set on foot & affidavits given in. No bible was to be found to swear upon. I lent mine, for the purpose, but never saw it after though I enquired diligently. These were called *witty*

tricks. Rumor gave that it was Benjamin Frobisher and [blank space] who bored the Kegs. It created an excessive bad feeling & led to retaliations some of which would have ended trajically but for providence, but nothing ever followed.[2]

Despite the frustrations of his professional life, Nelson's journals, letters, and reminiscences make an outstanding contribution to the record of fur-trade life and the culture of the American Indians.

The history and journals of Captain Meriwether Lewis (1774–1809) and his close friend, Second Lieutenant William Clark (1770–1838), which focus on their 1804–1806 expedition have already been mentioned several times in this book, but much more remains to be said about it. Officially known as the "Corps of Discovery Expedition," it is now the most famous expedition in American history and, indeed, it still stands high in the annals of world exploration.[3]

Why has this particular expedition captured the imagination of so many readers, while other equally exciting outdoor adventures have long been forgotten? Perhaps the best answer is the one given by the historian James P. Ronda, who has explained:

> The essential American experience has been the journey, the trek, the quest.... The Lewis and Clark Expedition has come to represent all American journeys. In the Corps of Discovery's progress across the continent, Americans see reflected thousands of individual passages into a new world.[4]

President Jefferson commissioned this expedition shortly after the 1803 Louisiana Purchase and gave it a variety of very difficult assignments. The chief of these were to map this newly-acquired territory; to find a practical route across the western half of what is now the United States; to establish an American presence there in order to deter Britain or other European powers from claiming it; to study the region's flora, fauna, geography, and climate; and, last but by no means least, to establish mutually-beneficial trade relationships with the local Indians.

Clark opened the journals of Lewis and Clark with the following sentence:

> I dispatched an express [i.e., a message sent by a fast rider] to Capt. Lewis at St. Louis, all our provisions Goods and equipage on Board a Boat of 22 oars a large Perouge of 71 oars a Second Perouge of 6 oars, Complete with Sails &c. &c. Men compd [i.e., they were furnished] with Powder [gunpowder] Cartragies and 100 Balls each, all in health and readiness to set out.[5]

Perhaps the easiest way to approach the Lewis and Clark expedition is simply to sketch out a brief chronology of its travels.[6] These details may help to give the modern reader a better understanding of the rewards and pitfalls of overland exploration through the North American frontier in the early 19th century.

12. The Great Lewis and Clark Expedition

First, it should be noted here that a contemporary chronicler—the lawyer and journalist Henry Marie Brackenridge, who had himself joined a fur trading expedition in 1811—set the stage quite well in just two sentences. This region was, he explained, truly a *terra incognita* to the common man:

> Before the memorable expedition of Lewis and Clark, none was found adventurous enough to penetrate that extensive portion of our continent [i.e., French Louisiana] more than a few hundred miles. It was almost as little known to us, as the interior of New Holland [i.e., Australia], and the deserts of Africa.[7]

The chronology for the Lewis and Clark expedition, mentioned above, follows here. It will give the reader an abbreviated but very clear summary of Lewis and Clark's adventures:

1803: The Lewis and Clark expedition sets off

In October 1803, the expedition assembles at Clarksville on the Ohio River. It then travels down the Ohio River to the Mississippi and thence upstream as far as Wood River, located just north of St. Louis. The winter of 1803–1804 is spent at Wood River.

1804: To the Indian villages near Bismarck, North Dakota

In May 1804, the expedition, manhandling a big keelboat and two big pirogues, ascends the Missouri and passes Saint Charles, Missouri, a riverside village. This event marks the formal beginning of the expedition's journey toward the Pacific.

In August 1804, after reaching the mouth of the Platte River in Nebraska, the members of the expedition see the first of the apparently endless buffalo herds roaming the Great Plains, and meet the local Indians, i.e., 250 members of the Otoe and Missouri tribes.

In October 1804, the expedition arrives at the villages of the Mandan and the Arikara Indians at the Great Bend of the Missouri, north of Bismarck, and spends the winter of 1804–1805 there. Cameahwait, the chief of a Northern Shoshone band that was camped along the Lemhi River in what is now Idaho, creates a three-dimensional map for Lewis and Clark, using piles of sand to depict the rugged topography of the mountains they now had to cross.[8]

1805: To the Pacific

In April 1805, Lewis and Clark send the keelboat downstream back to St. Louis, laden with biological specimens and Indian artifacts collected thus far. These will be forwarded to President Jefferson.

The expedition continues up-stream in two pirogues and six canoes. (Birch bark is not available in that region and in any case it would have been much too fragile for birch bark canoes to be used on snag-strewn streams, so the expedition will instead rely on sturdy, hollowed-out cottonwood trunks to make its vessels.)

By the end of April 1805, the explorers have reached the junction of the Missouri and Yellowstone rivers. In May 1805, Lewis climbs a bluff above the Missouri and, for the first time, he is able to see the high peaks of the Rockies.

By August 1805, his men having paddled and poled the canoes further upstream, Lewis climbs a local pass and reaches the Continental Divide. What he sees from there is a great disappointment for him. He had expected to be viewing an easily-traversed, gradual descent to the Columbia River and thence to the Pacific Ocean. What he sees instead are the Bitterroot Mountains. This is the first clear proof that there is in fact no navigable Passage to the Pacific. Moreover, the local Shoshone Indians confirm that a hard march of several days is needed to reach the headwaters of the Columbia.

In September 1805, after getting horses and guides from the Shoshones, the expedition crosses Lemhi Pass on the Montana-Idaho border and enters the Bitterroots. There is very heavy snow; game is scarce; and some horses have to be killed for meat. After 11 days and 160 miles of forced marches over the mountains, the expedition reaches a Nez Percé village in Idaho. It is there that Nez Percé hospitality saves the expedition from total failure due to exhaustion and lack of food and supplies.

In October 1805, embarking in Indian canoes, the explorers descend the Clearwater and the Snake rivers, eventually reaching the Columbia River. In November 1805, the expedition arrives at the Pacific Ocean, having come more than 4,000 miles from the mouth of the Missouri. It will spend the winter of 1805–1806 at a sopping-wet, cold, miserable camp which they name "Fort Clatsop" in honor of the local Indians.

1806: Heading home to St. Louis

With the coming of spring in March 1806, Lewis and Clark begin to make their way back to St. Louis. To maximize their knowledge of the region as a whole, in July 1806 they split the expedition into two groups for explorations north and south of main route home, Lewis leading one group and Clark the other. Blackfeet Indians attack Lewis's camp near the Marias River in Montana—a clash in which one Indian is killed and another is fatally wounded. This was the only armed conflict during the entire trip.

In August 1806, the two parties reunite at the mouth of the Yellowstone and then head down the Missouri. On 23 September 1806, the expedition finally reaches La Charette, a village not far from St. Louis, and Clark records the following in his journal:

12. The Great Lewis and Clark Expedition 85

> Every person, both French and americans seem to express great pleasure at seeing us return, they informed us that we were supposed to have been lost long sence, and were entirely given out [i.e., given up] by ever person &c.[9]

Lewis and Clark returned to St. Louis after a journey of nearly 6,000 miles. In their two-and-a-half years in the field, they made contact with more than 70 Indian tribes; produced 140 maps; and documented more than 200 new plant and animal species.

No modern account of the Lewis and Clark expedition would be complete, however, without paying tribute to the young Shoshone woman known as Sacagawea, who was the wife of the French fur trapper Toussaint Charbonneau.[10] (Spelling and punctuation below are as in the original.)

The first thing to note about this woman is how little is really known about her. Lewis and Clark recorded that she was a Shoshone girl who had been captured by the Hidatsa Indians in a war raid before she reached the age of puberty. Her captors later "sold her as a slave" to Charbonneau, who already had another Shoshone wife.

Lewis and Clark recorded her name (in various spellings) as "Sacagawea." They translated this as meaning "Bird Woman," which is what it meant in the Hidatsa language. Remarkably, during the course of the expedition they mentioned her in writing 73 times and were very impressed by her strong character. Lewis praised her "fortitude and resolution," while Clark noted her "patience truly admirable."

It does not appear from the writings of Lewis and Clark that Sacagawea played a major role as a pathfinder for their expedition. However, following her instructions, Clark's party did pass through "a low gap in the mountain" where Bozeman, Montana,[11] now lies, and arrived at the Yellowstone River just past the point where it emerges from "a high rugid mountain covered with Snow."

Her first-hand knowledge of the local topography, however, was indeed useful to the explorers. For example, she told Lewis that

> the point of a high plain to our right was not very distant from the summer retreat of her nation on a river beyond the mountains which runs to the west. this hill she says her nation calls the beaver's head from a conceived re[se]mblance of it's figure to the head of that animal. [The formation still known as the Beaverhead lies about eighteen miles north of what is now Dillon, Montana.] she assures us that we shall either find her people on this river or on the river immediately west of it's source; which from its present size cannot be very distant.[12]

13

"An atlas of the West"

Thomas James (1782–1847), a trapper and a hunter, was part of the Missouri Fur Company's expedition to escort the Mandan chief Shehaka back to his tribe, which lived along the upper Missouri River. This chief, in company with Lewis and Clark, had visited the "Great Father" (i.e., the U.S. president) in Washington, D.C., in 1807. Many years later, in 1846 James dictated his wilderness experiences in a book entitled *Three Years Among the Indians and Mexicans*.

Although he had some harsh things to say about the officers of the Missouri Fur Company, what is most remarkable (because he himself had suffered at the hands of Indians) is that he warmly praised the Mandans as "Chiefs with the dignity of Real Princes, and the eloquence of real orators, and Braves with the valor of the ancient Spartans."[1]

Walter B. Douglas, who edited James's book, described Shehaka in 1811 in the following candid, more skeptical terms:

> He is a fine looking Indian and very intelligent—his complexion fair, very little different from that of a white man much exposed to the sun. His wife had also accompanied him—[she] had a good complexion and agreeable features.
>
> They had returned home [from Washington, D.C.] loaded with presents, but have since fallen into disrepute from the extravagant tales which they related as to what they had witnessed; for the Mandans treated with ridicule the idea of there being a greater or more numerous people than themselves.
>
> He is a man of mild and gentle disposition—expressed a wish to come and live among the whites, and spoke sensibly of the insecurity, the ferocity of manners, and the ignorance of the state of society in which he was placed.
>
> He is rather inclined to corpulency, a little talkative, which is regarded among the Indians as a great defect; add to this his not being celebrated as a warrior; such celebrity can alone confer authority and importance or be regarded meritorious in this state of society.[2]

• • •

The first person of European descent known to have explored the Yellowstone region was the mountain man John Colter (c. 1774–1813).[3]

13. "An atlas of the West"

Colter's story is literally the stuff of legend, both because it is extremely interesting yet lightly documented. In trying to separate historical fact form adventuresome fiction, however, the modern historian is left with something like the following account[4]:

After serving as a hunter with the Lewis and Clark expedition from 1803 to 1806, Colter left the homeward-bound expedition on 15 August 1806 at the Mandan villages of what is now North Dakota. He had met two trappers—Joseph Dixon and Forest Hancock—who were following the expedition's outward route, hoping to find unexploited beaver-trapping areas. Eager to join them, Colter asked Lewis and Clark for an honorable discharge and received permission to join the trappers.

The next documented sighting of Colter was not until the spring of 1807, when he was seen paddling down the Missouri, alone, in a dugout canoe made from a cottonwood log. There was no information about Dixon, Hancock, or any beaver pelts, but when Colter reached the mouth of the Platte River (near today's Omaha, Nebraska) he met the first organized company of trappers to follow the Lewis and Clark journey toward the Rocky Mountains.

Led by the St. Louis entrepreneur Manuel Lisa, a native of Spanish Louisiana, this large group included three former members of the Lewis and Clark expedition, who encouraged Colter to join them in about October 1807. Legend has it that later on Colter set out, alone and on foot, on a remarkable 500-mile-long mission to trade with the Indians. In this process, he saw the geysers and the hot springs in a part of northern Wyoming that became known as "Colter's Hell" and which now is a portion of Yellowstone National Park.

In addition to being a skilled outdoorsman, he was also a gifted storyteller. When the English naturalist John Bradbury was traveling up the Missouri in 1811, he met Colter and from him heard this remarkable tale.

Colter told him that in the autumn of 1809 he had been captured by the Blackfeet Indians and, then barefoot and stripped naked, he had been forced to run for his life, after having been given a short head start, while the Indians chased him.

He explained that, when running hard as he could, he had survived only by stopping suddenly and unexpectedly. Then, instantly turning around, he had seized the spear of the closest and fastest-running Indian, and killed him by stabbing him with the spear. Colter added that he had then hidden in an abandoned beaver lodge until the other Indians got tired of looking for him and finally went away.

Bradbury ended his account, now known to historians as "Colter's Run," by writing laconically: "These were circumstances under which almost any man but an American hunter would have despaired." Colter himself retired to St. Louis in 1810 and spent his remaining years as a neighbor of the elderly frontiersman Daniel Boone, farming on the Missouri River frontier.

An interesting historical footnote here is that Colter often traveled alone in the wilderness. He could live off the land and carried only a single-shot muzzleloading rifle and an absolute minimum of other equipment. Much later, however, as the fame of Yellowstone slowly spread far and wide (it would become the first national park in the United States in 1872), the region began to attract explorers who deigned Colter-style bare bones equipment. For example, the September–October 1869 expedition of three experienced, self-reliant outdoorsmen from Helena, Montana—namely, David E. Folsom, Charles W. Cook, and William Peterson—is a good case in point here.

Their goal was to explore and document the Yellowstone region. Toward this end, their two-month-long expedition included the following items:

- The three men themselves
- Five horses
- A small arsenal of state-of-the-art firearms and ammunition
- Fishing tackle
- Two buffalo robes
- Five blankets
- 175 pounds of flour
- A dozen boxes of yeast powder
- 25 pounds of bacon
- 30 pounds of sugar
- 15 pounds of ground coffee
- A ham
- 10 pounds of salt
- 10 pounds of dried fruit
- 50 pounds of potatoes
- Prospecting gear
- Personal items[5]

• • •

The British trader Simon Fraser (1776–1862) was the first to descend the river that now bears his name, and also founded the earliest settlements in what is now central British Columbia.[6]

He joined the North West Company as a clerk in 1792. By 1801, he had risen to be a partner of the firm, after serving in the Athabasca region of today's northern Saskatchewan and Alberta. Fraser proved to be so able that in 1805 he was given responsibility for all the North West Company's operations beyond the Rockies, where he established the first settlements in today's British Columbia, i.e., Fort Fraser in 1806 and Fort George (now Prince George) in 1807. In the process, he traveled among Indian tribes that had never before seen a white man, and pioneered a route down what is now the Fraser River Canyon in 1808.

In so doing, Fraser had initially believed that he was following the Columbia River, but he was mistaken: he was in fact on the Fraser River. In any case, his travels down the Fraser River finally brought him to the Strait of Georgia opposite Vancouver Island. Local Indians had warned him about river whirlpools so strong that they would "swallow up canoes." This did not happen to him, but the passage was nevertheless so difficult that he wrote of it:

> A continual series of cascades, mixt with rocky fragments and bound by precipices and mountains that seemed at times to have no end. I scarcely ever saw any thing so dreary and seldom so dangerous in any country.[7]

The main lesson of Fraser's adventure was that the Fraser River was inherently unnavigable because of its precipitous drop from its headwaters to the ocean. As a result, the North West Company would now have to focus its trading energies on the Columbia River itself.

• • •

Manuel Lisa (1772–1820) was a real mover-and-shaker in the St. Louis fur trade during the first decade of the 19th century.[8] Working closely with his partner Andrew Henry, Lisa set up the Missouri Fur Company, an enterprise that financed a series of exploring expeditions in the wake of the successful Lewis and Clark expedition to open up the upper Missouri River watershed to American traders. An extremely intelligent and very active man, Lisa was the most successful fur trader along the frontier in his era, and was quick to hire some of the very best men who had been with Lewis and Clark.

The greatest single achievement of Lisa's Missouri Fur Company was that it managed to collect a great deal of new information on the geography and the economic prospects of the Rocky Mountains. These details would be important contributions to William Clark's master-map of the western frontier. Fittingly, in 1814, the U.S. Government rewarded Lisa for his private efforts on the nation's behalf by appointing him as the Indian agent for the tribes of the upper Missouri River.

Another important entrepreneur in the fur trade was the astute German immigrant John Jacob Astor, who had first made a name for himself in New York soon after the American Revolution, and then carved out a commercial empire based on the abundant fur resources of the Great Lakes region.[9]

By the spring of 1810, Astor had worked out arrangements for establishing a settlement he named "Astoria" which was to be the first outpost of his new Pacific Fur Company, located at the mouth of the Columbia River. As such, it would be the first American settlement on the Pacific Coast and would initiate the American land-based fur trade in the area. He then launched two expeditions—one by land, the other by sea—toward Astoria.[10]

Wilson Price Hunt, a St. Louis merchant working for Astor, was chosen to lead the overland expedition, even though he had no hands-on frontier experience whatsoever. This latter fact probably accounts for his mistaken decision to abandon the expedition's horses when he came to a ruined, i.e., unpopulated, fort on the Great Plains; to build dugout canoes there; and to try to reach Astoria by following first the Snake and then the Columbia rivers.

This was a serious error. As the modern historian Robert Utley explained,

> [His] waterborne overlanders soon discovered that the Snake River did not afford an easy descent to the Columbia. Cataracts, falls, and finally deep gorges with sheer walls forced laborious portages and ultimately abandonment of the canoes...
> In attempts to find a way to the Columbia, the company divided and subdivided, retraced trails that ended in impassible mountains or canyons, and grew weak from hunger, fatigue, and despair. Men drowned, starved, and lost their way in an unforgiving wilderness.[11]

Hunt's expedition finally did get to the Columbia River and at last to Astoria, where they met up with the Astorians who had arrived there by sea. One of the few bits of good news about Hunt's travels was that the route he pioneered would later become part of the famous Oregon Trail. In 1843, the missionary doctor Marcus Whitman would accompany the first major wagon train west along the Oregon Trail, thus proving the feasibility of this new route for later immigrants.[12]

The fur trader Robert Stuart (1785–1848), nephew of one of John Jacob Astor's "Scotsmen" partners, David Stuart, made the first documented crossing of South Pass in 1812, when he carried dispatches overland to New York from John Jacob Astor's trading post of Fort Astoria.[13]

South Pass, located on the Continental Divide between the Wind River Range and the Oregon Buttes in southwest Wyoming, was not a narrow mountain valley but was instead 20 miles wide. It consisted of a broad summit of gently-rising hills with a final elevation of 7,550 feet above sea level. This passageway would eventually become the Oregon Trail.

With six men in a canoe, Stuart embarked on an epic 3,768-mile journey to deliver the dispatches to Astor in New York City. They made a winter camp in early December 1812 along the North Platte River in central Wyoming. There was no shortage of buffalo: in fact, Stuart's men killed more than 30 on their first day of hunting.

This was of course far more than they needed or, indeed, could use by themselves. Such slaughter would later be repeated all over the Great Plains, reaching its high point in the 1870s when, due to the growing railroad industry and to the associated cattle boom, in less than 10 years the buffalo population would be dramatically reduced—nearly to the point of becoming an endangered species.

The main problem for the Stuart expedition, however, was not food but the report that the Arapaho Indians were on the warpath. As a result, in December 1812 Stuart decided to alter his march to the east, finally camping at a site near where the Oregon Trail would cross today's Nebraska-Wyoming border. His party lived so well there that Stuart could write:

> We destroyed [i.e., we consumed] an immoderate quantity of Buffalo Tongues, Puddings, the choicest of the meat. Our stock of Virginia weed [i.e., tobacco] being totally exhausted, McLellan's tobacco pouch was cut up and smoked as a substitute, in commemoration of the New Year.[14]

Stuart and his men arrived in St. Louis in mid–March 1813. He then traveled to New York City to give the dispatches to Astor, who treated them as proprietary commercial information and never publicized them. As a result, the South Pass portal to Oregon and California would remain "undiscovered" until frontiersman Jedediah Smith's expedition finally crossed it 1824.

• • •

In 1814, Stephen H. Long (1784–1864), a graduate of Dartmouth College, won a commission as lieutenant in the prestigious U.S. Army Corps of Engineers thanks to his mathematical abilities and his skill as a surveyor.[15] Two years later, he was appointed a major.

Major Long's first exploring expeditions took him up the Mississippi River in 1817 to the falls of St. Anthony, where Minneapolis now stands, and then up the Arkansas River in 1817–1818 to the site of the future Fort Smith. He did so well in these assignments that in 1818 the War Department selected him to lead an expedition into the Rockies.

His party, which included soldiers, scientists, and—most remarkably— two skilled artists from the Philadelphia area, namely, Titian Ramsay Peale and Samuel Seymour—ascended the Mississippi River and the Missouri River by steamboat to Council Bluffs. After spending the winter there, the expedition entered the Great Plains and then made the first recorded climb of 14,110-foot-high Pike's Peak, located south of present-day Denver.

Long tried hard, but he failed to find the Red River, which formed the boundary between American and Spanish territory. (Later, in 1852 another explorer—Captain Randolph B. Marcy—would find the Red River's headwaters.) Despite this setback, however, Long's expedition did yield some results.

Long's travels gave additional and useful information about the nature of the lands lying up the Platte River; along the Front Range of the Rocky Mountains; south to the Arkansas and Canadian rivers; and, finally, east to present-day Fort Smith, Arkansas.

For better or worse, Long repeated in his 1823 report an earlier and erroneous description, made by the explorer Zebulon Pike, that the Great Plains constituted nothing more or less than a "Great American Desert." If so, it followed, by implication, they were thus totally unsuited for any future settlement by American farmers.

On a more positive note, however, the fine work of the artists Peale (a naturalist-illustrator) and Seymour (a landscape painter) gave American and European readers their first detailed and accurate glimpses of this little-known part of the Western frontier.

Of these two artists, Peale is the more important today. He was a noted scientific illustrator whose sensitive paintings and drawings of wildlife are remarkable for their beauty and their accuracy. After accompanying Long's expedition to explore the Rocky Mountains, he then served on the United States Exploring Expedition of 1838–1842 and, later, became a pioneer American photographer.

Unlike the educated Stephen Long, the American frontiersman Jim Bridger (1804–1881) was one of the most famous explorers and mountain men. Although illiterate, his hands-on knowledge of the frontier was so extensive that the historian Bernard DeVoto would call him "an atlas of the West." Some highlights of Bridger's very colorful career are worth remembering here.[16]

For example, in a skirmish in 1832 at the Battle of Pierre's Hole, a valley on Idaho's Gallatin River lying north of Yellowstone National Park, a Blackfeet Indian shot an arrow into Bridger's back. The wooden shaft of the arrow snapped off, but the iron arrowhead, which was three inches long, remained lodged in his back for three years. Finally, at a rendezvous (an annual gathering of the mountain men), Marcus Whitman, a missionary doctor then en route to Oregon, dug out the arrowhead without benefit of any anesthesia.

A man who witnessed the operation later reported, "The doctor pursued the operation with great self-possession and perseverance," and that Bridger had "manifested equal firmness." It was said that when the doctor expressed his amazement that the severe wound made by the arrowhead had not become septic, Bridger replied cheerfully, "In the mountains, doctor, meat don't spoil!"[17]

Previously, in order to settle a bet, either late in 1824 or early in 1825 Bridger built a "bullboat" (a small round vessel made of deer or buffalo skin stretched tight over a wooden frame). In it, he floated down the Bear River in southeastern Idaho and thus became the first non-Indian to see the Great Salt Lake. When he tasted the water and found that it was very salty, he believed he had reached an arm of the Pacific Ocean. (Another account, however, depicts Bridger as traveling on horseback, not in a boat, when he tasted the salt water.)[18]

13. "An atlas of the West"

Even in middle age, Bridger's eyesight was still quite remarkable. In 1865, when he was guiding a U.S. Army expedition near the Tongue River in northeastern Wyoming, he called the attention of an Army officer to what he described as "a thin wisp of smoke in a saddle-shaped depression nearly 50 miles away."

The officer himself could not see the smoke, even with his binoculars, but his scouts, who had earlier been sent forward to reconnoiter, reported that the smoke was rising from an Indian village where campfires were burning. (In the clear air and strong sunlight of the northeastern Rocky Mountains, it was possible to see small objects at great distances. In 1884, for example, the wife of a rancher in Alberta, Canada, wrote that she was able to see rooftops 22 miles away.)

In 1904, a monument to Bridger was unveiled at the Kansas City Cemetery where he was buried. The epitaph on it gives a very good summary of his eventful life. It reads:

> 1804—James Bridger—1881
>
> Celebrated as a Hunter, Trapper, Fur Trader and Guide. Discovered Salt Lake, 1824; the South Pass [that broad gateway through the Rocky Mountains], 1827; visited Yellowstone Lake and Geysers, 1830; Founded Fort Bridger, 1843; Opened Overland Route by Bridger's Pass to Salt Lake. Was Guide for Exploring Expeditions, Albert Sidney Johnston's Army in 1857, and G.M. Dodge in U.P. [Union Pacific Railroad] Surveys and Indian Campaigns in 1865–66.[19]

14

Creating a "fur desert"

One of the most able explorers was the Canadian trapper Peter Skene Ogden (1790–1854), who was also a first-rate chronicler.[1]

Employed by the Hudson's Bay Company, Ogden led six separate expeditions between 1824 and 1830. They covered seven very different and very challenging areas, namely:

1. Most of the region between the Rocky Mountains and the Columbia River that was drained by the Snake River.

2. Both sides of the Cascade Range in what is now the state of Oregon.

3. Southern Idaho and northern Utah, e.g., the Bear Lake, Bear River, and Great Salt Lake regions.

4. Much of northern Utah and Nevada, e.g., the northern parts of the Great Basin and the valley of the Humboldt River.

5. Most of California north of San Francisco Bay, including the Klamath Lake and Mount Shasta regions.

6. The western side of the Great Basin, i.e., from the Humboldt Sink (near present-day Reno, Nevada) south to the Gulf of California in northern Mexico.

7. The southern end of the Sierra Nevada mountains and then northward through the Sacramento—San Joaquin Valley of California to Klamath Lake in southern Oregon.

This list of Ogden's explorations can usefully be fleshed out by adding details on some of them. In 1828, for example, Ogden led a party of trappers south from the Columbia River basin. In so doing, his overall goal was two-fold.[2]

First, he wanted to "trap out," as the frontier saying had it, the beaver-filled streams of the vaguely-defined Snake River country of the intermountain West. The Hudson's Bay Company had calculated that such a policy, if successful, would create a "fur desert" that would effectively discourage American trappers from pushing ever farther north, until they finally reached the Columbia River basin itself.

Second, as a gifted explorer, Ogden wanted to see with his own eyes the rivers and mountains of this promising but vast and little-known frontier region.

In November 1828 he reached a small river now known as the Little Humboldt and then, following it downstream, discovered the main branch of the Humboldt River itself. Since he knew neither its origin nor its destination, Ogden simply called this the "Unknown River." He must have liked what he saw before him, however, because the river was rich with beaver.

Ogden explored the river for several days, reaching the present site of Mill City, located about 30 miles downstream from Winnemucca, Nevada. Fine weather permitted his party to enjoy a few days of good trapping but then a sudden autumn blizzard forced them to retreat toward the Salt Lake City valley and their planned winter camp, later known as Ogden's Hole, in Utah.

They spent the winter of 1828–1829 in the Wasatch mountains of Utah, after which, in 1829, they returned to the Humboldt. The weather was good then, so Ogden was able to follow the river downstream. On 15 May 1829, he wrote in his diary:

> Started at dawn to escape the heat, the journey over beds of sand the horses sinking half leg deep, the country level tho' at distance hilly—course S.W. The Indians are not numerous in this quarter, but from the number of [camp]fires seen on the mountains are fully aware of our presence, and we must look out for our horses [i.e., to prevent them from being stolen by the Indians.]
>
> 75 traps produced 37 beaver. This is tolerable; for usually we receive only a third. The total number of American trappers in this region exceeds 80. I have only 28 trappers, 15 in two parties; and shall be well pleased if one of the two parties escapes [i.e., escapes an attack by the Indians.] The trappers now average 125 beaver a man and are greatly pleased by their success.[3]

Ogden and his men reached the very end of the Humboldt River, i.e., its sink or terminus, on 28 May 1829. He recorded that the Humboldt Sink was

> ...one continued swamp covered with frogs, toads and garter snakes... [but] wild fowl, although the country is well adapted for them, are not over numerous. Pelicans are however the reverse, particularly in the lower part of the river and they have noble sport pasturing on frogs and toads.[4]

After leaving this basin, Ogden and his expedition headed westward toward the Carson Sink, the Walker River, and, ultimately, California. His explorations of the Humboldt River basin were important because he was able to follow the river from "source to sink" and, in the process, produced the first maps and written descriptions of northern and central Nevada.

Moreover, while camped along the Humboldt River near present-day Lovelock, Nevada, Ogden had received the first description of two rivers lying further to the west, namely, the Carson River and the Truckee River. He decided not to explore them himself, however, because there was no evidence that they would be good trapping grounds for beaver. On the other hand, Ogden did eagerly search for—but of course failed to find—the long-sought but entirely mythical San Buenaventura River.

Ironically, Ogden's search for this non-existent body of water during his travels of 1829–1830 has put him solidly into the premier rank of the explorer-fur traders. Although his own journals for this trip were lost in a boat accident in a whirlpool on the Columbia River, modern scholars have retraced his likely route as follows, beginning and ending at Fort Vancouver, which was located on the present site of Portland, Oregon:

- From Fort Vancouver up the Deschutes River to near its head, and then south to Malheur Lake.
- From Malheur Lake south to the Humboldt River; up the Humboldt to the Humboldt Sink, then south to Walker Lake in western Nevada.
- From Walker Lake, up into the Sierra Nevada mountains, then south through the mountains until turning east to reach the Colorado River near Needles, California.
- South along the Colorado River to the Gulf of California, then back up the river for about 100 miles.
- From the Colorado River westward into California and its San Joaquin Valley.
- North through the San Joaquin Valley and the Sacramento Valley to the Pit River in northern California.
- Up the Pit River to Klamath Lake; the Deschutes River; the Columbia River; and, finally, Fort Vancouver.[5]

The journals and maps that resulted from Ogden's travels eventually found their way into the archives of the Hudson's Bay Company headquarters in London. There they could be studied by the eminent British mapmaker Aaron Arrowsmith.

The net result of Ogden's findings was that although an earlier (1810) map by Arrowsmith had indeed depicted the Buenaventura River as flowing into San Francisco Bay, this mythical stream soon became conspicuously absent on the most accurate maps of western North America.[6] Indeed, it has rightly been said that this was Ogden's major contribution to ever-increasing geographical knowledge of the western North American frontiers.[7]

After Ogden's heroic travels, the Hudson's Bay Company sent out many minor expeditions, but these did not have any dramatic results. Samuel Black, a well-traveled and very experienced member of the Company, was selected in 1824 to look for a will-o'-the-wisp known as the "Great River of the Northwest."[8]

British geographical thought at this time was still fixated on a variation of the concept of the Passage, in this case, the mistaken belief that numerous major rivers must arise in the western interior of North America and must then radiate out to both the Pacific Ocean and the Arctic Ocean.

Black's expedition was of course a failure: it has even been called, with a very nice turn of phrase, "an exercise in negative discovery."[9] It prompted the Hudson's Bay Company to turn its attention farther north and from 1821 to 1851 to explore Canada's "Far Northwest," e.g., the northwestern Rocky Mountains in what is now British Columbia and the Yukon Territory.

This was very difficult territory and, in the end, it served as the highwater mark in terms of British influence over the fur trade in western North America. The great British exploration achievement of this era would be Arrowsmith's 1854 map of British America, which laid out, very accurately, the complexities of the great rivers of Canada's Far Northwest. These included the Peel, the Liard, the Stikine, the Porcupine, the Yukon headwaters, the Pelly, and the Lewes.[10]

• • •

In 1829, Antonio Armijo, an astute New Mexican trader, was the first see the potential of a mutually-profitable livestock and woolen-goods trade between Abiquiu, New Mexico, and Santa Barbara, California. Indeed, he became its pioneer.

Armijo recognized that in California many of the livestock herds originally developed by Spanish missions and ranches but now wandering at will over vast open grasslands in a mild climate with an absence of large predators, had generated such a huge surplus of free-for-the-taking animals that they could easily be captured and traded along what would become known as the Old Spanish Trail.[11]

Deciding to act on this insight, Armijo decided to transport woolen items from New Mexico to California and to barter them there for horses and mules. He and his men would then drive these animals back to New Mexico for sale, either to buyers there or further east, e.g., in Missouri.

The official 1830 report by the Mexican government on Armijo's travels shows that his outbound journey had been hard indeed. The report read in part:

> It took [his party] three months less six days to arrive at the first village in California, which is Santa Barbara; they were delayed so [long] because the route was unknown and they had to make numerous detours of the impassible mountains and canyons which impeded a straight course...[12]

For example, at the ford of the Colorado River now known as the Crossing of the Fathers, Armijo's men had no recourse but to unpack their horses and mules and to carve steps into the steep canyon walls in order to provide safe footing down to the river for themselves and for their animals. Moreover, as part of this ordeal, they also had to carry on their own backs the trade goods, e.g., *serapes*, blankets, and quilts that were in such demand in California.

When Armijo's expedition finally reached San Gabriel, California, 86 days after setting on their travels, the Californians were astounded to learn that that these hardy traders were willing to exchange their very desirable woven goods for the horses and mules that were now so plentiful in California that they had almost no value.

As a result, the Californians hoped that a much shorter and much easier route to their markets would soon be found to help them get rid of their surplus animals.[13] No such new route was ever pioneered, however, but the trade continued and the Old Spanish Trail remained in use for years.

• • •

In 1830, the writer James O. Pattie (c. 1804–c. 1851)—a miner and an amateur physician who inoculated some residents of California with an anti-smallpox vaccine he had brought with him from the East—dictated to a reporter the remarkable story of his frontier adventures. While not without its shortcomings, his account is nevertheless full of local color and drama.

First published in 1831 and then reissued in 1930 with a useful introduction and notes, this book was sonorously entitled *The Personal Narrative of James O. Pattie of Kentucky During an Expedition from St. Louis through the Vast Regions between that Place and the Pacific Ocean, and then back through the City of Mexico to Vera Cruz. During Journeyings of Six Years, in which He and His Father, Who Accompanied him, Suffered Unheard of Hardships and Dangers, had Various Conflicts with the Indians, and Were Made Captives, in which Captivity His Father Died; Together with a Description of the Country, and the Various Nations through which They Passed.*

Pattie is believed to have died of cold and exposure when he left a camp in the Sierra Nevada mountains during the terrible winter of 1849–50. Before then, however, he had a number of near-death experiences in the field. The most dramatic of these was probably a bear hunt near what is now El Paso, Texas.

In his book, Pattie wrote:

> On a hunting trip [no date given] with a companion who was an American, he one morning saw fit to start out of bed, and to commence his hunt while I was yet asleep in bed. He had scarcely advanced a league, before he killed a deer on the top of a high ridge. He was so inadvertent as to commence skinning the animal before he had re-loaded his [muzzleloading single-shot rifle, a very time-consuming process]. Thus engaged, he did not perceive a bear with her cubs, which had advanced within a few feet of him. As soon as he saw his approaching companion [i.e., the bear], he left deer and rifle and ran for his life. The bear fell to work for a meal upon the deer, and did not pursue him…

Pattie and the other hunter then agreed to hide and not to shoot at the bear until it was very close. They did so but, the day being very damp, both their flintlock rifles misfired. The colleague's shot only wounded the bear in the belly and did not kill it. The enraged bear immediately charged both hunters.

Pattie was crouched in front of an unseen depression in the hillside. He held his own fire until the bear was only six feet away but his rifle "flashed in the pan," that is to say, the priming powder went off but did not ignite the main charge of powder, so no bullet came out of the barrel. Pattie writes:

> She [the bear] gave one growl and sprang at me with her mouth open. At two strides I leapt down the unperceived precipice. My jaw bone was split on a sharp rock, on which my chin had struck at the bottom. Here I lay senseless.
> When I regained collection, I found my companion had bled me with the point of his butcher knife [this was the early 19th century's normal "first aid" treatment], and was sitting beside me with his hat full of water, bathing my head and face…. My companion had cut a considerable orifice in my arm with his knife, which I deemed rather supererogation; for I judged that I had bled sufficiently at the chin…
> [Shortly thereafter] we ascended the ridge to where we had seen the bear lie down in the bushes. We fixed our guns so that we thought ourselves sure of their fire. We then climbed two trees, near where the bear was, and made a noise, that brought her out of her lair, and caused her to spring fiercely toward our trees. We fired together and killed her dead.[14]

15

How to Hunt Buffalo

In the summer of 1832, the artist and writer George Catlin (1796–1872) took the steamer *Yellow-Stone* up the Missouri River to its junction with the Yellowstone River, and spent three weeks with the Mandan Indians.[1]

All told, in fits and starts he would spend a total of eight years (1832–1839) traveling among what he described as "the wildest tribes of Indians of North America." His main achievement was to leave to his contemporary and future readers some extraordinary visual and literary records of the Plains Indians societies in their soon-to-vanish prime. Catlin's writing about the Indians was even better than his paintings.

Consider, for example, his lucid explanation of why the typical Blackfeet warrior was such a fine fighter. Indeed, at close range, a group of these warriors was often more than a match for a handful of Europeans or Americans, who were armed only with single-shot slow-to-load muskets or rifles. The Indians were also much better than the foreigners at "running buffalo," i.e., at hunting buffalo from horseback.

Catlin wrote:

> An Indian ... mounted on a fleet and well-trained horse, with his bow in his hand, and his quiver slung on his back, containing a hundred arrows, of which he can throw [i.e., can shoot from his bow] fifteen or twenty in a minute, is a formidable and dangerous enemy.
>
> Many of them also ride with a lance of twelve or fourteen feet in length ... with a blade of polished steel; and all of them (as a protection for their vital parts), with a shield or arrow-fender made of the [very thick] skin of a buffalo's neck, which has been smoked and hardened with glue extracted from hoofs.... These shields are arrow-proof, and will glance off a rifle-shot with perfect effect by being turned obliquely, which they do with great skill.[2]

Another good example of his writing skills are the colorful details that quickly bring to life the Mandan chieftain Mah-to-toh-pa ("Four Bears"). Catlin writes:

> This extraordinary man ... is undoubtedly the first and most popular man in the nation. Free, generous, elegant, and gentlemanly in his deportment—handsome, brave

and valiant; wearing a robe on his back, with the history of his battles emblazoned on it; which would fill a book of themselves, if properly translated. This, readers, is the most extraordinary man, perhaps, who lives at this day, in the atmosphere of Nature's noblemen; and I shall certainly tell you more of him anon.[3]

Catlin produced more than 500 paintings of the 48 different tribes he visited and tried to persuade Congress to buy some of them. He was much more successful, however, when he toured the United States and Europe with what he called "Catlin's Indian Gallery." This consisted of 310 oil paintings of Indians and 200 oils of other subjects, together with a large number of Indian ornamental shirts, robes, drums, headdresses, and other items.

Catlin published his extensive journals in two works: two volumes of his *Manners, Customs, and Conditions of the North American Indians* (1841), and one volume of his *Last Rambles Amongst the Indians of the Rocky Mountains and the Andes* (1867). He is also credited to have been the first American to put forward the concept of a national land preserve. In 1832, for example, he suggested the creation of "a nation's park, containing man and beast, in all the wild freshness of their nature's natural beauty."[4]

During this same period, in 1833 and 1834, the German Prince Maximilian of Wied-Neuwied, writer, ethnologist, naturalist, and explorer, together with his companion, a young Swiss artist named Karl Bodmer, made an epic journey up the Missouri River to the homelands of the Blackfeet Indians.[5]

The result of their travels was a world-famous multi-volume work, written by the Prince and profusely illustrated by Bodmer's 400 watercolors, pencil sketches, and field notes. Entitled *Travels in the Interior of North America, 1832–1834*, it has recently been reprinted in a modern format and is of surpassing historical and artistic interest.

Far from being a stodgy 19th century scientific treatise, *Travels* simply sparkles with excitement. Consider, for example, what the Prince wrote in his field journal on 28 August 1833:

> At break of day, we were awakened by musket-shot, and Doucette [the explorers' interpreter] entered our room, crying "Levez-vous, il faut nous battre" ["Get up: we have to fight!"], on which we rose in haste, dressed ourselves, and loaded our fowling-pieces with ball [i.e., they loaded their shotguns with heavy lead bullets rather than with the usual lighter and less-lethal birdshot].[6]

The explorers survived this day only because this battle was not, as the interpreter had feared, an assault on Fort Mackenzie itself, where they were staying, but rather a bloody fracas between rival Indian groups. A joint force of nearly 600 Assiniboins and 100 Crees attacked a small group of Blackfeet Indians who had pitched their tents just outside the fort. More than 14 Blackfeet Indians were killed and many others wounded; Assiniboin losses were estimated at three to six killed and more than 20 others seriously wounded.[7]

Also in 1832–1834, a Missouri-based 110-man expedition led by U.S. Army officer Benjamin Louis Eulalie de Bonneville, on official leave from the Army ostensibly to undertake a private fur trading and exploring mission, explored several major river systems in Wyoming, Idaho, Oregon, and Washington.[8] He also established an overland route to California that would later evolve into the famous California Trail.

Bonneville and his men set out from Fort Osage, Missouri, in 1832 on what was a semi-official exploring and trading expedition (apparently approved by the U.S. War Department) to learn more about the Oregon Country. This region was not well-defined, but it was certainly *large*. It was considered to include, in the United States, Oregon, Washington, and Idaho; western Montana and western Wyoming; and, in Canada, the province of British Columbia.[9]

It will never be entirely clear whether Bonneville was a spy but it seems that, for unexplained reasons, President Andrew Jackson himself personally interceded on his behalf to resolve a bureaucratic problem that was getting in Bonneville's way. In any case, Bonneville certainly agreed to provide the War Department with as much information as possible about the topography, climate, resources, and Indians of the frontier West.

In fact, however, his expedition did not fare very well in terms of fur trading: the competition from the more expert trappers of the American Fur Company was simply too great. Nevertheless, in the long run Bonneville scored a far more important geographic coup when he sent out the outstanding mountain man Joseph R. Walker (who was his field commander) in 1833–1834 to blaze a trail across the Great Basin of Utah and Nevada all the way to California.

Bonneville also became the first man to take heavily-loaded wagons across South Pass, Wyoming—the broad gap in the Rockies that would later become the major emigrant passageway to Oregon and California. Moreover, his maps would provide travelers with the most thorough and most accurate geographical information then available about the West. Finally, Bonneville achieved lasting literary fame in 1837 as the hero of Washington Irving's very colorful book about the West, entitled *The Adventures of Captain Bonneville*.

As already mentioned, Bonneville's field commander was Joseph Walker (1798–1876).[10] He was, in fact, the chief lieutenant of Captain Bonneville's party; both men were employed by the Hudson's Bay Company.

The Bonneville-Walker party was the last important exploration and fur-hunting expedition undertaken along Nevada's Humboldt River, which Walker, because of its arid surroundings, called the "Barren River." In 1833, his party traveled generally west along the Humboldt River; crossed the Carson Sink; ascended the Sierra Nevada range, following either the headwaters of the Carson River or the Walker River; and, finally, ended their long journey in California at Monterey Bay.

15. How to Hunt Buffalo

Their desert travel was also the first recorded east-to-west crossing through Nevada using the Humboldt River Valley. It proved that the Humboldt River route was in fact a viable passageway both for travelers and for their livestock. Its greatest virtue, however, aside from having a reliable supply of sometimes-barely-drinkable brackish water, was that it cut through the complex maze of the north-south-running desert hills that constitute the Basin and Range topography of the Great Basin.

Walker's journey was marked by one major bloody event, which is worth recounting in some detail for what it reveals of contemporary attitudes toward Indians.

In the first week of September 1833 at the Humboldt Sink, Walker and his party encountered a band of more than 400 Paiute Indians, who emerged from the reeds and began moving toward them in a hostile manner. The reason for the Indians' anger was that a few of the trappers, acting on their own and without any authorization from Walker, had shot and killed two or three Indians in retaliation for the Indians having stolen some of their beaver traps.

At the encounter at Humboldt Sink, Walker, using sign language, now indicated to the Indians that if any of them tried to enter his camp, they would be killed. The Paiutes simply laughed at this threat, however, and asked, again by signs, how the white men could possibly kill them at a distance.

Walker quickly realized that these Indians of the remote Nevada desert knew nothing at all about the destructive power of firearms. He therefore ordered some of his best marksmen to use their accurate, long-barreled, muzzleloading rifles to kill several of the ducks floating in a small pond nearby.[11] This they quickly did.

These results astonished the Indians, but they were much more impressed by the thunderous noise of the gunshots than by the dead ducks: upon hearing the shots, they threw themselves flat upon the ground. After their fright, however, the Indians quickly recovered their composure and even set up a beaver skin on the river bank for the mountain men to use as a target. They then disappeared into the night.

The next morning, Walker and his men broke camp before dawn, hoping that their shooting display would deter the Indians from any hostilities. This was not to be the case, however. The expedition's chronicler, Zenas Leonard, gives us the following account of what happened next:

> We now began to be a little stern with [the Indians], and gave them to understand that if they continued to trouble us they would do it at their own risk. [However] we were teased [by them] until a party of eighty or one hundred came forward, who appeared to be more saucy and bold than any others.
>
> This greatly excited Captain Walker, who was naturally of a very cool temperament, and he gave orders for the charge, saying that there was nothing equal to a good start

in such a case. This was sufficient [i.e., his men understood that Walker was ordering them to open fire]. A number of our men had never been engaged in any fighting with the Indians, and were anxious to try their skill. When our commander gave his consent to chastise these Indians, and give them an idea of our strength, 32 of us dismounted and prepared ourselves to give them a severe blow...

We closed in on them and fired, leaving thirty-nine dead on the field—which was nearly the half—the remainder were overwhelmed with dismay, running into the high grass in every direction, howling in the most lamentable manner. Captain Walker then gave orders to some of the men to take the bows of the fallen Indians and put the wounded out of misery [by shooting them].[12]

• • •

The first of the two books on the American frontier written by the German physician Dr. F.A. Wislizenus (1810–1889) was initially published in German in St. Louis in 1840. Entitled *A Journey to the Rocky Mountains in the Year 1839*, it vividly recounts his travels through Wyoming and Idaho on the Oregon Trail, and then into Colorado.

His next book, *Memoir of a Tour to Northern Mexico Connected with Col. Doniphan's Expedition in 1846 and 1847*, was published in English in Washington, D.C., in 1848. It focuses on his travels during the era of the Mexican-American War and, while competent and workmanlike, it is much more of a simple travelogue than its predecessor. Nevertheless, both volumes give the modern reader a perhaps more detached and prescient perspective on the American frontier.[13]

Much has been written about hunting buffalo, the animal that singlehandedly made the Plains Indians so formidable, but the account by Dr. Wislizenus remains one of the best, as the excerpts below will show.

He writes:

As to numbers, buffalo herds very greatly. One finds herds of fifty to a hundred head, but also of a thousand and of several thousands. Often many herds graze side by side and cover the country to such an extent that they are estimated not by the number of herds, but only by the *miles* they occupy...

Their real home now is the immense prairie between the boundary of the States and the Rocky Mountains ... many thousands are yearly killed by whites and Indians [but] their numbers are still incalculable. Should it, however, ever come to the extermination of these animals, then the whole of this country must necessarily assume some other shape; for to the inhabitant here the buffalo is far more important than his camel is to the Arab. It supplies his prime necessities: food, dwelling and clothing.

The hunt for buffalo is one of the grandest and most interesting of which I know. The hunting is done either a-foot by stalking, or on horseback by running...

Much more interesting than stalking is the hunt on horseback. This requires a skillful rider and a quick, well-trained horse. A good buffalo hunter prefers to ride without a saddle. He sticks one [single-shot] pistol in his belt, holds the other in his right hand, and starts off at top speed. He rushes into the midst of the fleeing herd, and for some minutes buffaloes and rider disappear in a thick cloud of dust. But suddenly he

15. How to Hunt Buffalo

reappears at one side close behind a buffalo which he has picked out for his prey and separated from the herd.

The hunted animal exerts all its strength to escape its pursuer; but the emulous horse [i.e., the horse, who is very eager to outrun the buffalo] races with him, following all his turnings, almost without guidance from the bridle. Now [the rider] has overtaken him; he is racing close to his left side; but the buffalo turns sharply and the horse shoots past him.

The race begins afresh. Again, the horse overtakes the buffalo; again they are running parallel, and the rider discharges his pistol point-blank in the buffalo's flank. He now gallops slowly after the exhausted animal, and, if necessary, gives him a second shot [after having reloaded one of his two pistols]. Often the wounded animal turns on the rider, who must rely on the swiftness of his horse for safety.[14]

The comments by Wislizenus on beaver trapping near the Wind River mountains of Colorado are equally enlightening. He writes:

> These trappers, the "Knights without fear and without reproach" [this is a medieval honorific], are such a peculiar set of people that it is necessary to say something about them.
>
> The name itself indicates their occupation. They either receive their outfit, consisting of horses, beaver traps, a gun, powder and lead, from trading companies, and trap for small wages, or else they act on their own account, and are then called freemen. The latter is more often the case.
>
> In small parties they roam through all the mountain passes. No rock is too steep for them; no stream too swift. Withal, they are in constant danger from hostile Indians, whose delight it is to ambush such small parties, and plunder them, and scalp them. Such victims fall every year.
>
> One of our fellow travelers, who had gone to the mountains for the first time nine years ago with about one hundred men, estimated that by this time half of the number had fallen victim to the tomahawks of the Indians. But this daily danger seems to exercise a magic attraction over most of them. Only with reluctance does a trapper abandon his dangerous craft; and a sort of serious home-sickness seizes him when he retires from his mountain life to civilization…
>
> Formerly single trappers [at the annual trappers' meeting known as a *rendezvous*] have often wasted a thousand dollars [on alcohol and gambling]. But their days of glory seem to be past, for constant hunting has very much reduced the number of beavers. Another decade perhaps and the original trapper will have disappeared from the mountains.[15]

This last sentence reflects the fact that men's fashions were changing by the 1830s: top hats were increasingly being made of silk, not of beaver fur. This fundamental shift in tastes, coupled with the shortage of beavers due to periodic over-trapping, led to a sharp collapse in beaver fur prices all along the frontier.

Finally, Wislizenus has some interesting things to say about (1) desert mirages in New Mexico (a mirage is a naturally-occurring optical phenomenon in which light rays bend to produce a displaced image of distant objects or the sky); (2) the infamous *Jornada del Muerto* (the "Day's Journey of the Dead Man," i.e., a potentially-fatal crossing of a waterless desert); and (3) the inevitable fate of the Indians.

Concerning mirages, he writes:

> But, for one quality this desert [in New Mexico] is distinguished. When your patience has been worn out by the long ride, and by the monotonous sameness of the scenery; when your lips are parched from thirst, and a friend at your side, in cruel consolation, reminds you of the luxuries of cultivated life—to all of which you would nevertheless prefer a refreshing draught of cold water—there emerges in the plain before your astonished eyes a beautiful lake.
>
> Its surface looks like crystal; the wind moves but slightly the wide sheet of water; but the faster you hurry forward, the nearer you approach it, the sooner you will be disenchanted; the lake disappears again before your presence; and when you arrive at the very spot, you perceive nothing but the same hard, dry, parched soil, over which you have travelled all day. This is the celebrated "*mirage*"....Though it also appears in other parts of the prairie, it is nowhere so common, so deceptive, and so well developed, as here.[16]

Of the *Jornada del Muerto*, Wislizenus says:

> [Its title] refers to an old tradition that the first traveller who attempted to cross it in one day perished in it. The word Jornada (journey performed in one day) is especially applied in Mexico to wide tracts of countryside without water, which for this reason must be crossed in one day...
>
> This awful Jornada, a distance of about 90 miles, with very little or without any water at all, has been resorted to because the Rio del Norte below Fray Cristobal [the last camping place before entering the waterless stretch of desert] takes not only a very continuous bend, but rough mountains, too, alongside of it, make it most difficult to follow the water-course. In the rainy season there is generally plenty of water in the Jornada, as everywhere else, but in the dry season often not a drop is found.[17]

The fate of the Indians of the North American frontier was already very clear to Dr. Wislizenus in 1839. He wrote:

> The ultimate destiny of these wild tribes, now hunting unrestrained through the Far West of the United States, can be foretold almost to a certainty, from the fate, already accomplished, of the eastern tribes, where in the contact of races, true civilization collides with the crude forces of nature, the latter must succumb. Civilization, steadily pressing forward toward the West, has driven the Indians step by step before it...
>
> So the waves of civilization will draw nearer and nearer from the East and from the West, till they cover the sandy plains, and cast their spray on the feet of the Rockies. The few fierce tribes who may have maintained themselves until that time in the mountains, may offer some resistance to the progress of the waves, but the swelling flood will rise higher and higher, till at last they are buried beneath it. The buffalo and the antelope will be buried with them; and the bloody tomahawk will be buried, too.[18]

16

Wanting to Become President of the United States

In his own eyes at least, John Charles Frémont (1813–1890), who will be mentioned again in later pages, was one of the greatest 19th century explorers.[1] Nicknamed and widely hailed by his many contemporary admirers as "the Pathfinder," Frémont was handsome, intelligent, energetic, and a showman—and one who would later be badly soiled by constantly trying to justify and promote himself.

In the short run, however, these weaknesses did not prevent him from being an excellent explorer. For example, in 1843 when near Klamath Lake, Oregon, he reported this of the Klamath tribe:

> The stream we had struck [i.e., the Pit River] issued from the mountain in an easterly direction, turning to the southward a short distance below; and, drawing a course upon the ground, they [the Indians] made us comprehend that it pursued its way in a long distance in that direction, uniting with many other streams, and gradually becoming a great river. Without the subsequent information, which confirmed the opinion, we became immediately satisfied that this water formed the principal stream of the Sacramento River.[2]

Here is a similar example of Frémont's pathfinding skill. In 1844, during the course of an expedition in the Far West, he interviewed the local Northern Paiute people at Pyramid Lake, Nevada, to find out precisely where he was. He later wrote:

> We could obtain from them but little information respecting the country. They made on the ground a drawing of the [Truckee] river which they represented as issuing from another lake [Lake Tahoe] in the mountains three or four days distant, in a direction a little west of south; beyond which they drew a mountain [the Sierra Nevada range]; and further still, two rivers [the Sacramento River and/or the American, Feather, or San Joaquin river], on one of which [probably the Sacramento] they told us that people like ourselves lived.[3]

When Frémont returned to Washington, D.C., at the end of his journey, he wrote this report on the expedition. Studded with tables of geographical data which he had calculated based on his own astronomical readings taken in the field, often done under very difficult conditions, it remains a narrative of very high literary quality.

This was in no small part due to the unflagging efforts of his wife Jessie, who not only edited her husband's work but who also played a key role in the drafting process by drawing out and helping shape his vivid memories of his remarkable travels and adventures. This report was published by the U.S. Senate in March 1843 and was read by a public eager to know more about—and, in many cases, eager to move to—the vast but still little-known American West.

Despite Jessie's literary efforts, Frémont did not fare so well at the hands of all his later biographers. In 1943, for example, the celebrated Pulitzer Prize and National Book Award-winning historian Bernard DeVoto had some scathing things to say about Frémont, i.e., that he was "an opportunist, an adventurer, and a blunderer on a truly dangerous scale."[4]

The real tragedy of Frémont's life was that, after carrying out a remarkable series of exploring expeditions in the 1840s, his enormous pride, his soaring ambitions (he wanted to become U.S. President), and his palpable eagerness to make money by lending his name to dishonest investment schemes all combined to destroy him. In the end, Frémont died alone in a New York City boarding house.

Modern readers, however, can still vicariously share in his experiences by reading the original reports of his expeditions of 1842–1845. These are entitled (1) "A Report on an Exploration of the Country Lying Between the Mississippi River and the Rocky Mountains, on the Line of the Kansas and Great Platte Rivers," and (2) "A Report of the Exploring Expedition to Oregon and North California, in the Years 1843–44."[5]

For example, Frémont wrote that, in 1844, when he and the men of his expedition were struggling through the deep snows of the Sierra Nevada mountains en route to the Sacramento Valley of California,

> ...I set out today with a reconnoitering party, on snow shoes. We marched all in single file, trampling the snow as heavily as we could. Crossing the open basin, in a march of about ten miles we reached the top of one of the peaks, to the left of the pass indicated by our guide [who was the famous frontiersman, scout, and U.S. government courier Christopher "Kit" Carson].
>
> Far below us, dimmed by the distance, was a large snowless valley, bounded on the western side, at a distance of about a hundred miles, by a low range of mountains, which Carson recognized with delight as the mountains bordering the coast. "There," said he, "is the little mountain—it is 15 years since I saw it; but I am as sure as if I had seen it yesterday."
>
> Between us, then, and this low coast range, was the valley of the Sacramento; and no one who had not accompanied us through the incidents of our life for the last few months could realize the delight with which we looked down upon it.[6]

16. Wanting to Become President of the United States

For better or for worse, Frémont will long be remembered, not only for the colorful details of his many adventures but also for the places in the United States that have since been named in his honor—for example, the city of Fremont, California; the Fremont Passes in the Sierra, Rockies, and Cascades; and the Fremont Peaks, the Fremont Glacier, and the Fremont Needle.[7]

In that same year (1844), led by the former mountain man and beaver trapper Caleb Greenwood, the Stephens-Townsend-Murphy party was the first wagon train to cross the Sierra Nevada into California. This party consisted of 11 wagons carrying 23 men, 8 women, and 15 children.

When they finally reached the Humboldt Sink in western Nevada, they met a very friendly Paiute Indian, now known to Western history as Old Winnemucca, who rode toward them repeatedly shouting a word that sounded to them like "Truckee." They assumed that this was his name, and therefore from then on they called him "Truckee." In fact, however, in the Paiute language, "Truckee" really means "Everything is all right!"

Having the great good luck to meet this Indian almost certainly saved the lives of the entire emigrant party. Truckee very carefully explained to Greenwood, by using sign language and by drawing diagrams drawn in the dust, that Greenwood and his party must immediately follow what later came to be known as the Truckee River route, rather than following a nearby trail that looked very promising but would have taken them much too far to the south.[8] If Greenwood had not understood or had not followed Truckee's advice, his party probably could not have crossed the Sierra Nevada before the snow began to fall. In that case, they would almost certainly have died there.[9]

• • •

During the mid-1800s, what has aptly been called a vibrant "sense of mission" to expand both the influence of the United States and its values seized U.S. government officials, explorers, and, the American people themselves. The best shorthand description of this sense of mission is the phrase "Manifest Destiny," which has been discussed briefly in earlier pages of this book and which also colors our perspective on the explorers themselves. During the early and mid-1800s, however, what we typically term the "frontiers" and know today as California, Nevada, Arizona, New Mexico, and Texas were actually part of Mexico. We might well ask, therefore, how well or poorly these "explorers," or more accurately, immigrants, were received by the local people.

An articulate spokesman was General Mariano Guadalupe Vallejo (1807–1890), who was one of brightest and most energetic *Californio* leaders.[10] (*Californio* is, first of all, a Spanish term that came into use in Alta California in the 1820s during the flourishing of the first generation of California-born

Mexicans. Later it included other Spanish speaking Roman Catholics, their descendants or those married to them.)

Without trying to describe Vallejo's long, eventful, and generally-successful career, it is useful to learn what he had to say about the growing wave of North American immigrants who were coming to Alta California in the 1840s, following the footsteps of the earliest explorers there.

Despite his own liberal leanings, Vallejo could not ignore his conservative duties as an officer of the Mexican army. For this reason, he pointedly warned the Ministry of War in Mexico City about the threat posed by the increasing flow of Americans into Alta California. In 1841, for example, he wrote:

> The total population of California does not exceed six thousand souls [here Vallejo was not including the Indians, who were never considered to be *Californios*], and of these two-thirds must be counted as women and children, leaving scarcely two thousand men. But we cannot count on the fifteen thousand Indians in the towns and missions, because they inspire more fear than confidence.
>
> Thus we have the lamentable situation in a country worthy of a better fate. And if the invasion which is taking place from all sides is carried out, all I can assure you is that the Californians will die; I cannot dare to assure you that California can saved. The people, loyal to their flag, will follow the same course and die.[11]

Vallejo also understood that these numerous, aggressive, and very energetic newcomers had skills that would be of value to California's agriculture and commerce. The *Californios* tradition-directed and frozen-in-time nature of their own society, however, did not value Yankee-style competition and upward-mobility.

Nevertheless, as Vallejo would explain years later in his memoirs,

> The arrival of so many people from the outside world was highly satisfying to us *arribeños* [i.e., northern *Californios*] who were ... gratified to see numerous parties of industrious individuals come and settle among us permanently.
>
> Although they were not possessed of wealth, they could be a powerful stimulus to our agriculture which, unfortunately, was still in a state of inactivity, owing to a lack of strong and intelligent workers...[12]

The idea of Manifest Destiny dovetailed well with United States' interests in further explorations of the American West. And thus, following orders to investigate areas that might be of political and economic interest to the United States, in 1838–1842, Navy Lieutenant Charles Wilkes led what is formally known as the U.S. Exploring Expedition but is now usually called the Wilkes Expedition.

After many far-flung adventures in other waters, the expedition's ships *Vincennes* and *Porpoise* arrived at the mouth of the Columbia River in 1841. However, the stormy conditions around the river's shallow bar (which had to be crossed in order to sail up-river) forced them to head for the Strait of

16. Wanting to Become President of the United States

Juan de Fuca instead. From there, Wilkes then organized several overland expeditions.

One exploring party, led by Lieutenant George Johnson, was to travel east across the Cascade Mountains and make its way to Fort Walla Walla, near the junction of the Columbia and Snake Rivers. Wilkes himself commanded another overland expedition, this time to the Hudson's Bay Company post at what was then known as Fort Vancouver (on the site of present-day Portland, Oregon). There he met Dr. John McLoughlin (1784–1857), the Chief Factor, i.e., the officer in charge, of all the western posts of the Hudson's Bay Company, who received him and his men very warmly.

McLoughlin was basically a physician and a trader, not an explorer *per se*, but he was so famous in the Pacific Northwest that he deserves mention here. Later known as the "Father of Oregon," he was a man of high energy and intelligence. He had a very striking appearance as well, being six feet, four inches tall, raw-boned, and extremely strong. He also had piercing eyes and a shoulder-length mane of prematurely white hair. He so impressed the local Indians, in fact, that they dubbed him the "White Headed Eagle." Given the fact that British and American authority on the ground in that region was shaky at best, McLoughlin and the Hudson's Bay Company enjoyed unrivaled power there.[13]

To return to the party led by Lieutenant Johnson, these men finally arrived at Fort Walla Walla, where they were the guests of Dr. Marcus Whitman, the American missionary doctor who had pioneered the U.S. settlement of the Oregon Country.

The subsequent travels of the members of the Wilkes expedition in the Pacific Northwest were extensive but are too detailed to justify discussion here. The interesting footnote was that in 1841 Wilkes selected several men, led by Lieutenant George Foster Emmons, to undertake an overland trip to San Francisco, which was then still a very small Mexican presidio.

Their goal was to determine whether a big river (other than the Columbia) ran into the Pacific Ocean and thus might offer a substantial harbor north of San Francisco Bay. During their trip, the men were threatened by a grizzly bear. Several men shot at the bear and could see (presumably from puffs of dust from the bear's hide) that their bullets were hitting it, but the bear did not fall down dead. This was a real disappointment to Emmons, who wanted to preserve its skin. In the same vein as many other explorers of the West, he wrote, "Among all the animals I have ever seen, I do not think I have witnessed so formidable an enemy."[14]

The Wilkes expedition pressed on to San Francisco and from there finally ended its travels in New York in 1842. Its program had been a clear success, marking the official entry of American explorers into the pursuit of international scientific knowledge. More specifically, the work of the expedition also helped to convince the American government that Puget Sound would in the long run be much more valuable to it than the Columbia River.

The U.S. Navy would continue to engage in exploration, though in a more modest way. The U.S. Army, for its part, would undertake both political and scientific exploration on an ambitious scale, with the twin objectives of (1) expanding American government influence deeper into the interior of North America, (2) and paving the way for an assertive use of the continent's natural resources to meet the demands of a demanding and expanding American population.[15]

Earlier, in 1838 the U.S. Army Corps of Topographical Engineers had been founded under the overall command of Colonel John J. Albert, who would be in charge of it for many years. It would become very active in the trans–Mississippi West, where Lieutenant John Charles Frémont would play a starring role.

In 1838, too, the French explorer Joseph Nicolas Nicollet (1786–1843), who had previously conducted a 59-day exploration of the north-central Minnesota wilderness looking for the source of the Mississippi River, sold to the Corps of Topographical Engineers his preliminary report and a map of his findings.[16] The Corps was sufficiently impressed by these results to name him to lead a well-equipped expedition westward to the Missouri River, with Frémont as his assistant.

Nicollet set out to follow the Minnesota River and to explore the upper waterways and lakes of this region. On his second expedition, in 1839, he was the first to make detailed studies of the Coteau watershed between the Missouri and Mississippi Rivers.

Acclaimed for all his work, Nicollet would spend his later years working out a masterful *Map of the Hydrological Basin of the Upper Mississippi*, which appeared in 1840 and was one of the first American-produced maps that showed, correctly, the nature of hydrographical or drainage basins. It was not until 1845, however, that the presence of a "great basin" lying between the Rocky Mountains and the Sierra Nevada range was clearly shown on a map—this one a joint undertaking by Frémont and the German cartographer Charles Preuss.

Since the War Department of the United States needed more maps, in 1845 the government set in motion three trans–Mississippi ventures to acquire them. All of these expeditions were directly related to two diplomatic crises: the first with Mexico over the independence of Texas and its annexation by the United States, and the second with Great Britain over the location of the boundary separating British and American territory in the Pacific Northwest.[17]

Colonel Stephen W. Kearney headed the first of these expeditions, leading a contingent of dragoons (i.e., heavy cavalry units) on a reconnaissance

16. Wanting to Become President of the United States 113

over the Oregon Trail to the South Pass and thence southward to Bent's Fort. Kearney's goals were three-fold: to impress the local Indians with American military power; to keep the Oregon Trail open for emigrants; to learn what natural resources the area had to offer to the United States; and, finally, to see how effective the dragoons were against the Indians of the western plains.

This expedition produced a better map of the Colorado River system (it was compiled in part from Frémont's own knowledge of the region) but otherwise broke no new ground. Frémont's star was in the ascendency, however, and he was put in charge of the next expedition, which was instructed to travel from Bent's Fort through the Colorado Rockies.

As part of this undertaking, Lieutenant James W. Albert (Colonel Albert's son) was to explore the southern Rockies and the regions south of the Arkansas River. He would accomplish all this in 1845 without running into any major problems. Frémont, in the meantime, was to finish his own work as soon as possible in the Colorado Rockies so that the information he acquired could be made available to Congress if military operations should become necessary, e.g., against Mexico.

However, there was nothing at all in Colonel Albert's own orders to Frémont to suggest that he (Frémont) had permission to lead a transcontinental military expedition to far-distant California. This, however, is precisely what Frémont did, simply to further his own career, even though his orders simply directed him to map the source of the Arkansas River.

This step led to his becoming deeply involved in the U.S.-Mexican war of 1846–1848 and, ultimately, to his own court-marshal in 1848 for disobeying a direct order from a superior officer. Although President Polk remitted his sentence, Frémont believed that his honor had been tarnished and that he was not guilty of anything. On these grounds, he left the official service of the U.S. government.[18]

17

Mountain Man Slang

The Oregon Trail, written by Bostonian Francis Parkman (1823–1893), is one of the best historical accounts ever written about the frontier West.[1] It dates from 1846 and can profitably be discussed here at some length.

This book contains many excellent descriptions of the lives of Indians and of fur trappers on the frontier. Parkman opens his famous work in these words:

> Last spring, 1846, was a busy season in the city of St. Louis…. Steamboats were leaving the levee and passing up the Missouri, crowded with passengers on their way to the frontier. On one of these, the "Radnor," since snagged and lost, my friend and relative, Quincy Adams Shaw, and myself, left St. Louis on the twenty-eighth of April [1846], on a tour of curiosity and amusement in the Rocky Mountains…[2]

Later, Parkman tells us about a camp of the Oglala Sioux, a Plains Indian tribe of South Dakota:

> The lodge of my host Kongra-Tonga, or the Big Crow, presented a picturesque spectacle that evening. A score or more Indians were seated around it in a circle, their dark naked forms just visible in the dull light of the smouldering fire in the middle. The pipe [Indian men smoked tobacco, often mixed with bark, for ritual purposes] glowed brightly in the gloom as it passed from hand to hand. Then a squaw would drop a piece of buffalo-fat on the dull embers.
>
> Instantly a bright flame would leap up, darting its light to the very apex of the tall conical structure [the tepee], where the tops of the slender poles that support the covering of [buffalo] hide were gathered together. It guilded the features of the Indians, as with animated gestures they sat around it, telling their endless stories of war and hunting, and displayed rude garments of skins that hung over the resting-place of the chief, and the rifles and powder-horns of the two white guests [i.e., Parkman and a fur trapper].
>
> For a moment all would be bright as day; then the flames would die out; fitful flashes from the embers would illumine the lodge, and then leave it in darkness. Then the light would wholly fade, and the lodge and all within it be involved again in obscurity.[3]

Parkman was full of praise for Henry Chatillon, his French-Canadian guide and buffalo hunter, who was, he wrote, "a man of extraordinary strength and hardihood." Chatillon was also an extraordinary hunter, as evidenced by Parkman's following description:

> Shaw [Parkman's travel companion] saw Henry standing erect upon the prairie, almost surrounded by the buffalo. Henry was in his element. Quite unconscious that anyone was looking at him, he stood the full height of his tall figure, one hand resting upon his side and the other arm leaning carelessly on the muzzle of his rifle.
>   His eye was ranging over the singular assemblage around him. Now and then he would select such a cow [i.e., a female buffalo, much tastier than a bull] as suited him, level his rifle, and shoot her dead; then, quietly reloading, he would resume his former position. The buffalo seemed no more to regard his presence than if he were one of themselves…
>   the buffalo showed no sign of fear; they remained gathered around their dead companions. Henry had already killed as many cows as we wanted for use, and Shaw, kneeling behind one of the carcasses, shot five bulls before the rest thought it necessary to disperse.
>   [Although the Indians dried much of the best meat of a buffalo and used the rest of the carcass for other purposes, Europeans and Americans did not have Indian wives and thus did not have the time or the labor needed to do this. As a result, they often took only the tongue, hump, and some of the most succulent ribs, leaving the rest of the animal to be devoured by the wolves.][4]

A somewhat different, and highly original personal account of the frontier is provided by the writer Lewis H. Garrard (1829–1887), who grew up in Cincinnati, was just 17 years old in 1846 when he received parental permission—and generous funding—for a trip into the frontier West.[5] From St. Louis, he traveled by river to Westport Landing (now Kansas City) and then overland to Bent's Fort, located on a branch of the Santa Fe Trail in the southwestern part of present-day Colorado.

His 1846 book *Wah-to-yah and the Trail*, is especially valuable today because it preserves some of the most unique and most remarkable slang used by the mountain men. The best example in Garrards's book is the one given below, which will be roughly translated into standard English as soon as it ends (the text given here is as in the original).

Garrard wrote:

> Though the wind was piercingly cold, Hatcher [a mountain man in Garrard's party] was up early making a fire, "for," said he, "this hos is no b'ar to stick his nose under cover all the robe season, an' lay round camp, like a darned Ned; but," he added in a undertone, as he looked to see if the government men were awake, "thar's two or three in this crowd—wagh!—howsomever, the *green* is 'rubbed out' a little."
>   This child hates an American what hasn't seen Injuns skulped, or doesn't know a Yute from a Khian mok'sin. Sometimes he thinks of makin' tracks for white settlement, but when he gets to Bent's big lodge, on the Arkansa, and sees the bugheways, an' the fellers from the States, how they roll their eyes at an Indian yell, worse nor if a village of Camanches was on 'em, an' pick up a beaver trap, to ask what it is—just shows what the niggurs had thar brungin' up—this child says—'a little bacca, if it's a plew a plug

an' Dupont an' Galena, a Green river or so,' and he leaves for the Bayou Salade. Darn the white diggings when thar's buffler in the mountains! Whoopee! shouted he to us, "are you for Touse? This hos is thar in one sun, wagh!"[6]

Approximate translation:

Although the wind was cold, Hatcher was up early, making a fire, for, he said, "I'm not like a bear to huddle in my robes and hang around camp like a darned pork-eating farmer..." but, he added, "there are two or three men in our own party who do have a little outdoors experience."

I myself [this child] hate to see an American who hasn't seen Indians scalped, or who can't tell the moccasin-print of one Indian tribe from another. Sometimes I think of leaving the wilderness and going to a white settlement, but when I get to Bent's Fort on the Arkansas River, and see the businessmen and the fellows from the United States there, how they roll their eyes, in fear, at an Indian yell—as frightened as they would be if a whole Comanche village was after them, or when they pick up a beaver trap and ask what it is, all this just shows where these fools were brought up.

I myself say: a little tobacco, even if it is very expensive, plus some gunpowder, some lead for bullets, and a couple of those excellent Green River brand hunting knives—with these few items I am entirely ready to leave for the best hunting grounds (i.e., the Bayou Salade, literally "Salt Valley," a Rocky Mountain valley teaming with big game because of its salty springs and soil). "Hurray!" he shouted to us, "Are you heading for Taos? I'll be there myself in one day, for sure!"

The mountain men enjoyed Taos very much. There they could get the rudimentary supplies they needed, thus saving themselves a long and difficult trip back to the Missouri settlements, and they could also enjoy the company of the often very pretty New Mexican women.

The best woman writer on the North American frontier was probably 18-year-old Susan Shelby Magoffin (1827–1855), who kept a detailed diary at a critical time, namely, 1846 and 1847, when her travels coincided with the early days of the Mexican-American War.[7]

Susan had married Samuel Magoffin, an older, wealthy, and highly-respected Santa Fe Trail trader. By the time of Susan's trip to New Mexico and northern Mexico in 1846, Samuel and his brother James had been involved in this trade for almost 20 years. On her travels, Susan was accompanied, as was fit and proper for a mid-19th-century gentlewoman of high economic and social status, not only by her husband but also by various servants and employees, plus her pet dog, Ring.

Susan was the first Anglo-American woman to travel west from Independence, Missouri, along the Santa Fe Trail and then south down El Camino Real de Tierra Adentro to Chihuahua, Mexico. Her party subsequently turned east off this latter trail and continued on to Matamoros, Mexico (located on the coast of the Gulf of Mexico, south of Brownsville, Texas).

Despite its human interest and its historical relevance, her diary was held privately by her family until 1926, when Stella Drumm, the librarian of the Missouri Historical Society, persuaded Susan's daughter to permit its publication that year. Drumm edited the diary and tells the modern reader, "In her simple and gentle way the young lady deftly raised the curtain from characters and events of great importance in American history."[8]

A good example of Susan's "soft" reporting follows here (text as in the original). Near the very end of her travels, Susan wrote, in Cerralvo, Mexico,

> At this place I made a *comadre* [a close friend] of an old woman witch, who brought eggs and bread down to the encampment to sell; she stopped at our tent door, she looked up at me, and said [in Spanish] take me with you to your country, "why," said I. "*le guerro V. los Americans*" [You are at war with the Americans]?
>
> She neither answered yes or no, but gave me a sharp pinch on my cheek, I suppose to see if the flesh and color were natural—and said, "*na guerro este*" [there is no war]. The pinch did not feel very comfortable, but I could but laugh at her cunning reply.[9]

• • •

The Corps of Topographical Engineers continued its work, naming First Lieutenant William Hemsley Emory as Brigadier Kearny's topographer.[10] This was an inspired choice because Emory had good experience (having worked on the Northeast Boundary Survey of 1843–1844 and on a map of Texas in 1844) and could count prominent astronomers, mathematicians, and geologists among his circle of friends. Emory and his associates did an excellent job in the field and made significant contributions to geographical knowledge.

For example, Emory's 1847 map of his travels was the first accurate map of the whole southwestern region. Based on 2,000 astronomical observations with an altitude profile of 357 separate barometric observations, this map completed the previous outlines of the geography of the trans–Mississippi West and corrected errors in earlier maps. Moreover, Emory and his colleagues studied the geology, the minerals, and the flora and fauna of the area. As if all this was not enough, their interest in the abandoned pueblos gave an important push to the study of Indian archeological remains. Emory's group could not determine the origins of the ruined pueblos, but its interest did provide a solid foundation for subsequent research on this subject.

• • •

The writer George Frederick Ruxton (1821–1848) was an English explorer and adventurer.[11] He became an officer in the British army and was posted to Ireland and Canada. Independently wealthy, he resigned from the army to become a professional big game hunter and traveled in Africa and Mexico before moving to the United States.

Ruxton was both a very fine outdoorsman and a very good writer. Traveling in Mexico in 1847, for example, he describes, in these simple but evocative terms, how silver was transported to the local mint:

> We met a *conducta* [i.e., in this context, a shipment] from the mines ... bearing bars of silver to the mint. The wagon in which it was carried was drawn by six mules galloping at their utmost speed. Eight or ten men, with muskets between their knees, sat in the wagon, facing outward, and as many more galloped alongside, armed to the teeth.[12]

Ruxton's literary reputation rests on his *Adventures in Mexico and the Rocky Mountains* in 1848, and his *Life in the Far West*, which first appeared as a magazine serial in 1848 and then in book form the next year. In 1966, both texts of both these books were combined and were published in the United States in 1966 in a single volume under the title of *Mountain Men*.

Unfortunately, despite surviving many death-or-glory episodes in the North American wilderness, Ruxton died of dysentery in St. Louis in 1848, at the age of only 27. However, readers today can get a good example of his life-style by reading about his travel along an exceptionally arid and therefore dangerous part of a New Mexico trail known in its entirety as El Camino Real de Tierra Adentro, i.e., the Royal Road of the Interior Land.

The dangerous section mentioned above was called the Jornada del Muerto, i.e., the Day's Journey of the Dead Man. Ruxton wrote of it:

> I was now at the edge of this formidable desert, where along the road the bleaching bones of mules and horses testify to the dangers to be apprehended from the want of water and pasture, and many human bones likewise tell their tale of Indian slaughter and assault...
>
> Near the Perillo [a tiny waterhole] is a point of rocks which abuts the road, and from which a large band of Apaches a few years ago pounced on a band of American trappers and entirely defeated them, killing several and carrying off all their animals. Behind these rocks they frequently lie in ambush shooting down the unwary traveler, whose first intimation of their presence is the puff of smoke [i.e., a gunshot] from the rocks, or the whiz of an arrow through the air. One of my mozos [muleteers], who was a New Mexican and knew the country well, warned me of the dangers of this spot, and before passing it I halted the mules and rode on to reconnoitre; but no Apache lurked behind it, and we passed unmolested...
>
> At sunrise [Ruxton and other travelers crossed this region at night to avoid the great heat and dryness of the day] we halted for a couple of hours on a patch of grass which afforded a bite to the tired animals, and about three in the afternoon had the satisfaction of reaching the river [the Rio Grande] at the watering place called Fray Cristoval, having performed the whole distance of the jornada, of ninety-five, or, as some say, one hundred miles in little more than twenty hours.[13]

Another excellent writer, George Douglas Brewerton (1827–1901) was a bright young U.S. Army lieutenant who accompanied Kit Carson when Kit left Los Angeles in early May of 1848 to carry official dispatches to Washington, D.C.

Brewerton's accounts of his travels with Carson appeared in installments in *Harper's* magazine, beginning in 1853, but were not published in book form until 1930, under the title of *Overland with Kit Carson*. A later (1993) edition of this book is the source of the comments given below.

17. Mountain Man Slang

Brewerton was very good at recounting death-or-glory frontier adventures, but he was even better at describing remarkable frontier landscapes for the benefit of stay-at-home readers who probably would never see them. He wrote, for example:

> As it was at the Mora [a river in central-eastern New Mexico] that I received my first impressions of the Great Plains, it may not be improper ... to attempt a description of the peculiarities of this region I was so soon to journey through...
>
> Clothed in the verdant livery of spring, or decked in the more luxuriant robes of early summer, they present the appearance of a sea of grass or flowers, save where some stream, fed by the mountain snows, stretches across the landscape, marked by the trees which fringe its banks and rear their wall of foliage above the otherwise almost unbroken level.
>
> Nor does a comparison between the prairies and the ocean cease with the great extent of surface presented to the eye: motion seems added to increase the delusion; each passing breeze, as it sweeps over the long grasses, gives an undulation to its ridges which is enhanced and heightened by the rapid succession of light and gloom derived from the shadows of flying clouds...
>
> Nor are these mighty wilds solitary or untenanted. The buffalo feed over them by the thousands; the timid deer or graceful antelope meet the eye at every turn; and the Indian makes them not only his hunting-ground but too frequently the theatre of scenes and conflicts the particulars of which but seldom reach the ears of the dwellers in our Atlantic cities...
>
> There is wild excitement, too, connected with the everyday life of the trapper and hunter in this section of the country. So intense is it, in fact, that more than one young man, whose talents and fortune would have fitted him for the occupancy of a brilliant position in the world of civilization, has turned his back upon society and its refinements to endure the oftentimes fearful hardships of this adventurous career.[14]

18

"Chastise them well"

In 1848, after the Mexican-American War was finally over, the news that gold had recently been discovered in California reached the east coast of the United States. By the end of 1849, more than 100,000 people from all over the world would flood into California by land or by sea to seek their fortunes in the Gold Rush.

There was thus a sudden and great surge of interest in learning more about the geography and resources of the American West. Frémont, still smarting from the humiliation of being court-martialed but still backed by his politically powerful father-in-law, Missouri Senator Thomas Hart Benton, now put himself forward eagerly in hopes of recouping his badly-tattered reputation.

In October 1848, Frémont therefore organized a 35-man expedition to California, designed to prove that a central route across the United States, i.e., a potential railroad route favored by Senator Benton, could be used by travelers even during the snow, ice, and bitter cold of a Rocky Mountain winter.

To make a long story short, however, this venture into the snows of the southern Colorado Rockies was an unmitigated disaster, largely thanks to Frémont's very bad judgment.[1] By 11 February 1849, the last remaining survivors had at last been brought to safety in Taos, New Mexico, but, like many other egocentric leaders before and after him, Frémont was very quick to blame others for his own failures.

In this case, he blamed the famous mountain man and guide Old Bill Williams, who had left the expedition before it reached its unhappy end and who, many days later, was found alone, with a fatal wound in his chest, frozen to death in the snow with his nearly-dead horse tied to tree not far from him. In any case, the bottom line was that, out of Frémont's initial group of 29 men, only 10 of them survived. It has been said that this disastrous expedition was an event from which Frémont would never recover, either personally or professionally.[2]

In this era, there were also some highly competent explorers who are less well known today because their activities were not as newsworthy as

18. "Chastise them well"

Frémont's. These men include in 1849 Captain Randolph B. Marcy (1812–1887) and his topographical engineer Lieutenant James H. Simpson (1813–1833), on the one hand, and Captain Howard Stansbury (leader of an 1849–1850 expedition looking for railroad passes through the Wasatch Mountains and the Rocky Mountains), who was assisted by Lieutenant James W. Gunnison, on the other.[3] A few words to summarize both the Marcy-Simpson expedition and the Stansbury-Gunnison venture may be useful here.

Marcy's expedition lasted for eight months and covered nearly 2,000 miles over some of the most difficult terrain in North America. He recommended to prospective emigrants a new route for wagon travel that shortened the distance between the Mississippi and the Pacific by 300 miles, and suggested, for the future, a route that, 33 years later, would become part of a southern transcontinental railroad line.

Moreover, Marcy was also an excellent writer and produced a truly outstanding guidebook, entitled *The Prairie Traveler* (1859), that was full of very practical "I-was-there" advice for cross-country travelers.[4] It gives specific, hands-on, guidance on more than 30 of the long distance trails; on how to cope with the logistics of long-distance overland travel in the Western frontier; and on how to deal with the local Indians, some of whom were extremely hostile.

Indeed, his book still makes interesting reading today. This, for example, is what he has to say about hostile Indians:

> The only way to make their merciless freebooters fear or respect the authority of our government is, when they misbehave, first of all to chastise them well by striking such a blow as will be felt for a long time, and thus show them we are superior to them in war. They will then respect us much more than when their good-will is purchased with presents.[5]
>
> A friend of mine, who has passed the last twenty-five years of his life among the Indians of the Rocky Mountains, corroborates the opinions I have advanced.... He says:
>
> '...they won't show fair fight, any way you can fix it [i.e., to avoid losing their own warriors, the Indians, who had few firearms, usually avoided pitched battles with the very well-armed whites]. Don't they kill and sculp a white man when-ar they get the better of him? The mean varmints, they'll never behave themselves until you give um a clean out and out licking...
>
> ...ef you treat um decently, they think you ar afeared. You may depend on it. Cap. [i.e., Captain, Marcy's rank], the only way to treat Indians is to thrash them well at first, then the balance will sorter take to you and behave themselves.[6] .

The Stansbury-Gunnison expedition reflected Senator Benton's belief that a railroad should be built between St. Louis and San Francisco. During his travels, Stansbury fell from his horse and was so badly hurt that the expedition had to end—but not before he was able to report that he had found a usable route through the Rocky Mountains that lay well to the south of the familiar South Pass route. This achievement was noteworthy because it saved many days of travel between Fort Laramie and the Mormon settlements of Utah. Indeed, the Overland Stage, the Pony Express, the Union Pacific Railroad, the Lincoln Highway (i.e., U.S. 30 from Philadelphia to Granger, Wyoming and U.S. 40 west of Salt Lake City and over Donner Pass), and Interstate 80 would all use part of the trail he blazed.

The Marcy and Stansbury expeditions would be the high point of the continental-scale explorations undertaken by the Corps of Topographical Engineers. Thereafter, the Corps focused on more modest regional studies, that is, trying to fill in the large gaps and blank spaces that still existed even on the best maps of the frontiers. A few examples are mentioned below.

In Texas, the Corps entered into a complicated web of *de facto* military, state, and commercial partnerships organized both to discover the economic potential of a given region and, and at the same time, to set up some defenses to deter any hostile Indians. None of these partnerships—in Texas or elsewhere—was of major historical importance. For this reason, they will not be discussed in detail here, but some points can usefully be made.[7]

Texas had managed to "solve" its Plains Indian problem simply by eradicating some of the southern Plains tribes as fighting forces. New Mexico itself, however, still needed either to set up effective defenses against its hostile Indians or, alternatively, to launch an offensive against them so powerful that, in its wake, defenses would not be necessary. There was no easy solution to this problem but, as the Ninth Army District of New Mexico wrestled with it, one positive result did emerge: detailed studies of the old, ruined Indian Pueblos were undertaken.

The topographical engineer in the case was Lieutenant James H. Simpson, who was assisted by the brothers Richard H. and Edward Kern. On one expedition, Simpson spent time at the populated pueblo of Jemez, located on the Rio Grande west of Santa Fe, where he studied the then-current way of life of the pueblo inhabitants and learned about their history and beliefs. The Kerns made drawings and watercolors, including sketches of the religious depictions that covered the walls of the *estufa* (a circular meeting room, often underground, that was common to all Pueblo tribes).

In 1849, Simpson and his helpers visited the Chaco Canyon ruins and later made copies of the names and dates seen, both in Spanish and in Latin, on Inscription Rock—some of them dating from 1606. Today, Simpson's fame rests not on his training as a topographical engineer but on his studies of the pueblos themselves. For example, his description of Indian languages suggested that there had once been six different linguistic groups among the tribes of the southwestern United States. It is said that his report on the pueblos he visited must still be referenced in any modern work on the ethnography of this region.[8]

• • •

18. "Chastise them well"

The world-famous frontiersman Kit Carson (1809–1868) was never hailed as a great literary figure—indeed, he was entirely illiterate and was barely able to sign his own name—but in 1856 he dictated to a friend a short but very readable memoir, entitled *Kit Carson's Autobiography*. It is the source for the following comments.

The *Autobiography* contains so many of Kit's remarkable true-life adventures that it is hard to single out just one to cite here, but his duel with a big, aggressive Frenchman named Shunar, which took place at the encampment of beaver trappers on Utah's Green River in the summer of 1835, is hard to surpass. Carson said that Shunar was

> an overbearing kind of man, and very strong. He made a practice of whipping every man that he was displeased with—and that was nearly all [men]. One day, after he had beaten two or three men, he said that he had no trouble to flog Frenchmen, and as for Americans, he would take a switch and switch them. [Shunar was thus implying that the Americans were merely children who could safely be whipped.]
>
> I did not like such talk from any man, so I told him that I was the worst American in camp. There were many who could thrash him but for the fact that they were afraid, and that if he used such expressions any more, I would rip his guts.
>
> He said nothing but started for his rifle, mounted his horse, and made his appearance in front of the camp. As soon as I saw this, I mounted my horse also, seized the first weapon I could get hold of, which was a pistol, and galloped up to him and demanded if I was the one he intended to shoot.
>
> Our horses were touching. He said no, drawing his gun at the same time [i.e., raising his rifle] so he could have a fair shot at me. I was prepared and allowed him to draw his gun. We both fired at the same time, and all present said that one report was heard [i.e., the two men fired at the same time].
>
> I shot him through the arm and his ball passed my head, cutting my hair and powder burning my eye, the muzzle of his gun being near my head when he fired. During the remainder of our stay in camp we had no more bother with this French bully.[9]

• • •

Before the U.S. Civil War, a 1857 map by Lieutenant Gouveurneur Kemble Warren became the culminating cartographic production of this Corps, It was one of the first maps to show the location and geographic nature of the Black Hills of South Dakota—as being distinct from the Laramie Range, which is a northern extension of the Front Range of the Colorado Rockies. (In 1863, the Corps of Topographical Engineers was disbanded by an Act of Congress and its duties were merged with those of the U.S. Army's Corps of Engineers.)[10]

Before its disbandedment, however, and because the 1848 Treaty of Guadalupe Hidalgo signed by the United States and Mexico at the end of the U.S.-Mexican War had not precisely defined the border between these two countries, a joint Mexican-American commission, which included members of the Corps of Topographical Engineers, was set up to do so. After various fits-and-starts, all the necessary documents were finally signed by both governments in 1857 and the field records of the Mexican Boundary Survey were officially closed.

This Survey essentially completed the formal geographical outline of the United States. Exploration did not then come to a full stop, of course, but the government and the American army now turned away from simply blazing trails in the wilderness and demarcating national boundaries. At the same time, however, the exploration of Canada continued apace.

In 1857, for example, joint British-Canadian exploring expeditions to the Canadian Northwest were headed by John Palliser (1818–1887) and George Gladman (1800–1863).[11]

These were unique undertakings because they were the last of the old-style expeditions, which had basically been geographic explorations with a light overlay of secondary scientific objectives, and the first of a new "hybrid" approach, in which science and geography played equally-important roles.

Palliser had proposed his journey to the Royal Geographical Society in London in order to explore the southern prairies and the Rocky Mountain passes of British North America. The British Colonial Office, for its part, wanted to know whether these lands could be accessed by Canada using a route entirely through British territory.

Thus from May 1857 until its return to England in June 1860, the Pallister expedition traveled several routes in the southern prairies, i.e., mainly between the northern and southern branches of the Saskatchewan River, and explored several passes through the Rocky Mountains. Pallister's verdict was that an all-British route was in fact feasible but that travel through the United States was very much easier, so an American route should be used instead.

The scientific results of this expedition were useful, too. The plants and trees of the region and its geology were carefully mapped. Coal supplies were noted and were judged to be adequate for future construction of a railroad through the prairies to the Pacific Ocean.

In 1857, the Canadian government sent out its own expedition under George Gladman to assess the agricultural potential of the area between Canada and a Red River settlement in what is now Manitoba. The geologist of this expedition would later (in 1860) write a book predicting that what he called the "sterile belt" of the northwestern United States would somehow force future population growth into Canada's Red River and Saskatchewan River valleys. Although without any factual basis, this theory did appeal to those who strongly favored the expansion of the Canadian way of life ever further into the Canadian west.

In the United States itself, a new and very challenging goal of exploration was *to support the settling of the trans-Mississippi West*—for example, by finding the best route for a transcontinental railroad.[12]

18. "Chastise them well"

Beginning in the late 1840s, this issue became of major importance to American business and political leaders alike; details of some of its key events are very briefly discussed in Appendix 3 on "The Railroad Surveys."

The most important fact here is that an expanding and restless American population was now established along the Western frontier, e.g., in the Oregon Country, California, Texas, and the Southwest. Regional frictions were building up between the North and the South, and a transcontinental railroad that would draw the Atlantic and Pacific coasts closer together now seemed to be a political necessity.

To find the best route, Congress therefore authorized a survey of all the practical train routes from the Mississippi to the Pacific. Previously, such a task would have fallen to the Corps of Topographical Engineers, but railroad exploration work was now placed under the control of Jefferson Davis, the secretary of war, who was to report to Congress by January 1854. A new Bureau of Explorations and Surveys was also set up to speed the work.

The reports of the transcontinental railroad surveys of 1853–1855 varied considerably, both in technical quality and in the political arguments put forward by their supporters. When a four-volume summary report finally appeared in 1857, however, Congress singularly *failed to decide on any route*, due to partisanship and regionalism. The search for a transcontinental railroad track therefore had to be put on hold.

19

A Nevada Outlaw Named Slade

The Canadian artist and writer Paul Kane (1810–1871) made two journeys, often by canoe, during the years 1845–1848 from Toronto (then known as York), Canada, to Vancouver's Island and Oregon through the Hudson's Bay Company's territory, and then back again. In so doing, he achieved his main objectives: to paint vivid landscapes and scenes of Indian life in Canada and the Pacific Northwest, and to describe them in print.

Kane's 1859 book, *Wanderings of an Artist Among the Indians of North America*, gives the reader good insights into Canadian frontier life and contains both color and black-and-white reproductions of Kane's art. It is the source of the quotations given below, which address a wide range of contemporary subjects and which have been chosen from different chapters of his book.

Kane wrote on a number of interesting topics, which are highlighted below in italics:

Traveling by canoe:

> It is usual to start every morning between 3 and 4 o'clock and proceed till 8 for breakfast, then continue steadily on until an hour before dark, so as to give the men time [at the camping-place] to prepare for the night.
>
> The only rest allowed [during the day] being at intervals of about an hour, when all hands stop two or three minutes to fill their pipes. It is quite a common way of expressing the distance from one place to another to say that it is so many pipes; and this, among those who have travelled in the interior gives a very good idea of the distance.[1]

Preparing the frontier food known as "pemmican":

> ...thin slices of dried meat are pounded between two stones until the fibres separate; about 50 pounds of this are put into a bag of buffalo skin, with about 40 pounds of melted [buffalo] fat, and mixed together while hot, and sewed up, forming a hard and compact mass.... One pound of this is considered equal to four pounds of ordinary meat, and the pemmican keeps for years perfectly good exposed to any weather.[2]

19. A Nevada Outlaw Named Slade

Pacific Ocean whaling:

[The Indians'] manner of catching the whale is ingenious.... Upon a whale being seen in the offing, they rush down to their large canoes, and push off with ten or twelve men each. Each canoe is furnished with a number of strong seal-skin bags filled with air, and made with great care and skill, capable of containing about ten gallons each.

To each bag is attached a barbed spear-head, made of bone or iron, when they can get it, by a strong string, eight or nine feet long, and in the socket of the spear-head is fitted a handle, seven or eight feet in length. Upon coming up [i.e., alongside] with the whale, the barbed heads with the bags attached are driven into him and the handles withdrawn.

The attack is continually renewed, until the whale is no longer able to sink from the buoyancy of the bags, when he is despatched and towed ashore. [The Indians] are sometimes led twenty to thirty miles out to sea in the chase, but such is the admirable construction of their canoes, and so skillfully are they managed, that an accident rarely happens.[3]

The annual salmon harvest:

Salmon is the only food used by the Indians on the Lower Columbia River, the two months of fishing affording a sufficient supply to last them the whole year round. The mode in which they cure them is by splitting them down the back, after which each half is again split, making them sufficiently thin to dry with facility, a process occupying in general from four to five days.

The salmon are afterwards sewed up in rush mats, containing about ninety or hundred pounds, and put up on scaffolds to keep the dogs from them. Infinitely greater numbers of salmon could readily be taken here, if it were so desired; but, as the chief considerately remarked to me, if he were to take all that came up, there would be none left for the Indians on the upper part of the river; so they content themselves with supplying [only] their own wants.[4]

• • •

An intelligent but uneducated lad who would later not only live with Indians, but also write about them was Elijah Nicholas ("Nick") Wilson (1842–1915). In 1850 "Nick" Wilson crossed the Great Plains by ox-team with his parents.[5] His family settled in Grantsville, a Mormon village just south of Utah's Great Salt Lake, but there was not very much to eat, the work was very hard, and the threat of Indian attacks kept the pioneers on a constant state of alert.

A few Goshute Indians hung around the town begging for a living; the settlers, deciding, "It is cheaper to feed them than too fight them," offered them some subsistence-level jobs. Wilson's father hired an Indian family to herd his small flock of sheep. A young Indian boy named Pantsuk, and Wilson, were ordered to become sheepherders.

Wilson learned the Goshute language fluently and remembered, "Pantsuk and I had great times together for two years. We trapped chipmunks and birds, shot rabbits with our bows and arrows, and had other kinds of papoose sport." Pantsuk soon died, however, and Wilson was so lonely and unhappy tending sheep all by himself that in 1856, at the age of 11, he ran away from home and joined a local tribe of Indians.

He later described his life in a 1910 book, *White Indian Boy*, from which the following account of how Indian women processed the buffalo killed by their men is taken. Wilson wrote:

> One morning I saw seven head of buffalo on the bench [of a local river] about a mile away. Ten Indians started after them [on horseback]. One having a wide spear with a long handle would ride up to a buffalo and cut the hamstrings of both legs and the other [i.e., another Indian] would come along and kill it.
>
> About fifteen squaws went up to skin the buffalos and get the meat.... The squaws would rip the animals down the back from head to tail and then rip them down the belly and take off the top half of the hide and cut all the meat on that side from the bones. They would then tie ropes to the feet of the buffaloes and turn them over with their ponies, and do the other side the same way.
>
> After they got the meat home, they would slice it up in thin pieces and hang it up to dry. When it was half dry they would take a piece at a time and pound it between two rocks until it was very soft, and then hang it up again to dry. The dried meat was put into a sack and the older it got the better it was.
>
> This was the way they did all of their buffalo meat. The meat was generally kept for use in the winter and during the general meetings of the tribe. I know that we had about five hundred pounds of it when we got to the place where the tribe was to assemble. It was about ... late August when the tribe had all assembled in Deer Lodge Valley, now in Montana.[6]

• • •

During 1859–1860, two government-sponsored expeditions in the Southwest used, of all things, *camels from the Middle East* as a unique means of transportation in Texas in order to locate supply routes for isolated military posts.[7]

These animals, led by experienced camel drivers, were transported from the Middle East with their handlers and were used in desert regions of Texas on an experimental basis. There were two high points in this remarkable process. During the first expedition in 1859, 24 camels were used, each carrying about 500 pounds of cargo. These "ships of the desert" were not easy to handle but performed so well that a second camel caravan, with 20 camels, 25 pack mules, and 20 infantrymen, was sent out in 1860. It, too, performed quite well.

Earlier, in 1857, camels had also been used to help build a wagon road in the Southwest under the provisions of the Pacific Wagon Road Program, which had been set up that same year to replace the failed Pacific Railroad Program. This 1857 experiment had been a success as well, and tests had shown that camels could even withstand the cold and snows of the high Sierra Nevada mountains.

The bad news, however, was that it was too hard for the U.S. government to find enough trained camel handlers and camel drivers, so camels would never come to play a major role in American frontier transportation. Nevertheless, they continued to be used from time to time in the Southwest until the 1880s.

• • •

In 1860, William H. Brewer, a very literate Yale-educated teacher of the natural sciences, eagerly accepted an offer from the famous geologist Josiah Whitney to take part in the first geological survey of California.[8]

Brewer was not a geologist himself but his background in agriculture and botany made him a very valuable member of Whitney's team. Moreover, Brewer also wrote exceptionally well, and spent much of his free time sending lively, detailed letters to his brother back east. These letters, later printed under the title of *Up and Down California in 1860–1864* and now the basic source for this section, give the reader a colorful first-hand glimpse of life and labor in California in those turbulent times.

Since this book is quite long (583 pages), only a tiny part of it can be discussed here. The following excerpt from the chapter on the Washoe mines of Nevada, where both gold and silver were discovered in 1850–1859, constitutes a good example.

Brewer writes that the rush to these mines got into high gear in 1860, when

> Thousands poured in from California, Oregon, the Colorado, the States—adventurers, gamblers, speculators, miners, prospectors, lawyers—in short, all of that numerous class that "makes haste to grow rich" who could get here. Mines were located [i.e., excavated] and opened, mills were built [to separate the gold and silver from the worthless rock in which it lay], towns were laid out and grew like mushrooms. Capital was active [i.e., the mines attracted a good deal of capital from outside Nevada].
>
> Some of the mines proved immensely rich, and as a consequence "wildcats" flourished in all their glory [i.e., highly speculative, fraudulent mines were in the spotlight, too]. A few mines turned out bullion at such a rate that statesmen and financiers feared that silver must fall in value. Last year [probably 1864] it culminated—when nearly *a ton a day* of gold and silver bullion was shipped from here; when more than five thousand teams were employed in bringing freights here [this part of Nevada was more of a desert, initially with very few people living in it, so everything had to be brought in by wagon trains]…when speculation ruled the day and in the streets were met men poor three years ago, now worth their hundreds of thousands—then, I say, the excitement raised and culminated—and this summer the vast bubble broke…
>
> As a consequence, thousands have been ruined, work has stopped on much "wildcat," and good mines must in the future be worked in a more healthy [i.e., a more rational] manner.[9]

A much better book by an even better writer, set in part in the same time and place as Brewer's book, is Mark Twain's *Roughing It*. Twain wrote this semi-humorous account in 1871; it discussed, among many other things, his experiences in Gold Rush California. His account of a Nevada outlaw named Slade is a fine example of Twain's accurate and sometimes tongue-in-cheek reporting.[10]

On a stagecoach ride through Nevada, wrote Twain, he had heard the drivers and conductors talk only about three things: "Californy," the Nevada silver mines, and the desperado Slade. What was most remarkable about Slade was that he held a very responsible job as a division agent, i.e., as a senior officer, of the stagecoach company, while at the same time he was also a cutthroat bandit. As Twain puts it,

> A high and efficient servant of the Overland [the stagecoach company], an outlaw among outlaws and yet their relentless scourge [because he killed so many of them himself], Slade was at once the most bloody, the most dangerous, and the most valuable citizen that inhabited the savage fastnesses of the mountains.[11]

Twain relates that when Slade was 26, he killed a man in a quarrel and had to flee from his native Illinois. In St. Joseph, Missouri, he joined one of the early California-bound wagon trains as its leader. One day on the plains, however, he got into a major argument with one of his wagon drivers. Both men drew their Colt revolvers,[12] but the driver was quicker and cocked his revolver first.

With this type of handgun, it is first necessary to pull the hammer back to cock the weapon before it can be fired. The driver was the better gunman. He cocked his Colt very rapidly, i.e., while he was drawing it from the leather holster, rather than drawing it first and then cocking the hammer a second or two later. His speed, however, did him little good. As Twain tells us,

> ...Slade said it was a pity to waste life on so small a matter, and proposed that the pistols be thrown on the ground and the quarrel be settled by a fist fight. The unsuspecting driver agreed, and threw down his pistol—whereupon Slade laughed at his simplicity and shot him dead![13]

Despite many warnings to Slade that if he continued his violent behavior he would soon be punished most severely, he paid no attention at all and continued to act just as he pleased. Eventually, however, his repeated outrages forced the local vigilante committee to order his execution. Twain reports that

> Everything being ready, the command was given, "Men, do your duty," and the box [on which Slade was standing under the gallows] being instantly slipped from beneath his feet, he died almost instantaneously.
> The body was cut down and carried to the Virginia Hotel, where, in a darkened room, it was scarcely laid out when the unfortunate bereaved companion of the deceased [i.e., Slade's wife] arrived, headlong speed [on horseback], to find that it was all over, and that she was a widow. Her grief and heart-piercing cries were terrible evidences of the depth of her attachment for her lost husband, and a considerable period elapsed before she could regain the command of her excited feelings.[14]

20

The Great Surveys

In the meantime, detailed scientific studies of the frontier West of the United States were being undertaken, beginning in 1867, through what became known in American history as the "Great Surveys." These expeditions are usually referred to now by the last names of their four leaders. Listed in the order in which the surveys began, they include the King Survey (1867–1878), the Powell Survey (1869–1879), the Hayden Survey (1871), and the Wheeler Survey (1872–1879). A few comments on some of them can usefully be offered here, though not necessarily in the order listed above.[1]

On balance, of the four Great Surveys, the 1871 "Geological and Geographical Survey of the Territories" led by the geologist Ferdinand Vandeveer Hayden, who had already worked in the area in 1870, probably had the greatest contemporary impact on the economic development and the settlement of the West. Its downside, however, was that since much of the Hayden Survey's work had been done in such haste, it came to be seen by some experts, who were judging by the more rigorous standards set by later geologists, as rather unpolished and crude.

In any case, the local Indians of the northern plains knew Hayden as the "Man Who Picks Up Stones Running" because of the speed with which he ranged over landscapes during his geological surveys. To fund the ambitious projects he had in mind, he was equally quick to cultivate "the great and the good," e.g., the powerful railroad interests, as well as average westerners he met in the field. His successes in these fields, coupled with excellent public relations, encouraged Congress to increase its appropriations for his work.

Hayden already knew something about the Yellowstone region, which he had visited in 1859–1860 as a surgeon-naturalist. In 1871 he advertised his decision to make Yellowstone his key area of operations. Congress first gave him $40,000 and then $75,000 to survey it. The culmination of his efforts there was the creation by Congress of Yellowstone National Park in 1872—the first such park in the United States.

Public and Congressional interest in this part of the West was whetted by the superb mountain panoramas drawn in 1876 by the Survey's artist, William H. Holmes. For example, his depictions of the San Juan Mountains, the Elk Mountains, the Pike's Peak group, and the La Plata Mountains are among the finest examples of terrain art ever done, being nearly photographic in their factual accuracy.

Hayden himself produced, in 1877, a well-received work entitled *Geological and Geographical Atlas of Colorado and Portions of Adjacent Territory*. Today, geologists still find this atlas useful when they are working in remote parts of the region.

The King Survey of 1867–1872 or, to give its formal name, the U.S. Geological Exploration of the Fortieth Parallel, focused on a 100-mile-wide strip of land running through northeastern California, Nevada, and eastern Wyoming. It was studied as a route for the transcontinental line of the Union Pacific Railroad and Central Pacific Railroad from Cheyenne, Wyoming, to the crest of the Sierra Nevada. There the King Survey would link up with the California Geological Survey.

This survey was led by the remarkably able geologist Clarence King, who was hailed by the historian and man of letters Henry Adams in his 1907 book, *The Education of Henry Adams*, as "the most remarkable man of our time."[2]

King published the results of his geological studies in a magisterial seven-volume *Report of the Fortieth Parallel Survey*, which appeared in installments in the 1870s, the last one in 1878. It quickly became a role model for other scientists to follow. Before then, however, King had won even wider acclaim by bringing to light the "Great Diamond Hoax" of 1872. This is such an interesting story that it deserves to be mentioned here.[3]

It must be remembered, to begin with, that explorers had in fact found significant amounts of gold in California in 1848 and significant amounts of silver in Nevada ten years later. As a result, in 1872 even very well-educated people were quite prepared to believe that significant amounts of other valuable minerals—*why not diamonds?*, for example—were quietly waiting to be discovered somewhere in the remote reaches of the frontier West.

To make a long story short, in 1872 two disheveled prospectors—the cousins Philip Arnold and John Slack—wandered into the Bank of California (the premier financial institution of the Far West) and confided to a bemused clerk that they had something of truly enormous value to deposit in the bank, namely, diamonds and other jewels.

Arnold and Slack were good actors and intelligent con-men who knew just enough about diamonds to spin an enticing story. They had previously bought, for $35,000, cheap cast-off diamonds in London and Amsterdam; had "salted" them (i.e., placed them judiciously around) their "mining claim" in the extreme northwest of Colorado's mountains; and had then spread the word that diamonds could be had for the taking, at a spot in the Far West that only they knew about.

20. The Great Surveys

This rumor had the same effect on some major financiers in San Francisco and New York as the scent of blood in the water is said to have on sharks. Prominent men lined up to buy the con-men's claim—but only after first taking the sensible precaution of hiring Henry Janin, a highly respected and professionally extremely conservative mining engineer in San Francisco, to inspect the site and to assure them that it was in fact genuine.

It did not take long for King and his men to hear about the alleged diamonds of the West. In their own careful scientific studies along the route of the Fortieth Parallel, they had never found a single diamond or ruby, nor had they found any geological formations in which these items might possibly exist. They were therefore understandably worried that both the Survey itself and their personal reputations would be permanently tarnished if the diamond story turned out to be true. They therefore decided to look into the matter quickly but thoroughly.

The upshot was that on 11 November 1872 King was in the Office of the U.S. Geological Survey in San Francisco and from there he wrote a 5-page damning letter to the Board of Directors of the San Francisco and New York Mining and Commercial Company, which had been set up to exploit the so-called diamond fields.

The gist of the letter is contained in its first two paragraphs, which read as follows:

Gentlemen:

I have hastened to San Francisco [King has just come from the diamond field] to lay before you the startling fact, that the New Diamond Fields, upon which are based such large investment and such brilliant hope, are utterly valueless, and yourselves and your engineer, Mr. Henry Janin, [are] the victims of unparalleled fraud.

Having convinced you verbally that my investigations have been made upon no other than your own ground, I beg herewith to give a brief statement of my mode of study and its unanswerable results.

Later in the letter, King went on to say:

This is the work of no common swindler, but of one who has known enough to select a spot where detection must be slow, and where every geological parallelism added a fresh probability of honesty. The selection of the geological locality is so astonishingly considered, the salting itself so cunning and artful, the choice of all conditions so fatally well made, I can feel no surprise that even so trustworthy an engineer as Mr. Janin should have brought home the belief he did [i.e., that the diamond fields were genuine], since, as his report states, he was not allowed [by the "prospectors"] to prospect exhaustively. Nor do I wonder that your second party of ten men brought back a confirmation of Mr. Janin's opinion, since they too were hurried from the ground without actually testing it.[4]

In 1872, King also wrote a dramatic account of his climbs in California's mountains. Entitled *Mountaineering in the Sierra Nevada*, this book has won a wide readership over the years, even though experienced climbers today will consider it rather overstated. That said, however, the fact remains King was one of the very few Americans of his day to want to climb remote, difficult peaks, and his successes entitle him to respect as eminent pioneer in American mountaineering.[5]

King's prompt, decisive whistle-blowing action certainly saved thousands of investors from investing in the Great Diamond Hoax and thus losing all their money. In addition, it led to the later publication, in 1913, of a now-obscure but still very readable historical source: *The Diamond Hoax and Other Stirring Incidents in the Life of Asbury Harpending*.

A very literate adventurer and a successful financier, Asbury Harpending (1839–1923) watched the whole Diamond Hoax unfold from start to finish. After Arnold and Slack took Henry Janin, Harpending, and other "fact-finders" to the alleged diamond fields, Harpending later wrote:

> [The second day at the diamond fields], prospecting was resumed and covered a wide range. Everywhere we found precious stones—principally diamonds—although a few sparkers of other kinds [e.g., rubies] were interspersed. It was quite wonderful how generally the gems were scattered over a territory of about a quarter of a mile square and of course we were only doing surface examinations. No one could tell what depth might produce.
>
> Accounts have been published to the effect that when we arrived at the diamond fields there were visible evidences of the ground having been tampered with and disturbed. This is absolutely false on its face. In the first place, any such evidence would have excited the suspicion of the keen-eyed Janin in a moment. Secondly, such a clumsy method of "salting" was unthinkable.
>
> Undoubtedly holes were made in the soil [by Arnold and Slack] with sharp iron rods, [and] gems were dropped in the holes, which were then closed by a hard stamp of the foot and the first winter's rain obliterated every trace that remained of human agency. [These "gems" were only coarse low-quality South African diamonds of almost no value.] Wherever we worked, the ground was "in place."
>
> Two days' work satisfied Janin of the absolutely genuineness of the diamond fields. He was wildly enthusiastic. It was useless, he said, to spend more time on that particular piece of property—that was proved [i.e., he himself was convinced that the diamond field was genuine].
>
> The important thing [Janin continued] was to determine how much similar land was in the neighborhood, and be able to seize on everything in sight, for Mr. Janin pointed out that this new field would certainly control the gem market of the world and that the all-essential part of the program was for one great corporation to have absolute control.[6]

One may well ask: what happened to Arnold and Slack, the two conmen, who were paid $600,000 (the equivalent of about $13.5 million today) for their fraudulent mining claim?

The answer is that Arnold later resurfaced in Elizabethtown, Kentucky, where he opened a bank with his share of the loot. Alas, he managed to of-fend a rival banker to such an extent that the latter opened fire on him with a shotgun, and Arnold died of pneumonia after being wounded in this attack. Slack, for his part, moved to St. Louis, where he lived quietly and owned a casket-making company. He later became a casket maker and undertaker in New Mexico, where he died in 1896 at the age of 76.

The Powell Survey was named after its one-armed director, John Wesley Powell, who had lost his right arm fighting in the Civil War. Its official name was the "U.S. Geographical and Geological Survey of the Rocky Mountain Region."

Thanks to both private and public financial support, Powell was able to plan and carry out in 1869 an exceptionally dangerous 1,500-mile-long descent of both the Green River and the Colorado, using four small but strongly-built boats. At the time, this was the last major unexplored region in the continental United States.

Two contemporary quotes—the first by Powell himself in his 1875 book, *Exploration of the Colorado River of the West and Its Tributaries*, and the second a 27 August 1869 journal entry by expedition member George Bradley—give readers a clear idea of the challenges faced by the Powell expedition.[7]

Powell wrote:

> We are now ready to start our way down the unknown.... We have but one month's rations remaining.... We are three quarters of a mile in the depths of the earth, and the great river shrinks into insignificance as it dashes its angry waves against the walls and cliffs that rise to the world above.
>
> We have an unknown distance yet to run; an unknown river to explore.

Bradley wrote:

> At noon we came to the worst rapid yet seen. The water dashes against the left bank and then is thrown furiously back against the right. The billows are huge and I fear our boats could not ride them [unless we can] keep them off the rocks...
>
> This is decidedly the darkest day of the trip but I don't despair yet.

Powell's Grand Canyon expedition won wide publicity and made him a national hero. A second expedition followed in 1872, this one being a topographical survey of the Canyonlands and plateaus of Colorado, Utah, and Arizona.

Powell was responsible for the creation of the U.S. Geological Survey in 1879; was its director from 1880 to 1894; and has been praised by modern historians both as "the greatest explorer-hero since the days of Frémont," and as "a prototype of the scientific entrepreneur, an advocate, and creator of government agencies devoted to scientific research, to be conducted for the public good."[8]

Named after its leader, First Lieutenant George Montague Wheeler, the fourth great expedition was officially named the "U.S. Geographical Surveys

West of the One Hundredth Meridian."[9] Historically, this meridian, which is located in the central Great Plains, has been considered to be the approximate boundary between the humid eastern United States and the much drier western United States. What this means in practice is that modern agriculture west of the meridian must rely heavily on large-scale irrigation.

Wheeler argued that the geological maps Hayden, King, and Powell had produced were not of much use to the U.S. Army. What the army really needed, he said, and what it alone could best produce, were wide-ranging *topographical* maps that showed the land as it was then—that is, with all its hills, mountains, canyons, valleys, river basins, streams, lakes, and—most especially—with all *the human imprints* on the land. This meant showing all the roads, towns, railroads, mines, farms, ranches, and factories.

Wheeler's point of view was accepted by General Andrew A. Humphries, who in 1871 gave him the following instructions:

> The main object of this exploration will be to obtain topographical knowledge of the country, and to prepare accurate maps. It is at the same time intended that you ascertain as far as practicable everything relating to the physical features of the country, the numbers, habits, and disposition of the Indians, the selection of such sites as may be of use for future military operations or occupation, and the facilities offered for making rail or common roads, to meet the wants of those who at some future period may occupy or traverse this part of the country.[10]

The successes of the Wheeler Survey included finding ancient rock beds in northern New Mexico, together with the remains of early animal life; a complete survey and mapping of Death Valley; a careful study of the Comstock Lode in Nevada, and of other mining districts there; and, finally, the remapping of the Lake Tahoe region in the Sierra Nevada mountains.[11]

But there was some bad news, too. Wheeler, who personally seems to have hated Indians and who opposed the U.S. government's Indian policy, was accused of mistreating the local Indians and even of killing or blinding them.

Moreover, the consolidation of the four Surveys into the U.S. Geological Survey in 1879 did not include the U.S. Army, which was purposively left out in the cold—probably because civilian scientists refused to be subject to military administration and authority.

In retrospect, this was a shame. If Wheeler had been allowed to complete his map-in-progress of the territories and states west of the Mississippi, all the later explorers and scientists would have had at their disposal a reasonably accurate map of about 1.5 million square miles of the American frontier.

21

A Famous Book:
The Big Bonanza

The Canadians, for their part, undertook major explorations of the western reaches of their own vast country between 1871 and 1904.[1]

In general, scientific modes of exploration, which had arrived in British North America thanks to the work of the University of Edinburgh, pervade geographical studies in the 1870s. There was no shortage of places where these new modes could quickly be put to work in the field.

In 1870, for example, Canada had acquired both Rupert's Land (the area drained by Hudson Bay) and the Northwestern Territory (present-day Manitoba, Saskatchewan, Alberta, the Yukon, and most of the Northwest Territories). Even as late as 1890, however, about one million square miles of Canada were still unknown to anyone but the Indians, trappers, loggers, and other hardy outdoorsmen.

Although much of the Canadian Northwest had first been explored during the heyday of the fur trade, Canadian government explorers took to the field again, with new objectives, in 1871. One of their first tasks after acquisition of Rupert's Land and the Northwestern Territory was surveying the international boundary line between the United States and Canada, i.e., from the Lake of the Woods to the Rocky Mountain. This assignment was given to the North American Boundary Commission Survey.

Although the boundary had been formally established by treaty in 1818, much survey work still needed to be done. The task of defining the boundary westward from the Red River began in 1873 and faced numerous hardships.

Given the prevalence of muskeg, i.e., the subarctic wetlands, some of the Boundary Commission's work had to be done in winter when the muskeg was frozen, but then the intense cold and heavy snowfalls often brought survey work to a standstill.

In other and very arid areas, however, survey workers had to contend with heat, dust, barren cactus-covered ground, and lack of water. Out on the endless grasslands, the Boundary Commission encountered great herds of buffalo that were being pursued by Indian and *métis* (i.e., "mixed race" Indian-Caucasian) hunting parties. Within 10 years, however, all the buffalo would be gone.

The work of the Boundary Commission ended in 1876 and was a clear success. Indeed, it was quite a feat of scientific precision, being based on the observation of 167 stars. It also provided the first photographic record of the country along the international boundary.

The Boundary Commission would be followed by several other major surveys of Canada, e.g., the Dominion Lands Surveys, the Canadian Pacific Railway Survey, and the Geological Survey of Canada. By the start of World War I, however, these big, government-organized explorations would be replaced with more specialized surveys that relied on smaller numbers of more highly trained personnel.

• • •

In 1876 the Nevada newspaperman William Wright (1829–1898), who used the penname Dan De Quille and who was a colleague of Mark Twain, wrote a definitive and often amusing book on silver and gold mining in Nevada. Entitling it *The Big Bonanza,* De Quille explained the contents in a long subtitle. It had something for almost every reader because it was, he wrote:

> An Authentic Account of the Discovery, History, and Working of the World Renowned Comstock Silver Lode of Nevada, Including Descriptions of the Various Mines Situated Thereon; Sketches of the Most Prominent Men Interested in Them; Incidents and Adventures Connected with Mining, the Indians, and the Country; Amusing Stories, Experiences, Anecdotes, etc., etc., and a Full Exposition of the Production of Pure Silver.[2]

One of the most interesting local characters that De Quille describes was a very eccentric prospector named Henry Thompkins Paige Comstock, who was better known to other miners as "Old Pancake" and whose last name would become immortalized as Nevada's world-famous "Comstock Lode." This was an exceptionally rich deposit of gold and silver ores.

De Quille tells us how he got this nickname:

> This name was given to him by his brother miners because he was never known to bake any bread. He always had—or imagined he had—so much [mining] business on hand that he could spare no time to fool away in making and baking bread. All his flour he worked up into pancakes. And even as, with spoon in hand, he stirred his pancake batter, it is said he kept one eye on the top of some distant peak and was lost in speculations with regard to the wealth in gold and silver that might rest somewhere below its rocky crest.[3]

Comstock and a few other miners got interested in some new "diggings" (prospecting locations) near them, even though their fellow miners did not think they would amount to very much. Comstock and his colleagues con-

21. A Famous Book: The Big Bonanza 139

tinued to work these diggings, however, and they soon reached "very rich dirt—much richer than Comstock had ever found in any part of his [earlier] claim." The end result was that, as De Quille explained,

> Thus was first discovered, located, and worked that portion of the Comstock Lode lying under the town of Gold Hill, and containing the Belcher, Crown Point, Yellow Jacket, Imperial, Empire, Kentuck, and other leading mines of the country—mines that have yielded millions upon millions in gold and silver bullion.[4]

• • •

The establishment of the U.S. Geological Survey in 1879 can profitably be discussed here to bring this book to a fitting end.[5]

In 1878, a slowdown in the American economy was creating problems in the ongoing process of mapping the West. The King survey had by this time completed its own reports, but those of the Hayden, Powell, and Wheeler surveys were still continuing in the field. Congress therefore asked the National Academy of Sciences to come up with a plan to survey and map the western reaches of the United States that would produce the best possible results at the lowest possible cost.

A committee of seven members was appointed by the National Academy and recommended that the U.S. Coast and Geodetic Survey be transferred from the Department of the Treasury to the Department of the Interior. It would then be renamed the "Coast and Interior Survey" and would be given responsibility for geodetic, topographic, and land-parceling surveys in addition to its existing work.

The Academy committee also recommended that an independent organization, to be known as the U.S. Geological Survey, should be set up within the Department of the Interior in order to study the geological structures and the economic resources of the lands in the public domain.

Accordingly, legislation to rename the Coast and Geodetic Survey, to transfer it to the Department of the Interior, and to establish the U.S. Geological Survey for "classification of the public lands, and examination of the geological structure, mineral resources, and products of the national domain" was included in the bill appropriating funds for the legislative, executive, and judicial expenses of the Federal Government for the fiscal year beginning July 1, 1879. In addition, an appropriation for the expenses of the new geological survey was included in the civil services bill.

This proposed transfer of land-parceling surveys in the west to the Federal Government in the east generated strong opposition from Congressmen from western states. The upshot was that the Democratic House and the Republican Senate were so far apart on some items of the bill that it was feared no agreement could be reached before Congress adjourned.

The legal details of this argument are not important here, but the bottom line certainly is. A compromise was finally reached and has been summarized by the U.S. Geological Survey in these words:

> Thus the U.S. Geological Survey was established, by a last-minute amendment, to classify the public lands—94 years after the Land Ordinance of 1785 first directed their surveying and classification—and to examine the geological structure, mineral resources, and products of the national domain.

The legislation also provided that the Hayden, Powell, and Wheeler surveys be discontinued as of June 30, 1879. Congress also established a public lands commission, of which the Director of the U.S. Geological Survey would be a member, to prepare a codification of the laws relating to the survey and disposition of the public domain, a system and standard of classification of public lands, a system of land-parceling surveys adapted to the economic uses of the several classes of lands, and recommendations for the disposal of the public lands in the western portion of the United States to actual settlers.[6]

22

Conclusions: Why the Explorations of the North American Frontiers Are So Important

Taken in their entirety, the international and national efforts to discover, understand, and then exploit the frontiers constitute a dramatic, long-running sequence of memorable people, places, and events. These efforts were never consistent or identical, but reflected instead important and frequently-changing local differences in culture, geography, politics, and economics.

It is impossible to sum up adequately, in one concluding chapter, the whole western North American frontier experience, but the events chronicled here do tell a riveting story. It includes the creation and defense of growing communities; of new uses for old lands; of the development of domestic and international markets; and, last but by no means least, the finding, merging, dislocation, and sometimes the obliteration of many different peoples and their cultures.[1]

Moreover, the modern historians Michael Golay and John Bowman make an excellent point when they warn the reader, in the first sentence of their excellent 2003 study of *North American Exploration*, that

> The narrative of North American discovery and exploration reads like a novel—a postmodern novel at that, in which definitions are elusive; claims are relative and subject to revision; and obscure, offstage characters are as vital to the outcome as those with documentable identities, personal histories, and catalogues of achievement.[2]

It is worth repeating here that the long history of European and American exploration of the North American frontiers has played a key role in Western European and American politics, economics, popular culture, literature, oral history, and iconography. For all these reasons, it still remains a rewarding and challenging field of study for scholars, historians, and students alike.

There are two very good reasons to learn something about all these explorations. The first, very simply put, is that they are intrinsically interesting because they involved so many different peoples who lived hard and worked hard along the frontiers as they created new societies.

The second reason, however, is more complicated and is ultimately more important. Exploration can now be seen not only as an adventuresome "death-or-glory" process but also as *a cultural process* that, on balance and over time, brought many advantages to the people living on the American, French-Canadian, Spanish-Mexican, and European-American frontiers. Some of these benefits are described below.

This is not to deny, of course, that great wrongs were also done during this long process, many of which can never be corrected. Examples here would have to include not only the obliteration of Indians themselves, but also the destruction of their cultures and traditional ways of life due to diseases and military-political factors, and the widespread damage to the environment and the wildlife of these frontiers.

Nevertheless, the *positive results* of the explorations must be well-understood, too. Although a great deal could be said about all of them, in the interest of brevity they are listed below only in a very condensed form[3]:

- Most of the mapping and defining of the North American frontiers was done by explorers, i.e., chiefly by men who, through their own travels, searched out new information. Without the insights they provided into the physical and cultural characteristics of these frontiers, most of the later developments there—e.g., the growth of towns, cities, agriculture, and industry—would not have been possible.
- Explorers discovered the mountain passes; crossed the rivers and lakes; and laid out the trails, wagon routes, and railroads that upward-mobile emigrants from more static societies would use to make new homes for themselves and their families.
- Explorers took the first steps in establishing the networks of commerce in the West and in shaping a "continental geopolitics." The French discovery of the Mississippi, and the later American exploration of the far-flung Mississippi-Missouri river system, are good cases to the point.
- On the Great Plains of both Canada and the United States, as in the Sacramento-San Joaquin Valley of central California, the travels of explorers were seeds that eventually permitted the United States and Canada to become "bread baskets to the world."
- Through their journeys and their writings, explorers made major direct or indirect contributions to the development of organized science in North America and abroad. Their comments on biology, geology,

22. Conclusions: Why the Explorations Are So Important

archeology, paleontology, anthropology, and linguistics all helped stay-at-home scholars to think more creatively about new and different kinds of time. These included historical time; prehistorical time; and "non-biblical time," that is, time that was not centered on the traditional biblical count of the world being only 4004 years old.

- Last but by no means least, explorers also opened a visual treasure-trove of new landscapes that would inspire generations of post–18th century artists and writers.

In 1879, when this book ends, what has aptly been termed "the Three Great Ages of Discovery" drew to a close, with the consolidation of the Great Surveys into the U.S. Geological Survey.[4]

During the First Great Age of Discovery, explorers such as Columbus pursued the twin goals of imperialism and international competition. In the Second Great Age, scientific thought flourished; Lewis and Clark, for example, were trying in large part to get a better understanding of the world they themselves were living in. The Third Great Age began with the Darwinian revolution, and focused on tracing biological and geological changes over long periods of time.

Annotated Chronology, 1492–1879

Further information on all these entries can be found in the text itself.

1492: Christopher Columbus discovers the West Indies while trying to find a passage to the riches of Asia.

1493: The papal bull *Inter Caetera* divides the unexplored world between Spain and Portugal.

1494: The Treaty of Tordesillas clarifies the respective boundaries of Spain and Portugal for exploration and colonization.

1528–1536: Looking for help, the shipwrecked Spanish explorer Álvar Núñez Cabeza de Vaca and his three companions begin an eight-year trek through the deserts of the American Southwest.

1539: Antonio de Mendoza, the viceroy of New Spain, sends out toward a Zuñi pueblo an ill-fated reconnaissance party protected by Spanish soldiers and led by Franciscan Friar Marcos de Niza. The glowing (and incorrect) report from Friar Marcos prompts Mendoza to follow up with the Coronado expedition (see 1540 below). Both this and a later expedition are marred by violence between Spaniards and Indians.

1534–1803: Heyday of New France, which includes what is now southern, northern, and eastern Canada, plus all of the central United States down to the Gulf Coast.

1535: Expanding the "northernmost frontier" of New Spain becomes a major goal of New Spain.

1540: The Spanish *conquistador* Francisco Vásquez de Coronado sets out from Mexico City to find the "Seven Cities of Gold."

1542: Juan Rodríguez Cabrillo becomes the first European to visit the Pacific shore of the United States.

1577: Sir Francis Drake sets out to find the Passage but ends up claiming (in 1579) all the lands of the Pacific Northwest north of the territory occupied by Spain, i.e., California.

1581–1598: Five Spanish pathfinding and exploration-settlement expeditions make their way into New Mexico and the Great Plains. The end result is the permanent Spanish occupation of New Mexico by Juan de Oñate in 1598.

1603: Sebastián Vizcaíno sends to the Spanish King a glowing report on Monterey, in what is now California, as an excellent port for the Spanish galleon trade.

1608: The founding of Quebec by Samuel de Champlain will open up, on the other side of the Lachine rapids, the vast, beaver-rich interior of New France.

1610–1629: Dozens of French-Canadian boys spend many months living with the Indians in order to learn their languages and cultures. The boys will then go on to play key roles in the French-Indian fur trade.

Late 1630s: The French explorer Jean Nicolet, who explores Lake Michigan, Mackinac Island, and Green Bay, and is the first European to set foot in what is now Michigan, is convinced that China is not very far from Green Bay, Wisconsin.

1659–1660: The French explorers Pierre-Esprit Radisson and Médard Chouart des Groseilliers open up for the Europeans a lucrative fur trade in the lands of the Cree Indians, i.e., in the western Great Lakes area and its northern wilderness. The local Indians may have told them about Grand Portage, which would become the easiest and best fur-trade canoe route into the far west of Canada.

1645–1711: Life of the Italian Jesuit explorer and missionary Eusebio Kino, who proves that California was not an island, despite the prevailing doctrine that it is. European cartographers remain divided on this issue, however, which was not finally settled until the expeditions of Juan Bautista de Anza in 1774–1776.

1660–1763: France and Great Britain work hard to expand their own access to fur-trading territories.

1665–1672: Jean Talon, the senior officer of New France, believes that the French should create a vast inland-waterway-based empire there and, in so doing might also discover the Passage.

1670: Founding of the Hudson's Bay Company, which would become a major player on the North American frontier.

1671: At Sault Sainte Marie, the French explorer Simon François D'Aumont claims for France all the lands west of Montreal.

1673: The French priest and the French explorer-trader Jacques Marquette and Louis Jolliet set out from Lake Michigan to explore the Mississippi River but turn around at the Arkansas River.

1681: The French explorer René-Robert Cavelier, better known to history by his title, "La Salle," leads another expedition down the Mississippi River and claims the Mississippi Valley for France.

1685: La Salle leads an expedition to the Mississippi River but his grave mistakes in the process result in the expedition's total failure.

1688: The French explorer Jacques de Noyen reaches Rainy Lake and possibly (the next year) Lake of the Woods as well, both of which lie northwest of Lake Superior in the border lakes area.

1690: On his most famous journey, the British explorer Henry Kelsey leaves York Factory to establish trade relations with the Indians living west of Hudson Bay. His epic explorations, however, would never be rewarded by his employer, the Hudson's Bay Company.

1699–1712: The French-Canadian explorer Pierre Le Moyne d'Iberville (known to history as "Iberville") and his family found the administrative district in New

France known as *La Louisiane* (Louisiana). He himself was a war hero and the discoverer of the mouth of the Mississippi River.

1708: French traders are said to have reached the foothills of the Rocky Mountains. The Spanish fear that the French now want to displace them and become the dominant power in the trans–Mississippi West.

1716: Iberville's younger brother, Jean-Baptiste Le Moyne, Sieur de Bienville, is himself a key figure in the exploration and colonization of French Louisiana. He founds Fort Rosalie (present-day Natchez), the first permanent European settlement on the Mississippi.

1717: The French-Canadian explorer, trader, Indian expert, and French spy Louis Juchereau de St. Denis falls in love with Manuela Sánchez, the young and beautiful granddaughter of the commander of a Spanish outpost on the Rio Grande. He marries her and tries to get official permission to remain in New Spain but, in the end, the couple has to retire to Louisiana.

1719: The first official French expedition to visit the Osage and Wichita Indians in what is now the American state of Kansas is led by the French army officer Claude Charles Du Tisne. He is quite impressed by the Osage men, who are often more than six feet tall and who wear their hair in a scalp-lock, i.e., a long tuft of hair on the crown of the otherwise-shaven head of a warrior

1724: The French explorer and trader Étienne de Veniard, Sieur de Bourgmont, writes about his explorations on the Mississippi River and the Platte River; draws up the first European maps of these regions; and in 1724 makes friends with the Apaches, thanks to his willingness (unlike the Spaniards) to offer them guns, powder, and lead for bullets.

C. 1736–1814: The major Spanish pathfinding expeditions of this era are now in regions near but not immediately on the Great Plains themselves. Expedition leaders include Juan Bautista de Anza; Fray Francisco Atansio Domínguez and Fray Silvestre Vélez de Escalante; and Pedro Vial.

1739: Two French-Canadian brothers—Pierre Antoine Mallet and Paul Mallet—are the first Europeans known to have crossed the Great Plains from east to west, i.e., from Illinois to New Mexico. In 1739, they lead the first of three trading expeditions to Santa Fe, but all of them end in failure.

1740s: The French-Canadian military officer Pierre Gaultier de Varrenes, Sieur de La Vérendrye, and his two sons (Francis and Louis-Joseph) explore the areas from Lake Superior to the mouth of the Saskatchewan River in Alberta, Canada, and the Black Hills of western South Dakota. Francis and Louis-Joseph bury an inscribed lead plate near present-day Fort Pierre, North Dakota, claiming the area for France. They may also go as far west as the Big Horn range in northern Wyoming.

1744: The French Jesuit priest, explorer of the Great Lakes François Xavier de Charlevoix publishes, in 1744, his *Journal Historique* (*Historical Journal*). This describes the North American lands he visited and the customs of the Indian tribes living there. Charlevoix is often considered to be first historian of New France.

1753: The French army officer, explorer, and Indian expert Jacques Legardeur de Saint-Pierre makes a very favorable impression on a young British Virginia major named George Washington.

1754: Working for the Hudson's Bay Company, the British trader Anthony Henday travels with a party of Cree Indians, partly by canoe and partly on foot, from York Factory to Red Deer, Alberta, where he could have seen the high peaks of the Rockies.

1763: Great Britain's victory in the Seven Years' War marks the end of the French Empire in continental North America.

1769: Gaspar de Portolá discovers San Francisco Bay and founds the settlements of San Diego and Monterey, California.

1774: Samuel Hearne, an English explorer, fur trader, writer, and naturalist, builds Cumberland House for the Hudson's Bay Company. This is the Company's first trading post located deep in the interior and is the first permanent settlement in Saskatchewan.

1774: In order to find a way to get by land to the California missions, the Franciscan priest and explorer Fray Francisco Thomás Garcés, guided by the Mojave Indians, travels along the Gila River in southern Arizona and reaches Mission San Gabriel Arcángel.

1774–1776: The expeditions of Juan Bautista de Anza between Sonora, Mexico, and the west coast of California prove that California is *not* an island.

1778: The dramatic rise of the Comanches to regional power in the American Southwest is reflected very clearly in a Spanish map of 1778.

1779–1784: The great smallpox epidemic kills tens of thousands of Indians in the West, but its impact is only very rarely recorded in American accounts.

1781–1782: Peter Pond—who was at different times an army officer, sailor, fur trader, explorer, map maker, and writer—is also an exceedingly violent and eccentric man. He kills a rival fur trader in a duel with pistols during the winter of 1781–1782. Later, during the winter of 1786–1787, he orders a Canadian trapper to kill another rival fur trader during a brawl.

1786–1792: Six early maritime expeditions explore the waters of the Pacific Northwest. The first of these, probably by James Hanna in 1786, puts Nootka Sound on the nautical map because of his success in trading iron bars for furs and skins. During the rest of the 1780s, more European and American trading ships call there.

1793: Pedro Vial, a French trader in the employ of Spain, pioneers the future route of the Santa Fe Trail, making a round trip estimated at 2,279 miles between Santa Fe and St. Louis. Had he not been captured by hostile Indians, he says, he could have made this trip in only 25 days.

1793: One of the greatest figures in the exploration of the Canadian West is Alexander Mackenzie, a Scottish explorer best known for achieving the first east-to-west crossing of North America north of Mexico. In 1793 he reaches the North Bentick Arm, an inlet of the Pacific Ocean, near the Bella Coola River.

1795–1797: A two-year expedition up the Missouri River, led by the Scotsman James Mackay and the Welshman John Thomas Evans is, in geographical terms, the most significant European or American venture out onto the northern Great Plain before the coming of Lewis and Clark. Using information provided by the Mandan Indians, Evans draws up a map that mentions, for the first time, both the Yellowstone River and the falls of the Missouri.

1802–1836: The young Englishman George Nelson works as a clerk for the XY

Company, a major Canadian fur trading company, but he greatly offends his domineering boss (Sir Alexander Mackenzie) by marrying the daughter of a local Ojibwa Indian leader. As a result, Nelson is never or only very rarely promoted, but his extensive 1802–1836 records of buying furs from and selling manufactured goods to the Indians are gold mines of information on the local fur trade.

1803: Napoleon Bonaparte sells Louisiana to the United States, thereby more than doubling its size.

1804–1806: Officially known as the "Corps of Discovery Expedition" and commonly referred to as the Lewis and Clark expedition, this is the most famous expedition in American history and still stands high in the annals of world exploration. Lewis and Clark travel nearly 6,000 miles and make contact with more than 70 Indian tribes. Their great adventure ushers in the era of the American beaver trappers and explorers known as "mountain men."

1804–1881: Life of Jim Bridger, one of the frontier's most celebrated explorers and mountain men, who was a hunter, trapper, fur trader, guide, and founder of Fort Bridger, Wyoming.

1808: A leader of the North West Company, Simon Fraser is given responsibility in 1805 for all the Company's operations beyond the Rocky Mountains. He establishes the first settlements in today's British Columbia; travels among Indian tribes that have never seen a Caucasian before; and, in 1808, runs the virtually-unnavigable Fraser River, thus proving that the North West Company would have to focus its trade on the Columbia River itself.

1810: One of the great success stories of the frontier is that of the German immigrant John Jacob Astor, whose Pacific Fur Company, located at the mouth of the Columbia River, is the initial American settlement on the Pacific Coast and begins the American land-based fur trade there. He names the settlement "Fort Astoria."

1811: The explorer David Thompson descends the Columbia River in 1811 and proves that it connects to the Pacific Ocean. By the end of his career, he will have explored an area of about 50,000 miles of western Canada and the northwestern United States; his maps will be the most detailed and most precise of the time.

1812: The fur trader Robert Stuart makes the first documented crossing of South Pass, when he carries dispatches overland from Fort Astoria to New York City.

1813: Death of the mountain man John Colter, the first person of European descent known to have explored the Yellowstone region and who, in his last years, farmed on the Missouri River frontier as a neighbor of the legendary frontiersman Daniel Boone.

1814: Manuel Lisa is a real mover-and-shaker in the St. Louis fur trade during the first decade of the 19th century. The greatest single achievement of his Missouri Fur Company is that it collects a great deal of new information on the geography and economic prospects of the Rocky Mountains.

1818: Major Stephen H. Long leads an expedition into the Rockies that includes two skilled artists from the Philadelphia area: Titian Ramsay Peale and Samuel Seymour. Their work gives American and European readers the first detailed and accurate glimpses of this little-known part of the Western frontier.

1824–1830: One of the West's most famous explorers is the Canadian trapper Peter

Skene Ogden, who between 1824 and 1830 leads six separate expeditions into seven very difficult areas, and who is also a first-rate chronicler. As a result of his travels, mythical waterways such as the Buenaventura River will no longer appear on the best British maps of North America.

1824: After Ogden's expeditions, the Hudson's Bay Company sends out many minor expeditions, but without any dramatic results. For example, the Company's explorer Samuel Black searches for but fails to find the mythical "Great River of the Northwest."

1829: The New Mexican trader Antonio Armijo pioneers the Old Spanish Trail to establish a mutually-profitable livestock and woolen-goods trade between Abiquiu, New Mexico, and Santa Barbara, California.

1830: The explorer, miner, and amateur physician James R. Pattie dictates to a reporter the story of his frontier adventures, e.g., a bear hunt near El Paso, Texas.

1832–1839: The artist, writer, and explorer George Catlin spends a total of eight years (1832–1839) among what he describes as "the wildest tribes of Indians of North America." His artistic and literary records of these Plains Indian societies at their prime are truly outstanding.

1832–1834: U.S. Army officer Benjamin Eulalie de Bonneville leads an expedition from Missouri to investigate the river systems of the West. He also establishes an overland route to California that will later evolve into the famous California Trail.

1833: One of the most memorable figures of Western exploration is the mountain man/explorer Joseph Walker, whose desert travel is the first recorded east-to-west crossing of Nevada using the Humboldt River Valley. This expedition is marred by a fight between Walker's party and the local Indians, in which 39 Indians are killed.

1833–1834: German Prince Maximilian of Wied-Neuwied, and Karl Bodmer, a young Swiss artist, make an epic journey up the Missouri River to the lands of the Blackfeet Indians. Their multi-volume work, *Travels in the Interior of North America, 1832–1834*, is of surpassing historical and artistic interest.

1838–1842: U.S. Navy Lieutenant Charles Wilkes leads the U.S. Exploring Expedition, better known as the Wilkes Expedition, which helps convince the American government that, in the long run, Puget Sound will be more valuable to it than the Columbia River.

1838–1845: U.S. Army officer John C. Frémont leads explorations into the Great Plains, the Great Basin, the Oregon Territory, and Mexico's Alta California.

1840: The French explorer Joseph Nicholas Nicollet produces one of the first American-made maps that correctly shows the nature of hydrographical basins, i.e., drainage basins.

1840 and 1848: The German physician Dr. F.A. Wislizenus publishes two instructive books, one on his travels in the Rocky Mountains (1840), and the other on his experiences during the Mexican-American War (1848).

1841: Mariano Guadalupe Vallejo, one of the brightest and most energetic leaders in California under Mexican rule, warns the Ministry of War about the threat posed by the increasing flow of Americans into Alta (i.e., Upper) California.

1843: The missionary doctor Marcus Whitman accompanies the first major wagon train west along the Oregon Trail, part of which has been blazed by William Price

Hunt, a merchant working for John Jacob Astor (see above). This proves the new trail is feasible for immigrants heading across the frontier West.

1844: Led by the former mountain man and beaver trapper Caleb Greenway, the Stephens-Townsend-Murphy party is the first wagon train to cross the Sierra Nevada mountains into California.

1844: The American merchant, explorer, naturalist, and author Josiah Gregg publishes his definitive two-volume work entitled *Commerce of the Prairies: Life on the Great Plains.*

1845: The doctrine of "Manifest Destiny" is the unilateral and self-proclaimed "right" of the United States to expand all the way to the Pacific Ocean—and even far beyond it.

1845: Since the U.S. government wants better maps of Texas and of the U.S.-Great Britain boundary line in the Pacific Northwest, it sets in motion three trans-Mississippi expeditions to acquire them.

1846: The trapper and hunter Thomas James dictates in 1846 a book on the Mandan chief Shehaka, praising the Mandans as "Chiefs with the dignity of Real Princes, and with the eloquence of real orators, and Braves with the valor of the ancient Spartans."

1846: Francis Parkman finishes *The Oregon Trail*, one of the best books ever written about the frontier because it contains so many "I was there" descriptions of the lives of the local Indians and fur trappers.

1846: Lewis H. Garrard's book *Wah-to-yah and the Taos Trail* is especially valuable today because it preserves some of the most unique and most memorable slang used by the mountain men.

1846–1847: The best woman writer on the North American frontier is probably 18-year-old Susan Shelby Magoffin, who keeps a detailed diary of her travels during the early days of the Mexican-American War.

1847: First Lieutenant William Hemsley Emory of the Corps of Topographical Engineers draws up the first accurate map of the whole southwestern region of the United States. His team also initiates the scholarly study of abandoned pueblos there.

1848: George Frederick Ruxton, an English explorer and adventurer, publishes two excellent books on his death-or-glory adventures in Mexico and the Rocky Mountains, before dying of dysentery in St. Louis at the age of 27.

1848: U.S. Army Lieutenant George Douglas Brewerton accompanies the famous outdoorsman Kit Carson from Los Angeles when Carson is assigned to carry official dispatches to Washington, D.C. Brewerton wrote very well, and his accounts of these travels are certainly worth reading today.

1848–1850: Other highly competent frontier explorations that are not well-known today include the Marcy-Simpson expedition of 1849 and the Stansbury-Gunnison expedition of 1849–1850.

1849: Lieutenant Simpson and his helpers visit the Chaco Canyon ruins in New Mexico. It is said that his report on the pueblos must still be referenced in any modern work on the ethnography of this region.

Mid–1800s: The vibrant "sense of mission" known as "Manifest Destiny" encourages the American government and the American people to expand their influence and value system westward to the Pacific Ocean.

1854: The great British exploration achievement of this era is Arrowsmith's 1854 map of British America, which lays out accurately the courses of the great rivers in Canada's Far Northwest.

1856: "Nick" Wilson runs away from the home of his pioneer family near the Great Salt Lake in Utah, and joins a Utah Indian tribe. His book, *White Indian Boy*, published in 1910, gives excellent "I was there" insights into Indian life.

1856: Kit Carson dictates to a friend a short but very readable memoir, entitled *Kit Carson's Autobiography*, which recounts, among many other adventures, Kit's 1835 duel with a big, aggressive Frenchman.

1857: The Mexican Boundary Survey, a joint Mexican-American geographical commission, defines the border between the two countries. This Survey essentially completes the formal "geographical outline" of the United States, but exploration of Canada continues apace.

1857: Joint British-Canadian expeditions to the Canadian Northwest, led by John Pallister and George Gladman, are the last of the old-style geographic explorations, and the first of a new "hybrid" approach stressing *both* geography and science.

1857: A four-volume summary report to Congress on feasible train routes from the Mississippi to the Pacific is finally published, but Congress fails to decide on any route. The search for a transcontinental railroad track therefore has to be put on hold.

1857–1880s: On an experimental basis, camels are imported from the Middle East, along with their handlers and drivers, to carry heavy burdens in the southwestern frontier. The camels do a very good job, but it is too hard to find enough qualified "camel men," so they never become widely used.

1859: Randolph W. Marcy publishes an outstanding book, *The Prairie Traveler*, which is full of practical advice on long-distance trails, the logistics of trail travel, and how to deal with very hostile Indians.

1859: A book by the Canadian artist and writer Paul Kane, entitled *Wanderings of an Artist Among the Indians of North America*, gives good insights into Canadian frontier life and also contains reproductions of Kane's art.

1860: William H. Brewer, a teacher of the natural sciences and a fine writer, eagerly accepts a job with the first geological survey of California. His book, *Up and Down California in 1860–1864*, gives accurate insights into contemporary gold and silver mining in Nevada.

1867–1879: The first detailed scientific studies of the American frontier West extend from 1867 to 1879, under the auspices of the four "Great Surveys." These successful expeditions are known today by the last names of their four leaders, namely, the King Survey, the Powell Survey, the Hayden Survey, and the Wheeler Survey.

1869: The mountain man John Colter (see 1813) explored the Yellowstone area alone and with very little equipment, but as Yellowstone's fame spreads the region begins to attract prosperous outdoorsmen who travel and camp out with a good deal of comfort.

1870–1871: In 1870, Canada had acquired both Rupert's Land, i.e., the area drained by Hudson Bay, and the Northwestern Territory, i.e., Manitoba, Saskatchewan, Alberta, the Yukon, and most of the Northwest Territories. One of the Canadian government's tasks in 1871 was to survey the boundary line between the United States and Canada, from the Lake of the Woods to the Rocky Mountains—a job given to the North American Boundary Commission Survey.

1871: Mark Twain's vivid, semi-humorous account of the Western frontier, published in 1871 under the title of *Roughing It*, reflects some of his experiences in Gold Rush California.

1872: In the Great Diamond Hoax, two larcenous prospectors claim to have found a fabulously valuable diamond field hidden in the American desert. Only the skill of the brilliant geologist Clarence King prevents many investors from losing a good deal of money.

1876: The Nevada newspaperman William Wright, who uses the penname Dan De Quille, writes a definitive and often amusing account on silver and gold mining in Nevada. It is entitled *The Big Bonanza*.

1879: The four "Great Surveys" in the United States are finally consolidated into the U.S. Geological Survey.

APPENDIX 1

The Fur Trade in New France

Since the fur trade was so important in the historical evolution of New France, it may be useful to distill and summarize it here.[1]

The lure of beaver fur—a very valuable and seemingly endless natural resource—initially prompted the French colonialists to establish a permanent presence in the St. Lawrence River Valley in the early 17th century. They then gradually spread out into the Great Lakes region; into the valleys of the Mississippi, Ohio, and Illinois rivers; and north and northwest into the huge Hudson Bay watershed. It was on this vast stage that the French played a dominant role in the very ambitious—and very successful—commercial enterprise designed to meet Europe's demand for prime furs.

This lucrative, adventuresome, complex, and long-running international undertaking has long been known simply as "the fur trade." However, it had very deep economic, social, and political dimensions which shaped the French colonial experience in many different ways. Although its annual earnings paled in comparison with the cod fisheries of the North Atlantic Ocean, the fur trade was in fact the economic powerhouse of New France. It financed new explorations, the spread of religion, and the development of settlements—all in the process enriching government officials, merchants, investors, and (very modestly, to be sure) the beaver trappers themselves.

The fur trade also helped dictate patterns of settlement in New France because of the need for a highly mobile, physically-strong, low-cost labor force, coupled with the need for small trading posts to keep them in business. Some of these posts—Quebec, Detroit, and Green Bay—would later become population centers.

There was another reality, too, in the fur trade. It forced the French colonialists into close and constant contact with the local Indians. Since there were only a handful of French colonists in the extensive rural regions of New France, they had no choice but to rely entirely on the Indians to harvest, process, and transport the furs, and to serve as their guides and cultural intermediaries. As a result, the French colonists became deeply enmeshed in Indian economies, societies, and politics. At the same time, they also lured the tribes, ever-deeper, into webs of European influence—for example, by buying furs from the Indians and then selling them firearms, ammunition, alcohol, and metal tools.

As an American historian noted in 2005,

> The trade between Native Americans and Europeans that evolved over a period of 300 years was based on a meshing of Native seasonal patterns of resource use and

production, on the one hand, and European commercial manufacturing and enterprise, on the other. The trade was dependent both on the continued production of furs and Native products, as well as on a continuing supply of goods produced in the East, in Europe, and elsewhere. Traders and Indian people were mutually dependent on exchanges that helped each other to survive and prosper in the environment of the Great Lakes region [and, of course, in other frontier regions, too].[2]

APPENDIX 2

Exploration by Canoe: The *Coureurs de Bois* and the *Voyageurs*

In order to survive—let alone *prosper*—in the fur trade, a man needed to master many skills, e.g., canoeing, hunting, fishing, and snowshoeing, and had to be able to get along very well with the local Indians.[1]

Trade with the Indians was usually marked by reciprocal and ceremonial gift-giving, which was the customary practice used to foster and to maintain trade alliances. In addition, sexual unions between Indian women and male fur traders were very common, too, and were mutually beneficial. These women played key roles as helpmates, translators, and cultural guides.

The hardy Europeans and Americans involved in the fur trade were variously known as *coureurs de bois* or as *voyageurs*—terms that now are often used interchangeably. The technical difference between them was that, in 1681, to curb the unregulated and therefore very profitable fur trade, the French "minister of marine" Jean-Baptiste Colbert created a system of issuing a relatively small number of licenses to fur traders. Over time, this system gradually replaced the unregulated *coureurs de bois* with "legal" voyageurs, but both groups continued to work side by side, as it were, for many years.

At first, both the *coureurs de bois* and the voyageurs worked on their own behalf or arranged small informal partnerships between themselves. After the fall of New France to the British in 1763 at the end of the Seven Years' War, however, the voyageurs tended to become the lower-status "hired hands" (or, more exactly, the "hired paddlers") of the big Montreal-based fur trading companies. In such companies, a *bourgeois* (i.e., a "master" in Canadian French) would hire wage-earning voyageurs to paddle his trade goods west to the Indians and then to paddle the Indians' furs back to Montreal.

French-Canadian canoemen would explore their way up the St. Lawrence River; through the Great Lakes and the Illinois Country; and then down the Mississippi to Louisiana and the Gulf of Mexico. In the process, they would often be the first Europeans make contact with many of the Indian tribes living and working along these inland waterways. In this appendix, descriptions from four contemporary sources are offered in chronological order on the men themselves.

The first thing that must be said is that the *coureurs de bois* led a life of extremes.

Consider, for example, these excerpts taken from a letter of 10 August 1688 from Governor Jacques-René de Brisay de Denonville to the French navy minister, the Marquis of Seignelay.

The governor wrote in part:

> ...one of the greatest ailments of Canada ... [is] the abuse of alcohol, which is so excessive that I fear the country will be lost...
>
> I have noticed that, with the strain of crossing rapids, it is common for our tired Canadian men to drink up to a pint of alcohol directly from the barrel, in order to regain some strength. Those who hold back still drink a half-septier [i.e., a considerable amount], often on an empty stomach. Afterwards, feeling strong, they cross the rapids and then fall asleep, without a thought for food, having no appetite until the evening, when the vapors of alcohol had dissipated.
>
> In the drinking establishments, Monsieur, all the drinkers, of whom there are many, usually drink a pint or a quart of alcohol after drinking wine.... What ravages these mixtures can do to a stomach! And how can a man stand up to the slightest bout of illness after this manner of abuse? Indeed, many have died this year.[2]

In a 1691 memoir written in Quebec by Jean Bouchart de Champigny, the sixth Intendant of New France, he explained why he did not want the young Frenchmen to become fur traders. There were two good reasons for this policy.

First, he believed that young men should stay in their home regions and become farmers there: if they disappeared to trap beaver, this would seriously reduce the local labor supply.

Second, the free-spirited coueurs de bois never paid the tithes or seigniorial duties levied on farmers. This reduced the incomes of both the civil and the religious authorities of New France.

In his memoir, Jean Bouchart therefore wrote as follows:

> It is regrettable that our vigorous, never-tiring Canadian youth are attracted to nothing but these kind of journeys, where they live in the woods like savages, spending two or three years without receiving the sacraments [of the Catholic Church], in idleness and often extraordinary misery. Once accustomed to this life, they find it hard to dedicate themselves to cultivating the land, and they live in extreme poverty because they spend much upon their return.
>
> On the other hand, those who settle and add value to the land are rich or, at least, live comfortably with their fields and fish ponds around their houses, as well as considerable numbers of cattle...[3]

During the heyday of the Canadian fur trade from the 1650s to the late 19th century, two different kinds of birchbark canoes were in frequent use. One was the big 36-foot-long, six feet wide *canot de maître* ("canoe of the leader"), also known as a Montreal canoe. The other was the smaller 25-foot-long, four to four and a half feet wide *canot du nord* ("canoe of the north").[4]

In either case, there was never much room in canoes for the paddlers themselves (most of the limited space was taken up by cargo), so Canadian canoemen tended to be short, wiry men with deep chests, muscular arms and shoulders, and remarkable powers of endurance.

Thomas McKenney, an American who traveled with them in the 1820s, reported that

A Canadian, if born to be a laborer, deems himself to be very unfortunate if he should chance to grow over five feet five, or six inches;—and if he shall reach five foot ten or eleven, it forever excludes him from the privilege of becoming a *voyageur*.

There is no room for the legs of such people, in these canoes. But if he shall stop growing at about five feet four inches, and be gifted with a good voice, and lungs that never tire, he is considered to have been born under a most favourable star.[5]

Despite its hardships and dangers, life as a *coureur de bois* was always much more exciting than farming. Alexander Ross, author of the 1855 book *Fur Hunters of the West*, tells his readers why.

In this account, Ross is reporting what an old man—a retired *coureur de bois*— had to say about his life. This old man was speaking in French, which Ross translated as follows (his long account has been shortened here):

"I have now," said the old man, "been forty-two years in this country [i.e., along the Red River of the North, which now forms part of the boundary between Minnesota and North Dakota.] For twenty-four I was a light canoeman. I required but little sleep, but sometimes got less than I required. No portage was too long for me: all portages were alike. My end of the canoe never touched the ground until I saw the end [i.e., the end of the portage.]

"Fifty songs a day were nothing to me. I could carry, paddle, walk and sing with any man I ever saw. During that period I saved the lives of ten *bourgeois* [the leaders of canoe expeditions], and was their favorite because the others stopped to carry at a bad step [i.e., at a place where it was very difficult to keep one's footing while carrying a canoe] and lost time, I pushed on—over rapids, over cascades, over chutes: all were the same to me. No water, no weather ever stopped the paddle or the song.

"I have had twenty [Indian] wives in the country [he did not marry any of them, but simply lived with them 'in the custom of the country,' as these informal relationships were described]; and was once possessed of fifty horses and six running dogs [sled dogs] trimmed in the first style. I was then like a *bourgeois*, rich and happy.... Five hundred [British] pounds have twice passed through my hands, although now I have not a spare shirt on my back or a penny to buy one.

"Yet, were I young I should glory in commencing the same career. I would spend another half-century in the same fields of enjoyment. There is no life so happy as a *voyageur*'s life; none is so independent; no place where a man enjoys so much variety and freedom as in the Indian country. *Huzzah, hussah pour le pays sauvage*! ['Hip, hip, hurray for the wild country!']"[6]

APPENDIX 3

The Railroad Surveys

The following comments are drawn from a National Park Survey article on "Railroad Surveys" (see Bibliography) and from a book on *Western Rivers and Lakes of the Great Basin* by coauthors Janin and Carlson. Both sources have been used here to add details to the railroad-related points already made earlier in the text of the present book.

The era of railroad explorations and surveys was spurred on by the end of the U.S.-Mexican War in 1848 and by the flourishing of gold mining in California in 1849 and thereafter. As will be seen below, it progressed only by fits and starts.

In 1848, for example, Senator Thomas Hart Benton persuaded three St. Louis businessmen to finance the exploration of a proposed central, i.e., a 38th parallel, route that would link St. Louis and San Francisco. If successful, this project would ensure that any later transcontinental route would have to run through St. Louis.

The explorer John Charles Frémont was then hired to lead an exploration party westward in order to find the best route over the Rocky Mountains near Cochetopa Pass in Colorado. In December 1848, Frémont's party went through the 12,327-foot-high Bill Williams Pass in the San Juan Mountains. By 17 December 1848 the men and animals were huddled on top of Pool Table Mesa in Colorado, but it was so cold there that both men and mules were freezing fast.

An advance party was therefore sent out to find help, but some of these men died en route, while others had to resort to cannibalism in order to survive. Frémont then sent out another relief party, which located the first party and led it out of the mountains. Thanks to help from the Ute Indians, this second relief party managed to reach Taos, New Mexico, but Frémont now abandoned Taos to work for his own political glory in California, leaving his men to fend for themselves as best they could.

Subsequent relief parties, led by the mountain man Old Bill Williams, worked until January 1849 to get all the survivors out of the mountains but, nevertheless, a total of 10 men died in the process. Contemporary observers considered this expedition to have been a complete fiasco. They blamed it, correctly, on self-serving Frémont himself. As mentioned earlier in this text, Frémont blamed Williams, who was then dead, for failures that were entirely his own fault.

In 1849, Colonel John F. Albert of the Topographical Engineers urged that, in order to avoid the deep snows of the Rocky Mountains, the railroad should follow the 32nd parallel along the Gila River. Albert therefore dispatched Colonel Randolph March to explore this route.

The Railroad Surveys

In 1850–1852, however, Colonel Joseph E. Johnston led a special task force across Texas to find and to map the existing military and emigrant roads, as well as to look for possible future railroad routes.

Congress now decided to take a hand in this important national matter. In 1853, it authorized a U.S. government survey of all the contending Pacific Railroad routes to determine which one was the most promising. Toward this end, four main exploring parties were sent out into the field in 1853. They looked at four or more different routes:

1. A northern route between the 47th and 49th parallels. It would run from the Great Lakes, i.e., from Chicago, to Puget Sound.

2. The Cochetopa Pass route. Senator Benton tried hard to persuade Congress to let Frémont (his son-in-law) lead this expedition but the Army sent Captain John W. Gunnison instead. Not being a politician ready to take "no" for an answer, however, Benton sent Frémont out anyway, on a privately-funded expedition. Both Frémont and Gunnison soon came to grief. Frémont lost one of his men in the snows of the San Juan Mountains, and his party had to be rescued. Gunnison's own party was attacked by the Paiutes; Gunnison and most of his men were killed. His deputy, Lieutenant Beckwith, then took over the party and successfully explored the region into 1854. Indeed, his explorations laid out the actual route later used by the Union Pacific railway company for the transcontinental railroad.

3. The 35th parallel route expedition, led by Lieutenant Amiel Weeks Whipple, was sponsored by a Missouri Congressman. This expedition was a success and the route that Whipple had chosen was in fact quite viable. A major problem, however, was that he had vastly overestimated the cost of building a railroad along this route (his estimate was double what the real figure would be). Because of this error, Congress paid little attention to his route.

4. The 32nd parallel route was studied by two exploratory expeditions, i.e., one by Lieutenant John G. Parke from the west, and the other by Captain John Pope from the east. The only fault of this route was that the explorers were not able to find a good pass *in American territory* that would be suitable for using San Diego as the destination for a railroad line. The option of laying tracks in Mexico itself was a non-starter for political reasons.

By 1860, a transcontinental railroad had become a political necessity, especially for the more than 300,000 inhabitants of California. In 1861 the Central Pacific Railroad Company was formed in San Francisco. By 1862, railroad financiers were finally able to push a transcontinental railroad bill through Congress. Since Senator Benton had lost power to influence railroad matters, and since the southern states were now out of the Union due to the Civil War, the Beckwith route (a northern) route was chosen.

Thus this line, which would become known as the Overland Route, was built between 1863 and 1869. It linked the previously-existing rail network, which had ended at Council Bluffs, Iowa, with San Francisco Bay on the Pacific coast. As one of the three private companies involved in building the Overland Route, the Central Pacific Railroad Company laid 690 miles of track eastward, over the Sierra Nevada mountains, from Sacramento, California, to Promontory Summit, Utah Territory.

A sister company, the Union Pacific, laid track from Council Bluffs, Iowa, westward toward Utah. Work on these western parts of the transcontinental line began in 1863 and did not end until 1869, with shifts working day and night—at a total cost of about $100 million in contemporary prices, which would be about $2.4 billion in today's dollars.

Because of the enormous difficulty of building a railroad line over the Sierra Nevada mountains, it is important now to say a further word about this process.

Federal explorers and surveyors had decided earlier that any trans-Sierra railroad should follow the course of the Truckee River in California. Thus in 1868 the Central Pacific connected, via the upper Truckee River canyon route, the hamlet of Truckee with the growing city of Reno. This was the first rail transportation corridor that followed the part of the river between these two small communities. Further east, the Central Pacific would also use the Humboldt River as part of its route.

The great railroad engineer Theodore Judah was instrumental in the decision to lay the Central Pacific's tracks through the Truckee River gorge. In the 1850s, Judah was nicknamed "Crazy Judah" by his compatriots for one very good reason: he strongly believed that a railroad line could in fact be built over both the Rocky Mountains and over the Sierra Nevada, thus linking California to the East Coast.

Events proved him right. Thanks in no small part to his own foresight and determination, the east and west coasts of the United States would soon be linked by bands of steel: overland migration would no longer be the long, slow, and often dangerous undertaking it had been in the past.

Before Judah appeared on the scene, the Truckee River route had been the choice of many overland travelers, either on horseback, in covered wagons, or even afoot, pushing handcarts. However, the Truckee River route had gradually fallen out of popularity because travelers now found it easier to use the now-improved Carson River route or other trails.

Judah himself did not pay much attention to the Truckee River route until 1860, when a local pharmacist and promoter named Daniel Strong, who was working in the mining boomtown of Dutch Flat, California, told him about an old, now-abandoned wagon road that ran through Donner Pass. Strong took Judah on a mule-back exploratory trip to the pass.

From this high vantage point, Judah could see that if a rail line was laid through the Truckee River gorge, the Dutch Flat route would allow the track to rise steadily to a single summit—one at the very manageable (in engineering terms) grade of no more than 105 feet to a mile.

Judah and Strong soon met with a group of wealthy Californians who would become famous as the "Big Four": Collis Huntington, Charles Crocker, Leland Stanford, and Mark Hopkins. They agreed to organize the Central Pacific Railroad and to fund a survey needed to convince Congress to approve the western portion of the first transcontinental railroad.

Appendix 4

Early Explorations of the Yellowstone Region, 1797–1871

Because the Yellowstone region is so unique, its early explorations merit a brief and very informal survey here.[1]

David Thompson, the celebrated early explorer and geographer in the British fur trade of the Pacific Northwest, used the words "Yellow Stone" in notes he wrote in 1797–1798 when he was visiting the Mandan villages on the Upper Missouri. It is not known how these words originated, but the canyon walls that tower over the river near its headwaters do have the appearance of "yellow rock."

During their 1805–1806 expedition, Lewis and Clark heard distant volcanic explosions in the Yellowstone region that sounded much like thunder and made the earth tremble, but they did not investigate these sounds.

As mentioned earlier, John Colter, who had been with the Lewis and Clark expedition, was probably, in 1808, the first non-Indian to get a good glimpse of Yellowstone. The earliest newspaper account of the Yellowstone region, however, only appeared in a Philadelphia newspaper in 1827. At about the same time, the trapper Daniel T. Potts wrote one of the earliest letters about what is now Yellowstone Park, describing its thermal features. The trapper Joe Meek, for his part, came across what is now known as the Norris Geyser basin area in 1829, but no one believed his remarkable stories of seeing "fire and brimstone" there.

This same lack of belief greeted the stories of mountain man Jim Bridger, who began exploring the Yellowstone region in the 1830s. He was famous as a spinner of tall tales, and no one accepted his outlandish accounts of waterfalls sprouting upwards and of petrified "birds and trees."

In 1834, Warren Angus Ferris, a clerk of the American Fur Company, visited what is now Yellowstone Park purely out of curiosity. He made a name for himself, however, by being the first person to provide an accurate description of a geyser, and was perhaps the first to apply the word "geyser" (a term that originated in Iceland) to Yellowstone's thermal features.

In 1835–1839, the trapper Osborne Russell traveled into the Yellowstone three times, exploring the shores of Yellowstone Lake and many of the thermal areas and the smaller lakes south of Yellowstone Lake. In 1842, the former trapper Warren Ferris published an account in the *Western Literary Messenger* that described Yellowstone's geysers.

In the years that followed, the struggles in the United States over slavery; the ups and downs of the American Civil War; and the skirmishes with western Indians all deterred the U.S. Government from sending any official exploration party into the Yellowstone region.

An unofficial party of prospectors, led by Walter Washington deLacy, explored the southern portion of Yellowstone Park in 1863 and saw some thermal features there. A few years later, the name "deLacy Lake" appeared on a local map of the area, but this was later changed to the present-day Shoshone Lake.

In 1865, a group of Piegan Indians guided Father Francis Xavier Kuppens, a young Jesuit priest serving near Great Falls, Montana, to present-day Yellowstone Park. Among other places, he visited the Grand Canyon of the Yellowstone and the geysers of the Firehole Basin. Later that same year, Kuppens described his travels to Acting Territorial Governor Thomas Francis Meagher, who suggested that if this place of wonders really did exist, it should be preserved as a national park.

Frederick and Philip Bottler became, in 1868, the first settlers between Bozeman, Montana, and the present Park. The Bottler Ranch was at first a starting-point for hunting and prospecting in the area.

Three mine workers—David E. Folsom, Charles W. Cook, and William Petersen—set out in 1869 to explore the Yellowstone region. They went to the Grand Canyon of the Yellowstone; saw the teeming wildlife of the region; and looked at the geysers and boiling pools. These experiences led them to conclude that the whole area needed to be preserved from commercialization, so after returning from their explorations, they wrote articles about what they had seen. Reputable magazines, however, refused to publish what they considered to be totally unreliable stories.

In 1870, after years of enticing rumors about the Yellowstone region, a group of gold prospectors, curious private citizens, and U.S. Government surveyors went into the Yellowstone region. As a result of what they saw there, they decided to do their best to make sure that the region was preserved from development so that all Americans (and foreign visitors) could have the opportunity to enjoy its wonders.

The most famous of the parties that explored the Yellowstone region in 1876 was led by Henry D. Washburn, surveyor-general of the Montana territory. First Lieutenant Gustavus C. Doane, who commanded the military escort that accompanied the Washburn group, had no camera or artist to record his impressions. He was thus forced to rely on his own journal to record, for posterity, his own sense of wonder at the Jackson Hole region.

He wrote, movingly:

> The moonlight view was one of unspeakable grandeur. There are twenty-two summits in the line [of mountains], all of them mighty mountains, with the gleaming spire of Mount Hayden rising in a pinnacle above all.
> There are no foothills to the Tetons. They rise suddenly in rugged majesty from the rock strewn plain. Masses of heavy forest appear on the glacial debris and in the parks behind the curve of the lower slopes, but the general field of vision is glittering glacial rock. The soft light floods the great expanse of the valley, the winding silvery river and the resplendent deeply carved mountain walls.[2]

Doane also drafted the official report of the expedition. His report was so good that it encouraged Congress to authorize an official exploration of the region in 1871, led by Ferdinand V. Hayden. This adventure was staffed (among many very competent people) by artist Thomas Moran and photographer William H. Jackson, whose watercolors and photographs appeared in Hayden's 500-page report to Congress and made a very positive impression there.

Lobbying to make Yellowstone a "national park" therefore began very soon and on March 1, 1872, President Ulysses Grant signed into law the world's first national park. In Yellowstone National Park, 2.2 million acres of wilderness were "set apart as public park or pleasuring ground for the benefit and enjoyment of the people." Nathaniel Langford, one of the most outspoken advocates of the national park idea, was appointed the first superintendent of the Park.

The above expeditions, coupled with later expeditions, ultimately led Congress and the Federal Government to adopt strong laws to protect the Park and its resources. These legal efforts culminated in the Lacey Act of 1894, designed "To protect the birds and animals in Yellowstone National Park, and to punish crimes in said park." This Act would become the cornerstone of future law enforcement policies there.

Chapter Notes

Chapter 1

1. After a personal communication of 31 December 2018 from Dr. Timothy P. Foran, Curator of British North America, in the Canadian Museum of History in Gatineau, Canada.
2. Some of these comments are drawn from Janin, *Claiming the American Wilderness*, pp. 48–49.
3. Quoted in Janin, *Claiming the American Wilderness*, p. 48.
4. After Allen, *A Continent Defined*, p. 1.
5. After Kessell, *Kiva, Cross, and Crown*, p. 2.
6. After Kessell, *Spain in the Southwest*, p. xiv.
7. For concise introductions to the history of the French in the frontier West, see Janin, "The French: Lords of Rivers and Lakes" in Janin, *Claiming the American Wilderness*, pp. 96–126; and Taylor, "French America, 1650–1750," in *American Colonies*, pp. 362–395.
8. See Calloway, *One Vast Winter Count*, pp. 367–426.
9. After Golay and Bowman, *North American Exploration*, p. 3.
10. The Oregon Treaty of 1846 would resolve a decades-long dispute over possession of the Oregon Country by extending the original boundary between the United States and British North America further west to the Pacific Ocean, with all of Vancouver Island being retained by the British.
11. After Allen, "Canadian Fur Trade and Exploration of Western North America," pp. 78–79.
12. After Nichols, *Indians in the United States and Canada*, pp. xv, 2.
13. After Taylor, *American Colonies*, p. 40.
14. Quoted in Taylor, *American Colonies*, p. 364.
15. Quoted in Calloway, *One Vast Winter Count*, p. 236.
16. After a private communication of 12 October 2018 from Professor Roger Nichols.
17. Gilman, *Lewis and Clark*, p. 142. Italics have been added to the sentence reading "They were visual narratives."
18. After Calloway, *One Vast Winter Count*, pp. 10–13.
19. After Russell, "Trade Muskets and Rifles Supplied to the Indians," pp. 104–105.
20. After Allen, "Canadian Fur Trade and Exploration of Western North America," p. 76.
21. Although the two terms "Canada" and "New France" are sometimes used interchangeably in the historical literature, "New France" actually covered a much broader swath of North American territory than the Great Lakes-St. Lawrence colony of Canada did.
22. Quoted in Janin, *Claiming the American Wilderness*, pp. 96–97.
23. Quoted in Janin, *Claiming the American Wilderness*, p. 104.
24. After Conrad, *A Concise History of Canada*, p. 59, 60.
25. After Allen, *Western Rivermen*, p. 17.
26. After Janin, *Claiming the American Wilderness*, p. 205.
27. After Janin, *Claiming the American Wilderness*, p. 106.
28. Quoted in Janin, *Claiming the American Wilderness*, p. 69.
29. Quoted in Janin, *Claiming the American Wilderness*, p. 69.
30. Quoted in Calloway, *One Vast Winter Count*, p. 337.

Chapter 2

1. After Janin, *Claiming the American Wilderness*, pp. 182–202.
2. Adapted from Calloway, *One Vast Winter Count*, p. 315.
3. Quoted in Brown, *Bury My Heart at Wounded Knee*, pp. 209–210.
4. After Janin, *Claiming the American Wilderness*, p. 7.
5. Quoted in Kukla, *A Wilderness So Immense*, p. 118.
6. After Conrad, *a Concise History of Canada*, p. 79.
7. After Feigenbaum, *Jefferson's America & Napoleon's France*, p. 1.
8. Quoted in Kukla, *A Wilderness So Immense*, opposite title page.
9. Quoted in Janin, *Claiming the American Wilderness*, pp. 199–200.

Chapter 3

1. The chronological sequence given below is drawn from Janin, *Claiming the American Wilderness*, pp. 203–213; some of the comments also come from the same source. Other information is drawn from Golay and Bowman, *North American Exploration*; Allen, *A Continent Defined*; Blumenthal, *The Early Exploration of Inland Washington Waters*; and Cabrillo National Monument Foundation, *The Voyage of Juan Rodrígues Cabrillo*.
2. Quoted by Janin, *Claiming the American Wilderness*, p. 128.
3. Quoted by Janin, *Claiming the American Wilderness*, p. 129.
4. Quoted by Janin, *Claiming the American Wilderness*, p. 66.
5. Quoted by Janin, *Claiming the American Wilderness*, p. 76.
6. After Blumenthal, *The Early Exploration of Inland Washington Waters*, full text.
7. Quoted by Blumenthal, *The Early Exploration of Inland Washington Waters*, pp. 19–22.
8. After Golay and Bowman, *North American Exploration*, pp. 234–235.
9. After Blumenthal, *The Early Exploration of Inland Washington Waters*, pp. 46–72.
10. After Golay and Bowman, *North American Exploration*, pp. 242–243; and Blumenthal, *The Early Exploration of Inland Washington Waters*, pp. 73–101.
11. This section draws on Golay and Bowman, *North American Exploration*, p. 389; Allen, *A Continent Defined*, pp. 381–391; Blumenthal, *The Early Explorations of Inland Washington Waters*, pp. 102–194; and Janin, *Claiming the American Wilderness*, pp. 146–149.
12. Quoted by Gibson, "The Exploration of the Pacific Coast," p. 383.

Chapter 4

1. Quoted by Janin, *Claiming the American Wilderness*, p. 51.
2. Quoted by Janin, *Trails of Historic New Mexico*, p. 26.
3. This chapter draws on a number of sources, including Calloway, *One Vast Winter Count*, pp. 133–142; Golay and Bowman, pp. 73–75; John, *Storms Brewed in Other Men's Worlds*, pp. 13–24; Weber, *The Spanish Frontier in North America*, pp. 46–49; Kessell, *Kiva, Cross, and Crown*, pp. 18–25; Janin and Carlson, *Trails of Historic New Mexico*, pp. 29–33; and Janin, *Claiming the American Wilderness*, pp. 55–58.
4. Pedro de Castañeda of Nájera, *Narrative of the Coronado Expedition*, p. 37.
5. Quoted in Golay and Bowman, *North American Exploration*, p. 101, citing Fray de Niza, *Relación*, 1540.
6. Quoted in Golay and Bowman, *North American Exploration*, p. 75, citing Coronado, Letter to Antonio de Mendoza, Viceroy of New Spain, August 1540.
7. Pedro de Castañeda of Nájera, *Narrative of the Colorado Expedition*, p. 135.
8. Quoted in Weber, *The Spanish Frontier in North America*, p. 49, citing Coronado to the king, October 20, 1541, in Hammond and Rey, eds. and trans., *Coronado Expedition*, 189, and Castañeda, "Narrative," 241. Weber also notes it is conceivable that El Turco was in fact acting in good faith but either did not understand Coronado or was himself simply lost. Since there were no landmarks of any kind on the open plains, hunters could not easily find their way back to camp, and a Spanish scouting party was forced to rely on a "sea-compass" in order to travel safely.
9. Castañeda, *Narrative of the Coronado Expedition*, pp.135–137.
10. Castañeda, *Narrative of the Coronado Expedition*, pp. 43–45, 367–369.

11. After Jones, "Spanish Penetrations to the North of New Spain, pp. 41–42.

Chapter 5

1. The following discussion of these five expeditions is drawn in large part from Jones, "Spanish Penetration to the North of New Spain," pp. 42–48.
2. After John, *Storms Brewed in Other Men's Worlds*, p. 28.
3. After John, *Storms Brewed in Other Men's Worlds*, p. 25.
4. After Golay and Bowman, *North American Exploration*, pp. 115–116.
5. Quoted in Janin, *Trails of Historic New Mexico*, p. 37.
6. Quoted in Weber, *Spanish Frontier*, p. 79.
7. After Golay and Bowman, *North American Exploration*, pp. 107–109, John, *Storms Brewed in Other Men's Worlds*, pp. 36–56; Simmons, *The Last Conquistador*, entire text; and Janin, *Claiming the American Wilderness*, pp. 63–65.
8. Simmons, *The Last Conquistador*, p. xiv.
9. Quoted by Christine Preston, *The Royal Road*, no page number given.
10. This account follows John, *Storms Brewed in Other Men's Worlds*, pp. 48–50.
11. After Calloway, *One Vast Winter Count*, p. 10.
12. Quoted in Janin, *Claiming the American Wilderness*, p. 64.
13. This section draws on Golay and Bowman, *North American Exploration*, pp. 280–281; Janin, *Claiming the American Wilderness*, pp. 131, 205; and Conrad, *A Concise History of Canada*, p. 49.
14. Rupert's Land was operated by the Hudson's Bay Company from 1670 to 1870. It was mostly located in present-day Canada, with a small part in what is now the United States. It included the whole of Manitoba; most of Saskatchewan; southern Alberta; southern Nunavut; northern parts of Ontario and Quebec; and, in the United States, small parts of Minnesota, North Dakota, Montana, and South Dakota.
15. Quoted in Janin *Claiming the American Wilderness*, p. 131.
16. After Janin, *Claiming the American Wilderness*," p. 131.

17. Quoted in Saunt, *West of the Revolution*, p. 126.

Chapter 6

1. After Jones, "Spanish Penetrations to the North of New Spain," p. 48, and Janin and Carlson, *Trails of Historic New Mexico*, pp. 52–53.
2. This account follows Janin and Carlson, *Trails of Historic New Mexico*, pp. 49–52.
3. Quoted in Janin, *Trails of Historic New Mexico*, p. 51.
4. This section draws on Hague, *Road to California*, all pages; and on Janin and Carlson, *Trails of Historic New Mexico*, pp. 165–170.
5. This section is drawn from Gregg, *Commerce of the Prairies*, full text (two volumes in one edition).
6. Quoted in Janin, *Trails of Historic New Mexico*, p. 52.
7. Gregg, *Commerce of the Prairies*, pp. 37–38.
8. This account follows Janin and Carlson, *Trails of Historic New Mexico*, pp. 52–56, and Warner, *The Domínguez-Escalante Journal*, pp. 53, 89–90.
9. After *The Domínguez-Escalante Journal*, p. xv.
10. Warner, *The Domínguez-Escalante Journal*, p. 84.
11. After Hafen and Hafen, *Old Spanish Trail*, pp. 19, 362.

Chapter 7

1. After Janin, "The French: Lords of Rivers and Lakes" in Janin, *Claiming the American Wilderness*, pp. 96–126.
2. After John, *Storms Brewed in Other Men's Worlds*, p. 158.
3. After Heidenreich, "Early French Explorers in the North American Interior," in Allen, *A Continent Defined* pp. 76–77.
4. This account follows Janin, *Claiming the American Wilderness*, p. 131, and Golay and Bowman, *North American Exploration*, pp. 280–281.
5. After Heidenreich, "Early French Exploration in the North American Interior," p. 112.
6. Sources used in this section include Janin, *Claiming the American Wilderness*, pp. 68–69.

7. For numerous good examples of maps showing California as an island, see Hayes, *Historical Atlas of California*, pp. 28–35.

8. Quoted in Janin, *Claiming the American Wilderness*, pp. 68–69.

9. This account is drawn from Golay and Bowman, *North American Exploration*, pp. 249 and 287–288; Janin, *Claiming the American Wilderness*, pp. 106–108; and Allen, *A Continent Divided*, pp. 126–130.

10. Quoted in Janin, *Claiming the American Wilderness*, p. 107.

Chapter 8

1. This account is drawn in part from Golay and Bowman, *North American Exploration*, pp. 291–293.

2. After Calloway, *One Vast Winter Count*, p. 10.

3. Quoted in Golay and Bowman, *North American Exploration*, p. 292, citing Zenobius Membré, "Narrative of La Salle's Voyage Down the Mississippi."

4. The "border lakes" include the lakes strung out along the Pigeon River and Rainy River, as well as the outlying Lac des Milles Lacs, Dog Lake, Lac Seul, and Lake Nipigon. After White, *Grand Portage as a Trading Post*, p. iv.

5. After Golay and Bowman, *North American Exploration*, p. 301.

6. This account variously follows Golay and Bowman, *North American Exploration*, p. 289; Janin, *Claiming the American Wilderness*, pp. 132–133; and Allen, *A Continent Defined*, pp. 215–218.

7. Quoted in Janin, *Claiming the American Wilderness*, p. 132.

8. Quoted in Calloway, *One Vast Winter Count*, p. 246.

9. This account follows Golay and Bowman, *North American Exploration*, pp. 283–284, and John, *Storms Brewed in Other Men's Worlds*, pp. 164, 196–197, 199, 215.

10. After John, *Storms Brewed in Other Men's Worlds*, p. 196.

11. This account is drawn from Golay and Bowman, *North American Exploration*, pp. 254–255; and Janin, *Claiming the American Wilderness*, p .113.

12. Quoted in Janin, *Claiming the American Wilderness*, p. 113.

13. This section draws on Golay and Bowman, *North American Exploration*, pp. 276–277; John, *Storms Brewed in Other Men's Worlds*, pp. 211, 214–215, 217–219, 247, 255, 304–306; and Allen, *A Continent Defined*, pp. 160–161, 164.

14. This account is drawn from Chipman and Lemée, "St. Denis, Louis Juchereau de," pp. 1–3; Janin, *Claiming the American Wilderness*, pp. 22, 114; Weber, *The Spanish Frontier in North America*, pp. 160–163, 167, 172–174, 184, 186, 196, 223, 309; DeVoto, *The Course of Empire*, pp. 173, 176; Allen, *A Continent Defined*, pp. 162–164; Golay and Bowman, *North American*, pp. 254, 259, 271, 306; and John, *Storms Brewed in Other Men's Worlds*, pp. 198–205, 207–213, 221–222, 342–344, 367.

Chapter 9

1. Some of these observations are drawn from Janin, *Claiming the American Wilderness*, pp. 115–118; DeVoto, *The Course of Empire*, pp. 177, 182, 184–185, 186; Allen, *A Continent Defined*, pp. 165–172; Golay and Bowman, *North American Exploration*, pp. 320–321; John, *Storms Brewed in Other Men's Worlds*, pp. 219–220; Kessell, *Kiva, Cross, and Crown*, p. 387; Calloway, *One Vast Winter Count*, pp. 260, 272; Weber, *The Spanish Frontier in North America*, p. 196.

2. Quoted in Calloway, *One Vast Winter Count*, p. 260.

3. Sources used in this section include Golay and Bowman, *North American Exploration*, p. 263; Calloway, *One Vast Winter Count*, p. 218; Allen, *A Continent Divided*, pp. 175–178..

4. After Allen, *A Continent Divided*, p. 178.

5. After Calloway, *One Vast Winter Count*, p. 218.

6. This section draws on Janin, *Claiming the American Wilderness*, pp. 36, 89, 118–120.

7. After Taylor, *American Colonies*, pp. 417–419.

8. After Janin, *Claiming the American Wilderness*, p. 120.

9. Sources for these pages include Janin, *Claiming the American Wilderness*, pp. 120–122, and Blakeslee, "Mallet Brothers" in *Encyclopedia of the Great Plains*.

10. After Gregg, *Commerce of the Prairies*, p. 13.

11. Quoted by Calloway, *One Vast Winter Count*, pp. 285-286.
12. Sources used in this section include Chaput "Legardeur de Saint-Pierre, Jacques" in *Dictionary of Canadian Biography*; Allen, *A Continent Defined*, pp. 189-195; and DeVoto, *The Course of Empire*, pp. 205, 217-218, 220.
13. Quoted in Chaput, "Legardeur de Saint Pierre, Jacques," p. 3.
14. Quoted in Chaput, "Legardeur de Saint-Pierre, Jacques," p. 1.

Chapter 10

1. Sources used in the following pages include Golay and Bowman, *North American Exploration*, pp. 313-314, 343-344, 347; Calloway, *One Vast Winter Count*, pp. 275, 297, 299; Allen, *A Continent Defined*, pp. 226, 227, 228-230; DeVoto, *The Course of Empire*, pp. 218, 219-220.
2. After Calloway, *One Vast Winter Count*, p. 275.
3. Some of the points in this section are drawn from Janin, *Claiming the American Wilderness*, pp. 137-138, and from Marsh and Panneton, "Samuel Hearne," pp. 1-3.
4. After Calloway, *One Vast Winter Count*, p. 10.
N5. After Janin, *Claiming the American Wilderness*, pp. 137-138.
6. The most concise sources used in this section are Golay and Bowman, *North American Exploration*, pp. 231-233; and Janin, *Claiming the American Wilderness*, pp. 13-16.
7. The missions in California relied on the forced labor of the local Indians in order to survive and to prosper. Foreign visitors to the missions often had very negative things to say. In 1786, for example, the French navigator Jean-Francois Galaup, Comte de La Pérouse, reported as follows: "The government is a veritable theocracy for the Indians; they believe that their superiors [i.e., the missionaries] are in immediate and continual communication with God...The friars, more occupied with heavenly than temporal interests, have neglected the introduction of the most common arts...With pain we say it, the resemblance [to slavery] is so perfect that we have seen men and women in irons or in the stocks; even the sound of the lash might have struck our ears..." (Quoted by Golay and Bowman, *North American Exploration*, p. 221.)
8. Quoted in Janin, *Claiming the American Wilderness*, p. 76.
9. Quoted in Heizer, "Aboriginal California and Great Basin Cartography," p. 460.
10. Quoted in Hafen and Hafen, *Old Spanish Trail*, p. 32.
11. Quoted in Hafen and Hafen, *Old Spanish Trail*, p. 55.
12. This section draws from Janin and Carlson, *Trails of Historic New Mexico*, pp. 73-75; Golay and Bowman, *North American Exploration*, pp. 216-217; Allen, *A Continent Defined*, pp. 347, 348, 349; Weber, *The Spanish Frontier in North America*, pp. 251-254, 256-258, 265; Calloway, *One Vast Winter Count*, pp. 390, 391; DeVoto, *The Course of Empire*, pp. 288-290; John, *Storms Brewed in Other Men's Worlds*, pp. 558-561, 564-566, 568, 570-571, 575-576, 578, 582, 593, 606-609.
13. After Janin, *Trails of Historic New Mexico*, p. 74.
14. Quoted in Janin, *Trails of Historic New Mexico*, pp. 74-75.
15. Some of the information presented here variously comes from Gough, "Pond, Peter"; Janin, *Claiming the American Wilderness*, pp. 171-173; Golay and Bowman, *North American Exploration*, pp. 377-378; and Tanner, *The Canadians*, pp. 23-29.
16. Quoted in Gough, "Pond, Peter," p. 1.
17. After Gough, "Pond, Peter," p. 4.
18. After Janin, *Claiming the American Wilderness*, p. 171.

Chapter 11

1. Sources used here include Loomis and Nasatir, *Pedro Vial and the Roads to Santa Fe*, pp. 262-287, 316-407; Janin, *Claiming the American Wilderness*, p. 33; Janin and Carlson, *Trails of Historic New Mexico*, pp. 56-58. The last source has been used extensively in this account because it was not possible to improve it without running on at too great a length.
2. Quoted in Janin, *Claiming the American Wilderness*, p. 33.
3. The main source used in this section is Schwantes, *The Pacific Northwest*, p. 46 ff.
4. After Schwantes, *The Pacific Northwest*, pp. 46-47.
5. Sources used in this section include

Golay and Bowman, *North American Exploration*, pp. 361–365

6. After Calloway, *One Vast Winter Count*, p. 10.

7. Quoted in Golay and Bowman, *North American Exploration*, p. 364, citing Alexander Mackenzie, "Journal of a Voyage from Fort Chipewyan to the Pacific Ocean in 1793," in Mackenzie's *Voyages* (1801).

8. Both quotes are cited by Golay and Bowman, *North American Exploration*, p. 364.

9. Quoted in DeVoto, *The Course of Empire*, p. 421.

10. This section draws on the full text of Wood, *Prologue to Lewis & Clark*, as well as Janin, *Claiming the American Wilderness*, pp. 89–93;

11. Today, a pirogue is a small, light, flat-bottomed boat used for duck hunting in marshes and very shallow waters. In the 19th century, however, a pirogue was often a large, heavy, flat-bottomed, masted rowboat built from planks.

12. Quoted in Janin, *Claiming the American Wilderness*, p. 92.

13. Information in this section comes from Golay and Bowman, *North American Exploration*, pp. 386–388; Janin, *Claiming the American Wilderness*, pp. 3, 154–155, 171; Conrad, *A Concise History of Canada*, p. 103; and Allen, "Canadian Fur Trade and Exploration of Western North America," pp. 81–84.

14. Quoted in Janin, *Claiming the American Wilderness*, following p. viii.

15. There was an extensive intra-Indian trade at The Dalles and an active international trade as well. For example, a wide range of relatively inexpensive English, American, Russian, and Spanish goods (beads, kettles, cloth, metal, and guns) were all for sale here.

16. Quoted in Golay and Bowman, *North American Exploration*, p. 387.

Chapter 12

1. The major source for this section is Nelson, *My First Years in the Fur Trade*, full text.

2. Nelson, *My First Years in the Fur Trade*, pp. 42–43.

3. The Lewis and Clark Expedition is now so famous and so thoroughly documented that it is not feasible here to list all the sources used in this section. The most important ones, however, include Golay and Bowman, *North American Exploration*, pp. 354–358; Janin, *Claiming the American Wilderness*, especially Appendix 1, pp. 215–219; and the full text of Bergon, *The Journals of Lewis and Clark*.

4. Quoted in Janin, *Claiming the American Wilderness*, p. 219.

5. Lewis and Clark, *The Journals of Lewis and Clark*, p. 1.

6. Adapted from Ambrose, *Undaunted Courage*, pp. 108, 479–480, and from the "Timelines" in "Lewis & Clark's Historic Trail" (see bibliography).

7. Quoted in Janin, *Claiming the American Wilderness*, p. 216, citing Brackenridge, *Journal*, p. 27.

8. After Calloway, *One Vast Winter Count*, p. 11.

9. Quoted in Janin, *Claiming the American Wilderness*, p. 219, quoting Bergon, *Journals*, p. 486.

10. The following accounts are drawn from Gilman, *Across the Divide*, pp. 118, 181, 282; Bergon, *The Journals of Lewis and Clark*, p. 218; and Allen, *Lewis and Clark and the Image of the American Northwest*, p. 389.

11. In 1863, John Bozeman would lead a group of 2,000 settlers along the Bozeman Trail, a new cutoff route connecting the Oregon Trail with the gold fields of southwestern Montana. Bozeman and his colleague John Jacobs would blaze this cutoff route in 1862.

12. Quoted in Bergon, *The Journals of Lewis and Clark*, p. 218.

Chapter 13

1. After James, *Three Years Among the Indians and Mexicans*, p. vi.

2. After James, *Three Years Among the Indians and Mexicans*, pp. 209–210.

3. Sources used in this section include the full text of Harris, *John Colter*; Golay and Bowman, *North American Exploration*, pp. 325–326; and DeVoto, *The Course of Empire*, pp. 491–493.

4. Some of the following information is drawn from David Lavender's Introduction to the Bison Book Edition of Burton Harris's book, *John Colter: His Years in the Rockies*, pp. xi–xvii.

5. After Preston, "Nature's Boundaries," p. 14.
6. Sources used in this section include Golay and Bowman, *North American Exploration*, pp. 334–335, and Allen, *A Continent Defined*, pp. 266–267.
7. Quoted in Golay and Bowman, *North American Exploration*. p. 335.
8. Good if short sources on Manuel Lisa include Golay and Bowman, *North American Exploration*, pp. 358–359; Utley, *A Life Wild and Perilous*, pp. 11–12;
9. Good sources for this section include Utley, *A Life Wild and Perilous*, pp. 25–30; and Allen, *A Continent Comprehended*, pp. 59, 60–62, 137.
10. By the end of 1813, however, Astoria was sold to the North West Company and was also captured by a British ship as a prize during the War of 1812.
11. After Utley, *A Life Wild and Perilous*, p. 29.
12. In 1847, 15 Oregon missionaries, including Dr. Whitman and his wife Narcissa, were murdered by Cayuse Indians who believed that Whitman had deliberately poisoned Indians during an outbreak of measles. In 1850, five Cayuse Indians were hanged in Oregon City for their role in this massacre.
13. This account follows Golay and Bowman, *North American Exploration*, pp. 384–385.
14. Quoted in Golay and Bowman, *North American Exploration*, p. 385.
15. Sources used in this section include Allen, *A Continent Comprehended*, pp. 64–74; Utley, *A Life Wild and Perilous*, pp. 70; Golay and Bowman, *North American Exploration*, pp. 359–360.
16. Sources used in this section include Gilbert, *The Trailblazers*, pp. 64–68, 214; Golay and Bowman, *North American Exploration*, p. 322; and Janin, *Fort Bridger, Wyoming*, pp. 14–18.
17. Quoted in Janin, *Fort Bridger, Wyoming*, p. 14.
18. Both accounts are quoted in Janin, *Fort Bridger, Wyoming*, p. 15.
19. Quoted in Janin, *Fort Bridger, Wyoming*, pp. 17–18.

Chapter 14

1. Sources used here include Allen, "Canadian Fur Trade and Exploration of Western North America," pp. 100–131; and a forthcoming book by Janin and Carlson on the history of the Lake Tahoe region of California and Nevada.
2. After "Peter Skene Ogden (1790–1854)," p. 1.
3. Quoted in "Journal of Peter Skene Ogden; Snake River Expedition, 1828–1829," p. 15.
4. Ogden is quoted in State of Nevada Division of Water Resources, "Humboldt River Chronology," pp. II-6. Some of the other comments about the Humboldt here are also drawn from this same source.
5. After Allen, "Canadian Fur Trade and Exploration of Western North America," p. 104.
6. See Hayes, *Historical Atlas of California*, p. 56, for the Arrowsmith map.
7. After Allen, "Canadian Fur Trade and Exploration of Western North America." p. 105.
8. After Allen, "Canadian Fur Trade and Exploration of Western North America," p. 111.
9. After Allen, "Canadian Fur Trade and Exploration of Western North America," pp. 113.
10. After Allen, "Canadian Fur Trade and Exploration of Western North America," p. 131.
11. Some of the comments in this section are drawn from Janin and Carlson, *Trails of Historic New Mexico*, pp. 75–76, and from Hafen and Hafen, *Old Spanish Trail*, pp. 155–170.
12. Quoted in Janin and Carlson, *Trails of Historic New Mexico*, p. 75.
13. After Janin and Carlson, *Trails of Historic New Mexico*, pp. 75–76, citing Hafen and Hafen, *Old Spanish Trail*, pp. 156–158.
14. Pattie, *The Personal Narrative of James O. Pattie*, pp. 145–147.

Chapter 15

1. Sources for this discussion include Janin, *Claiming the American Wilderness*, pp. 45–46, 220–221; Catlin, *North American Indians*; and Catlin, *The North American Indians*, vol. 1, full text.
2. Quoted by Janin, *Claiming the American Wilderness*, pp. 45–46.
3. Quoted by Janin, *Claiming the American Wilderness*, pp. 220–221.

4. Quoted by Preston, "Nature's Boundaries: The Greater Yellowstone Ecosystem," p. 13.
5. This section is drawn in part from Janin and Faircloth, "A Sense of Wonder," and from Karl Bodmer's book, *Bodmer's America*.
6. Quoted in Janin and Faircloth in "A Sense of Wonder," p. 6.
7. After Janin and Faircloth, "A Sense of Wonder," p. 6.
8. Sources used in this section include Golay and Bowman, *North American Exploration*, pp, 319–320; Gilbert, *The Trailblazers*, pp. 94–95; and Allen, *A Continent Comprehended*, pp. 170–171, 176, 180.
9. After Whaley, *Oregon and the Collapse of Illahee*, p. 6.
10. Some of the sources used in this section include Gilbert, *Westering Man: The Life of Joseph Walker*; Gilbert, *The Trailblazers*, p. 91; Janin and Carlson, *Historic Nevada Waters*; and Allen, *A Continent Comprehended*, pp. 171–173.
11. Muzzleloading rifles could fire either a relatively heavy lead ball or much lighter but numerous pellets of lead birdshot. A good shot using a ball could probably have been sure of hitting a sitting duck out to, say, 45 yards. Using birdshot he could have been sure of a kill at about 25 yards.
12. Quoted in Gilbert, *Westering Man*, p. 131.
13. The main sources used for this section are the full texts of both books.
14. Wislizenus, *A Journey to the Rocky Mountains in the Year 1839*, pp. 47–50.
15. Wislizenus, *A Journey to the Rocky Mountains in the Year 1839*, p. 88.
16. Wislizenus, *A Memoir of a Tour to Northern Mexico*, p, 12.
17. Wislizenus, *A Memoir of a Tour in Northern Mexico*, p. 38.
18. Wislizenus, *A Journey to the Rocky Mountains in the Year 1839*, pp. 159–160.

Chapter 16

1. Sources used in this section include Janin and Carlson, *The California Campaigns of the U.S.-Mexican War*, numerous entries pp. 73–200; Frémont, *Frémont's First Impressions*, whole text; Golay and Bowman, *North American Exploration*, pp. 336–339; and Harlow, *California Conquered*, numerous entries pp. 42–339.

2. Quoted in Heizer, "Aboriginal California and Great Basin Cartography," pp. 460–461.
3. Quoted in Heizer, "Aboriginal California and Great Basin Cartography," p. 460.
4. Quoted in Janin and Carlson, *The California Campaigns of the U.S.-Mexican War*, p. 78.
5. See *Frémont's First Impressions* in the Bibliography.
6. Frémont, *First Impressions*, p. 281.
7. After Ann F. Hyde in her Introduction to *Frémont's First Impressions*, p. xxiv.
8. This trail is now known as the Walker Trail.
9. After Fey, *Emigrant Shadows*, pp. 41–42.
10. This section draws on Janin and Carlson, *The Californios*, full text, and on Rosenus, *General Vallejo and the Advent of the Americans*, full text.
11. Quoted in Janin and Carlson, *The Californios*, p. 118.
12. Quoted in Janin and Carlson, *The Californios*, p. 118.
13. After Schwantes, *The Pacific Northwest*, p. 72.
14. Quoted in Ponko, 'Military Explorers of the American West,' p. 339.
15. After Ponko, "Military Explorers of the American West," pp. 341–342.
16. This section is drawn from Golay and Bowman, *North American Exploration*, pp. 299–300.
17. Some of the following comments follow Ponko, "Military Explorers of the American West," pp .353–365.
18. Frémont's rise and fall is fully documented in many sources, e.g., in Janin and Carlson, *The California Campaigns of the U.S-Mexican War*. In the interest of brevity, it will not be repeated here.

Chapter 17

1. The main source for this section is Parkman's *The Oregon Trail*, full text.
2. Parkman, *The Oregon Trail*, p. 15.
3. Parkman, *The Oregon Trail*, p. 136.
4. Parkman, *The Oregon Trail*, pp. 230–231.
5. Sources used here include Garrard, *Wah-to-yah and the Taos Trail*, full text.
6. Garrard, *Wah-to-yah and the Taos Trail*," pp. 161–162.

7. Sources used here include Janin and Carlson, *Trails of Historic New Mexico*, pp. 117-120; and Magoffin, *Down the Santa Fe Trail and into Mexico*, full text.
8. Quoted in *Down the Santa Fe Trail and into Mexico*, pp. xi-xii.
9. Quoted in *Down the Santa Fe Trail and into Mexico*, p. 259.
10. This section is drawn in part from Ponko, "Military Explorers of the American West," pp. 359-365.
11. Sources used here include Janin and Carlson, *Trails of Historic New Mexico*, pp.107-109; and Ruxton, *Mountain Men*, full text.
12. Quoted by Christine Preston, *The Royal Road*, no page number given.
13. Quoted in Janin and Carlson, *Trails of Historic New Mexico*, p. 108.
14. Brewerton, *Overland with Kit Carson.*, pp. 220-222.

Chapter 18

1. After Ponko, 'Military Explorers of the American West,' pp. 365-368.
2. After Ponko, "Military Explorers of the American West," p. 368.
3. This section reflects Ponko, "Military Explorers of the American West," pp. 368-373.
4. See Marcy, *The Prairie Traveler*, whole text.
5. At an 1847 peace council held in central Texas, Comanche chiefs granted a right-of-way through their lands in exchange for presents worth $3,000. This agreement, however, hastened their own downfall by persuading would-be settlers that the Comanches could easily be bought off and thus need not be feared any more. (After Capps, *The Great Chiefs*, pp. 110-111.)
6. Marcy, *The Prairie Traveler*, pp. 211-212.
7. Details on these partnerships can be found in Ponko, "Military Explorers of the American West," pp. 374-389.
8. After Ponko, "Military Explorers of the American West," p. 381.
9. Carson, *Autobiography*, pp. 42-44.
10. After Ponko, "Military Explorers of the American West," pp. 409, 411.
11. After Zeller, "Nature's Gullivers and Crusoes," pp. 232-235.
12. This discussion largely follows Ponko, "Military Explorers of the American West," pp. 389-395.

Chapter 19

1. Kane, *Wanderings of an Artist*, p. 45.
2. Kane, *Wanderings of an Artist*, pp. 52-53.
3. Kane, *Wanderings of an Artist*, p. 160.
4. Kane, *Wanderings of an Artist*, pp. 219-220.
5. This section follows Wilson, *White Indian Boy*, full text.
6. Wilson, *White Indian Boy*, pp. 23-24.
7. After Ponko, "Military Explorers of the American West," pp. 404-406.
8. After Brewer, *Up and Down California in 1860-1864*, back cover of book.
9. Brewer, *Up and Down California*, pp. 553-554.
10. See Twain, *Roughing It*, pp. 69-83.
11. Twain, *Roughing It*, p. 70.
12. A single action revolver is one that must be cocked manually, i.e., first by pulling the hammer back with a thumb, and then squeezing the trigger by using an index finger, for each shot. By using two hands, e.g., by what is known as "slip-shooting," or by "fanning," an expert can do this very rapidly at very close range. The famous Colt Single Action Army revolver, first manufactured in 1872, is still being made today with only minor changes.
13. Twain, *Roughing It*, pp. 70-71.
14. Twain, *Roughing It*, p. 82.

Chapter 20

1. Some of these comments on the Great Surveys are drawn from Bartlett, "Scientific Exploration of the American West," pp. 467-515.
2. Quoted in Golay and Bowman, *North American Exploration*, p. 351.
3. A disclaimer is needed here: Henry Janin was the paternal grandfather of Hunt Janin, one of the authors of the book you now have in your hands.
4. Sources used here include Allen, *A Continent Comprehended*, pp. 495-497; "The Great Diamond Hoax of 1872"; and Henry Janin, "A brief statement of my part in the unfortunate diamond affair [of 1872]."
5. After Farquhar's Preface in King's *Mountaineering in the Sierra Nevada*, p. 17.

6. Harpending, *The Great Diamond Hoax*, pp. 215–216.
7. Both these quotes are from Golay and Bowman, *North American Exploration*, pp. 378, 379
8. This section has been drawn in part from Golay and Bowman, *North American Exploration*, pp. 378–380.
9. Sources used in this section include Bartlett, "Scientific Exploration of the American West," pp. 509–513; and Golay and Bowman, *North American Exploration*, pp. 390–391.
10. Quoted in Golay and Bowman, *North American Exploration*, p. 391.
11. The last paragraphs of this section are variously drawn from Golay and Bowman, *North American Exploration*, p. 391; and Bartlett, "Scientific Exploration of the American West," pp. 512–513, 520.

Chapter 21

1. Some of these comments are drawn from Waiser, "The Government Explorer in Canada, 1870-1914" and from Zeller, "Nature's Gullivers and Crusoes," p. 243.
2. Dan De Quille, *The Big Bonanza*, title page.
3. Dan De Quille, *The Big Bonanza*, p. 45.
4. Dan De Quille, *The Big Bonanza*, p. 47.
5. This section is drawn from USGS, "Establishment of the U.S. Geological Survey," pp. 1–3.
6. U.S Geological Survey, "Establishment of the U.S. Geological Survey," p. 3.

Chapter 22

1. After Hine and Faragher, *The American West*, p. 10.
2. Golay and Bowman, *North American Exploration*, p. 1.
3. Some of the following comments are drawn from Goetzmann's chapter on "A 'Capacity for Wonder': The Meaning of Exploration" (see Bibliography).

4. After Allen, "Introduction to Volume 3," p. 6.

Appendix 1

1. Many of these comments are drawn from a lightly edited private communication of 18 March 2019 from Dr. Timothy P. Foran, Curator of British North America, in the Canadian Museum of History in Gatineau, Canada.
2. White, *Grand Portage as a Trading Post*, p. 6. This excerpt has been lightly edited to improve readability.

Appendix 2

1. This appendix is drawn in part from Janin, *Claiming the American Wilderness*, pp. 104–105, 236–240.
2. Quoted in Janin, *Claiming the American Wilderness*, pp. 236–237.
3. Quoted in Janin, *Claiming the American Wilderness*, p. 237.
4. At its headquarters on Hudson Bay, in about 1774 the Hudson's Bay Company developed a new kind of boat for the fur trade. Known as the York Boat, it could be paddled, poled, rowed, or sailed. It was not a canoe, however, so it will not be discussed in this book.
5. Quoted in Janin, *Claiming the American Wilderness*, p. 236.
6. Quoted in Janin, *Claiming the American Wilderness*, pp. 237–238.

Appendix 4

1. Sources used here on Yellowstone include Gourley, "Historical Timeline."
2. Doane, quoted in Holdsworth and Craighead, *A Portrait of Jackson Hole & The Tetons*, p. 5.

Bibliography

Allen, John Logan. "Introduction to Volume 3: A Continent Comprehended" in John Logan Allen, *North American Exploration*. Lincoln and London: University of Nebraska Press, 1997, pp. 1–7.

———. *Lewis and Clark and the Image of the American Northwest*. New York: Dover, 1975.

———. *North American Exploration: A Continent Divided*. Vol. 2. Lincoln and London: University of Nebraska Press, 1997.

———. *North American Exploration: A Continent Comprehended*. Vol. 3. Lincoln and London: University of Nebraska Press, 1997.

———, ed. "The Canadian Fur Trade and the Exploration of Western North America, 1797–1851" in John Logan Allen, *North American Exploration: A Continent Comprehended*. Vol. 3. Lincoln and London: University of Nebraska Press, 1997, pp. 75–131.

Allen, Michael. *Western Rivermen, 1763–1861: Ohio and Mississippi Boatmen and the Myth of the Alligator Horse*. Baton Rouge and London: Louisiana State University Press, 1990.

Ambrose, Stephen E. *Undoubted Courage: Meriwether Lewis, Thomas Jefferson, and the Opening of the American West*. New York: Touchstone, 1996.

American Rivers. "Missouri: America's Longest River." https:www.americanrivers.org/river/Missouri-river/. Accessed 29 April 2019.

Armstrong, Virginia Irving, ed. *I Have Spoken: American History Through the Voices of Indians*. New York: Swallow Press, 1971.

Bartlett, Richard A. "Scientific Exploration of the American West" in John Logan Allen, *A Continent Comprehended*, Lincoln and London: University Press, 1997, pp. 461–520.

Bergon, Frank, ed. *The Journals of Lewis and Clark*. New York: Penguin, 2003.

Blakeslee, Donald J. "Mallet Brothers" in *Encyclopedia of the Great Plains*. Lincoln: University of Nebraska Press, 2011.

Blumenthal, Ricard W., ed. *The Early Exploration of Inland Washington Waters: Journals and Logs from Six Expeditions, 1786–1792*. Jefferson, NC: McFarland, 2004.

Bodmer, Karl. *Bodmer's America: Karl Bodmer's Illustrations to Prince Maximilian of Wied-Neuwied's Travels in the Interior of North America 1832–1834*. London: Joselyn Art Museum and Editions Alecto, 1991.

———. *Bodmer's America*. London and Omaha: Joslyn Art Museum and Editions Alecto, 1991.

Brewer, William H. *Up and Down California in 1860–1864. The Journal of William H. Brewer* (4th ed.) (Francis P. Farquhar and William Bright, eds.). Berkeley, Los Angeles and London: University of California Press, 2003.

Brewerton, George Douglas. *Overland with Kit Carson: A Narrative of the Old Spanish Trail in '48* (Marc Simmons, ed.). Lincoln and London: University of Nebraska Press, 1993.

Brown, Dee. *Bury My Heart at Wounded Knee: An Indian History of the American West*. New York: Henry Holt, 1970.

Buck, Solon J. "The Story of the Grand Portage." Duluth: Minnesota Historical Society, 1922.

Cabeza de Vaca, Alvar Núñez. *Chronicle of the Narváez Expedition* (Fanny Bandelier, Harold Augenbraum, and Ilan Stavans, eds.). New York: Penguin, 2002.

Cabrillo National Monument Foundation

(James D. Nauman, ed.). *An Account of the Voyage of Juan Rodríguez Cabrillo.* San Diego: Cabrillo National Monument Foundation, 1999.

Calloway, Colin G. *One Vast Winter Count: The Native American West Before Lewis and Clark.* Lincoln and London: University of Nebraska Press, 2003.

Canfield, Gae Whitney. *Sarah Winnemucca of the Northern Paiutes.* Norman: University of Oklahoma Press, 1983.

Capps, Benjamin. *The Great Chiefs.* Alexandria: Time-Life Books, 1975.

———. *The Indians.* New York: Time-Life Books 1973.

Carson, Kit. *Kit Carson's Autobiography* (Milo Milton Quaife, ed.). Lincoln: University of Nebraska Press, 193

Castañeda of Nájera, Pedro de. *Narrative of the Coronado Expedition* (John Miller Morris, ed.). Chicago: Lakeside Classica, Donnelley, 2002.

Catlin, George. *North American Indians* (Peter Matthiessen, ed.). New York: Penguin, 2004.

———. *The North American Indians.* Vol. 1. Edinburgh: John Grant, 1903.

Chaput, Donald. "Leguardeur de Saint-Pierre, Jacques," in *Dictionary of Canadian Biography*, vol. 3, University of Toronto/Université Laval, 2003, accessed May 19, 2018.

Child, Brenda J. "Women of the Great Lakes and Mississippi" in *Holding Our World Together: Ojibwe Women and the Survival of Community.* New York: Penguin, 2013.

Chipman, Donald E., and Patricia L. Lemée. "St. Denis, Louis Juchereau de" in "The Handbook of Texas Online." Texas State Historical Association." https://tshaonline.org/handbook/online/articles/fst01. Accessed May 13, 2018.

Conrad, Margaret. *A Concise History of Canada.* New York: Cambridge University Press, 2012.

Cook, James. *The Journals* (Philip Edwards, ed.). London: Penguin, 1999.

De Quille, Dan (Pen name of William Wright). *History of the Big Bonanza* (Introduction by Mark Twain.) Los Angeles: Peruse Press, 2013.

DeVoto, Barnard. *The Course of Empire.* Boston and New York: Houghton Mifflin, 1998.

Feigenbaum, Gail. *Jefferson's America & Napoleon's France: An Exhibition for the Louisiana Purchase Bicentennial* (Victoria Cook, ed.). Seattle and London: New Orleans Museum of Art In Association with University of Washington Press, 2003.

Fey, Marshall, R. Joe King, and Jack Lepisto. *Emigrant Shadows: A History and Guide to the California Trail.* Virginia City: Western Trails Research Association, 2002.

Frémont, John C. *Frémont's First Impressions: The Original Report of His Exploring Expeditions.* Introduction to the Bison Books edition by Anne F. Hyde. Lincoln and London: University of Nebraska Press, 2012.

"The French: Lords of Rivers and Lakes" in Hunt Janin, *Claiming the American Wilderness: International Rivalry in the Trans-Mississippi West, 1528–1803.* Jefferson, NC: McFarland, 2006, pp. 96–125.

Garrard, Lewis H. *Wah-to-yah and the Taos Trail* (A.B. Guthrie, Jr., ed.). Norman: University of Oklahoma Press, 1955.

Gibson, James R. "The Exploration of the Pacific Coast" in John Logan Allen, *North American Exploration: A Continent Divided.* Lincoln and London: University of Nebraska Press, 1997, pp. 328–396.

———. *Otter Skins, Boston Ships, and China Goods: The Maritime Fur Trade of the Northwest Coast, 1785–1841.* Seattle, Montreal, Kingston, and London: University of Washington Press and McGill-Queen's University Press, 1999.

Gilbert, Bil [sic]. *The Trailblazers.* Alexandria: Time/Life, 1973.

———. *Westering Man: The Life of Joseph Walker.* Norman: University of Oklahoma Press, 1985.

Gilman, Carolyn. *Lewis and Clark: Across the Divide.* Washington and London: Smithsonian Books in association with the Missouri Historical Society, 2003.

Goetzmann, William H. "A 'Capacity for Wonder': The Meanings of Exploration" in John Logan Allen, *North American Exploration: A Continent Comprehended*, Volume 3. Lincoln and London: University of Nebraska Press, 1997, pp. 521–545.

Golay, Michael, and John S. Bowman, *North American Exploration.* Hoboken: Wiley, 2003.

Gough, Barry. *First Across the Continent: Sir Alexander Mackenzie.* Norman and London: University of Oklahoma Press, 1997.

———. "Peter Pond" in *Dictionary of Cana-*

dian Biography. University of Toronto/ Université Laval, 1983.
Gourley, Bruce. "Yellowstone History: Historical Timeline." https://yellowstone.net/history/timeline, 2019. The references cited in this timeline, which covers the years 1795 to 2006, are ultimately sourced to Aubrey L. Haines, *The Yellowstone Story*, Vols. 1 and 2, published in 1977. Accessed 18/04/2019.
"The Great Diamond Hoax of 1872." (University of Minnesota handout for a geology course.) http://www.geo.umn.edu/courses/1081/handouts1081_SS2006_Diamond_Hoax_Hndt.htm. Accessed May 6, 2007.
Gregg, Josiah. *Commerce of the Prairies: Life on the Great Plains in the 1830s and 1840s*. Santa Barbara: Narrative Press, 2001.
Hafen, Leroy R., and Ann W. Hafen. *Old Spanish Trail: Santa Fe to Los Angeles*. Lincoln and London: University of Nebraska Press, 1993.
Hague, Harlan. *Road to California: The Search for a Southern Overland Route, 1540–1848*. San Jose, New York, Lincoln, Shanghai: Authors Choice Press, 2001.
Hämäläinen, Pekka. *The Comanche Empire*. New Haven and London: Yale University Press, 2008.
Harlow, Neal. *California Conquered: The Annexation of a Mexican Province, 1846–1850*. Berkeley, Los Angeles, and London: University of California Press, 1982.
Harpenden, Asbury. *The Great Diamond Hoax and Other Stirring Incidents in the Life of Asbury Harpenden* (James H. Wilkins, ed.). San Francisco: James H. Barry Co., 1913.
Harris, Burton. *John Colter: His Years in the Rockies* (Introduction by David Lavender.) Lincoln and London: University of Nebraska Press, 1993.
Hayes, Derek. *Historical Atlas of California with Original Maps*. Berkeley, Los Angeles, and London: University of California Press, 2007.
Heidenreich, Conrad. "Early French Exploration in the North American Interior" in Allen, John Logan, *A Continent Defined*. Lincoln and London, 1997, pp. 76–77.
Heizer, Robert F. "Aboriginal California and Great Basin Cartography" in R.F. Heizer and M.A. Whipple. *The California Indians: A Source Book*. Berkeley and Los Angeles (2nd ed.), 1971, pp. 459–471.
____, and M.A. Whipple. *The California Indians: A Source Book* (2nd ed.) Berkeley, Los Angeles and London: University of California Press, 1971.
Hine, Robert V., and John Mack Faragher. *The American West: A New Interpretive History*. New Haven: Yale University Press, 2000.
Hoig, Stan. *Beyond the Frontier: Exploring the Indian Country*. Norman: University of Oklahoma Press, 1998.
Holdsworth, Henry H., and Charlie Craighead. *A Portrait of Jackson Hole & The Tetons*. Helena: Farcountry Press, 2007.
Holling, Clancy. *Tree in the Trail*. Boston: Houghton Mifflin, 1942.
Hopkins, Sarah Winnemucca. *Life Among the Piutes*. Reno and Las Vegas: University of Nevada Press, 1994.
Howard, Thomas Frederick. *Sierra Crossing: First Roads to California*. Berkeley, Los Angeles and London: University of California Press, 1998.
Hunt, David C. "Bodmer's America: Karl Bodmer's Illustrations to Prince Maximilian of Wied-Neuwied's Travels to the Interior of North America, 1832–1834" in *Bodmer's America*, Joslyn Art Museum and Editions Alecto Limited, London and Omaha, 1991.
Inman, Colonel Henry. *The Old Santa Fe Trail: The Story of a Great Highway*. London: Macmillan, 1897.
James, Thomas. *Three Years Among the Indians and Mexicans* (Walter B. Douglas, ed.). St. Louis: St. Louis Missouri Historical Society, 1916.
James-abra, Erin. "Exploration." The Canada Encyclopedia, Updated on May 21, 2015. https://www.thecanadianencyclopedia.ca/index.php/en/article/exploration. Accessed 15 October 2018.
Janin, Henry. "A brief statement on my part in the unfortunate diamond affair [of 1872]. Printed for Private Distribution outside of San Francisco." Dated January 5th 1873; original text held by the Huntington Library in San Marino, California.
Janin, Hunt. *Claiming the American Wilderness: International Rivalry in the Trans–Mississippi West, 1528–1803*. Jefferson, NC: McFarland, 2006.
____. *Fort Bridger: Trading Post for Indians, Mountain Men and Westward Migrants*. Jefferson, NC: McFarland, 2001.
____. "The French: Lords of Rivers and Lakes" in Hunt Janin, *Claiming the Amer-*

ican Wilderness: International Rivalry in the Trans–Mississippi West, 1528–1803.* Jefferson, NC: McFarland, 2006, pp. 96–126.
_____, and Nicki Faircloth. "A Sense of Wonder: The Indian Engravings of Karl Bodmer" in *Persimmon Hill*, A Publication of the National Cowboy Hall of Fame. Volume 21, Number 4, Winter 1993, pp. 6–13.
_____, and Ursula Carlson. *The California Campaigns of the U.S.-Mexican War, 1846–1848.* Jefferson, NC : McFarland, 2015
_____. and _____. *The Californios: A History, 1769–1890.* Jefferson, NC: McFarland. 2017.
_____. and _____. *Historic Nevada Waters: Four Rivers, Three Lakes, Past and Present.* Jefferson, NC: McFarland. 2019.
_____. and _____. *Trails of Historic New Mexico: Routes Used by Indian, Spanish and American Travelers through 1886.* Jefferson, NC: McFarland, 2010.
John, Elizabeth A.H. *Storms Brewed in Other Men's Worlds: The Confrontation of the Indians, Spanish, and French in the Southwest, 1510–1795* (2nd ed.). Norman and London: University of Oklahoma Press, 1996.
Jones, Oakah L., Jr. "Spanish Penetrations to the North of New Spain" in John Logan Allen, *North American Exploration.* Vol. 2, *A Continent Divided.* Lincoln and London: University of Nebraska Press, 1997, pp. 41–42.
The Journals of Lewis and Clark (Frank Bergon, ed.) New York: Penguin, 2003.
Kane, Paul. *Wanderings of an Artist Among the Indians of North America.* Mineola: Dover Publications, 1996.
Kessell, John L. *Kiva, Cross, and Crown: The Pecos Indians and New Mexico 1549–1840.* Albuquerque: University of New Mexico Press, 1990.
_____. *Spain in the Southwest.* Norman: University of Oklahoma Press, 2002.
King, Clarence. *Mountaineering in the Sierra Nevada* (Francis P. Farquhar, ed.). Lincoln and London: University of Nebraska Press, 1997.
Kroeber, A.L. *Handbook of the Indians of California.* New York: Dover, 1923.
Kukla, Jon. *A Wilderness So Immense: The Louisiana Purchase and the Destiny of America.* New York: Knopf, 2003.
Larson, T.A. *History of Wyoming.* Second edition, revised. Lincoln and London: University of Nebraska Press, 1990.

Lewis and Clark's Historic Trail. "Timelines." https://lewisclark.net. Accessed 6 June 2
Loomis, Noel M. and Abraham P. Nasatir. *Pedro Vial and the Roads to Santa Fe.* Norman. University of Oklahoma Press, 1967.
Magoffin, Susan Shelby. *Down the Santa Fe Trail and into Mexico: The Diary of Susan Shelby Magoffin, 1846–1847* (Stella M. Drum, ed.). Lincoln and London: University of Nebraska Press, 1982.
Marcy, Randolph B. *The Prairie Traveler: A Handbook for Overland Expeditions, with Maps, Illustrations, and Itineraries of the Principal Routes Between the Mississippi and the Pacific.* Old Saybrook: Applewood Books, Globe Pequot Press, book originally published in 1859.
Marsh, James H., and Daniel Penneton. "Samuel Hearne" in *The Canadian Encyclopedia*, December 17, 2015. http://thecanadianeycyclopedia.ca/en/article/samuel-hearne. Accessed 21 May 2018.
McNeese, Tim. *The St. Lawrence River.* Philadelphia: Chelsea House, 2005.
Moore, Bob. Pike National Trail Association. "Pike—The Real Pathfinder." https://www.zebulonpike.org/pike-hardluck-explorer.htm. Accessed 10 June 2018.
National Park Service. "Railroad Surveys." https://web.archive.org.web/20090118171121/http://www.nps.gov:80/archive/jeff/lew... Accessed 25 December 2018.
Nelson, George. *My First Years in the Fur Trade: The Journals of George Nelson, 1802–1804.* St. Paul: Minnesota Historical Society, 2002.
Newell, Olive. *Tail of the Elephant: The Emigrant Experience on the Truckee Route of the California Trail, 1844–1852.* Nevada City: Nevada County Historical Society, 1997.
Nichols, Roger L. *Indians in the United States and Canada: A Comparative History.* 2nd ed. Lincoln and London: University of Nebraska Press, 2018.
Parkman, Francis. *The Oregon Trail* (James K. Smith, ed.) New York: Airmont, 1964.
_____. *Pioneers of France in the New World.* Lincoln and London: University of Nebraska Press, 1996.
Pattie, James O. *The Personal Narrative of James O. Pattie* (Timothy Flint and Milo Milton Quaife, eds.). Santa Barbara: The Narrative Press, 2001.

Ponko, Vincent, Jr. "The Military Explorers of the American West, 1838–1860" in John Logan Allen, *A Continent Comprehended*. Lincoln and London: University of Nebraska Press, Vol. 3, 1997, pp. 332–411.

Preston, Charles R. "Nature's Boundaries: The Greater Yellowstone Ecosystem" in *Spectacular Yellowstone and Grand Teton National Parks* (Letitia O'Conner, Dana Levy, and Paul Vucetich, eds.). New York: Universe Publishing, 2008, pp. 12–19.

Preston, Christine; Douglas Preston; and José Antonio Esquibel. *The Royal Road: El Camino Real from Mexico City to Santa Fe*. Albuquerque: University of New Mexico Press, 1998.

Rosenus, Alan. *General Vallejo and the Advent of the Americans*. Berkeley: Heyday Press, 1999.

Russell, Carl P. "Trade Muskets and Rifles Supplied to the Indians" in *Guns on the Early Frontiers: A History of Firearms from Colonial Times Through the Years of the Western Fur Trade*. Lincoln and London: University of Nebraska Press, 1957, pp. 103–141.

Ruxton, George Frederick. *Mountain Men: George Frederick Ruxton's Firsthand Accounts of Fur Trappers and Indians in the Rockies* (Glen Rounds, ed.). New York: Holiday House, 1966.

Saunt, Claudio. "A Forest Transformed: The Hudson's Bay Company and Cumberland House" in Claudio Saunt, *West of the Revolution*. New York and London: Norton, 2014, pp. 124–147.

Schwantes, Carlos Arnaldo. *The Pacific Northwest: An Interpretive History*. 2nd ed. Lincoln and London: University of Nebraska Press, 1996.

Simmons, Marc. *The Last Conquistador: Juan de Oñate and the Settling of the Far Southwest*. Norman: University of Oklahoma Press, 1991.

Stewart, Omer C. *Forgotten Fires: Native Americans and the Transient Wilderness* (Henry T. Lewis and M. Kat Anderson, eds.). Norman: University of Oklahoma Press, 2002.

Tanner, Ogden. *The Canadians*. Alexandria: Time-Life Books, 1977.

Taylor, Alan. *America's Colonies: The Settling of North America*. New York: Penguin, 2001.

———. "French America, 1650–1750" in Alan Taylor, *America's Colonies: The Settling of North America*. New York: Penguin, 2001, pp. 363–395.

Twain, Mark. *Roughing It* (Leonard Kriegel, ed.). New York and Scarborough, Ontario: New American Library, 1962.

United States Geological Survey. "Establishment of the U.S. Geological Survey. https://pubs.usgs.gov/circ/c1050/establish.htm. Accessed 29 December 2012.

U.S. Statutes at Large. *The Lacey Act of 1894*. Vol. 28, p. 73. "Chap. 72—An Act to protect the birds and animals in Yellowstone Park, and to punish crimes in said park, and for other purposes." Approved, May 7, 1894.

Utley, Robert M. *A Life Wild and Perilous: Mountain Men and the Paths to the Pacific*. New York: Henry Holt, 1997.

Waiser, William A. "The Government Explorer in Canada, 1870–1914" in John Logan Allen, *North American Exploration: A Continent Comprehended*. Lincoln and London: University of Nebraska Press, 1997, pp. 412–460.

Warner, Ted J. *The Domínguez-Escalante Journal: Their Expedition Through Colorado, Utah, Arizona, and New Mexico in 1776* (Ted J. Warner, ed.; Fray Angelico Chavez, trans.). Salt Lake City: University of Utah Press, 1995.

Weber, David J. *The Spanish Frontier in North America*. New Haven and London: Yale University Press, 1992.

———. *The Taos Trappers: The Fur Trade in the Far Southwest, 1540–1846*. Norman and London: University of Oklahoma Press, 1982.

Whaley, Gray H. *Oregon and the Collapse of Illahee*. Chapel Hill: University of North Carolina Press, 2010.

White, Bruce M. *Grand Portage as a Trading Post: Patterns of Trade at "The Great Carrying Place."* St. Paul: Grand Portage National Monument, National Park Service, Grand Marais, Minnesota, Turnstone Historical Research, 2005.

Whitebrook, Robert Ballard. *Coastal Exploration of Washington* (Henry R. Wagner, ed.). Palo Alto: Pacific Books, 1959.

Wilson, Elijah Nicholas. *White Indian Boy: My Life Among the Shoshones* (Howard R. Driggs, ed.). 4th edition. Colorado Springs: Piccadilly Books, 2009.

Wislizenus, F.A. *A Journey to the Rocky Mountains in the Year 1839* (Frederick

A. Wislizenus, ed.). New York: Cosimo Classics, 2005.

_____. *Memoir of a Tour to Northern Mexico, Connected with Col. Doniphan's Expedition, in 1846 and 1847* (Jack D. Rittenhouse, ed.) Albuquerque: Calvin Horn, 1969.

Wood, W. Raymond. *Prologue to Lewis & Clark: The Mackay and Evans Expedition.* Norman: University of Oklahoma Press, 2003.

Zanjani, Sally. *Sarah Winnemucca.* Lincoln and London: University of Nebraska Press, 2001.

Zeller, Susanne. "Nature's Gullivers and Crusoes: The Scientific Exploration of British North America, 1800–1870" in John Logan Allen, *North American Exploration: A Continent Comprehended.* Lincoln and London: University of Nebraska Press, 1997, pp. 190–243.

Index

Albert, Col. John J. 112, 160
Albert, Lt. James W. 113
Anza, Capt. Juan Bautista de 41, 42, 43, 44, 45, 52
Armijo, Antonio 97, 98
Astor, John Jacob 79, 89, 90, 91

Bingham, George Caleb 13
Black, Samuel 96, 97
Bodmer, Karl 101
Bonilla, Capt. Francisco Leyva de 36
Bonneville, Benjamin Louis Eulalie de 102
Bradbury, John 187
Brewer, William H. 129
Brewerton George Douglas 118, 119
Bridger, Jim 21, 92, 93
Brûlé, Étienne 49

Cabeza de Vaca, Álvar Núñez 3, 28, 29
Cabrillo, Juan Rodríguez 22
Carondelet, Baron 18, 19
Carson, Kit 21, 95, 96, 102, 108, 118, 123
Cartier, Jacques 12, 19
Castañeda, Pedro de 30, 31, 32
Castaño de Sosa, Gaspar 36
Catlin, George 100, 101
Cavelier, René-Robert (Sieur de La Salle; better known as "La Salle") 64
Champlain, Samuel de 12, 13, 48, 49
Chamuscado, Capt. Francisco Sánchez 34
Charbonneau, Toussaint 85
Charlevoix, François Xavier de 62, 63
Chatillon, Henry 114, 115
Chouart, Médard (Sieur de Groseilliers) 7, 39
Clark, 2nd Lt. William 8, 16, 21, 28, 75, 77, 80, 82, 83, 84, 85, 86, 87, 89, 143
Cochise (Apache chieftain) 17
Colter, John 21, 86, 87
Columbus, Christopher 3, 4, 143
Comanches 41, 42, 43, 44, 65, 66, 74, 75
Coronado, Francisco Vásquez de 6, 30, 31, 32, 33
coureur de bois (French fur trader-explorer) 49, 62, 159

Crespi, Father Juan 25, 70, 71
Cumberland House 69

DeVoto, Bernard 21, 92, 108
Domínguez, Father Francisco Atanasio 41, 45, 46, 47
Drake, Sir Francis 22, 23
Du Tisne, Claude Charles 58, 59

El Turco ("The Turk") 31, 32
Emory, William Hemsley 117
Escalante, Fray Silvestre Vélez de 41, 45, 46, 47
Espejo, Antonio de 35
Estevánico (a Moor guide) 28, 29, 30
Evans, Thomas 77
expeditions 5, 7, 8, 22, 25, 33, 34, 36, 39, 41, 51, 52, 56, 57, 64, 68, 69, 76, 89, 90, 91, 93, 94, 96, 108, 111, 112, 122, 124, 128, 131
explorers 1, 2, 5, 6, 7, 8, 10, 11, 12, 14, 15, 17, 19, 20, 21, 22, 24, 25, 27, 28, 29, 35, 38, 39, 41, 44, 45, 46, 48, 49, 51, 52, 54, 56, 57, 59, 61, 62, 63, 66, 68, 69, 70, 71, 72, 74, 75, 78, 84, 85, 88, 91, 92, 94, 95, 96, 101, 102, 107, 109, 110, 111, 112, 117, 120, 132, 135, 136, 137, 142, 143

Fiddler, Peter 11
Folsom-Cook-Peterson expedition 88, 164
Fraser, Simon 88, 89
Frémont, John Charles 8, 107, 108, 109, 112, 113, 120, 121, 135
frontier (frontiers) 1, 2, 3, 4, 5, 6, , 8, 9, 10, 11, 13, 15, 17, 18, 19, 21, 22, 25, 28, 29, 41, 43, 44, 48, 51, 59, 61, 62, 63, 66, 68, 71, 77, 82, 87, 89, 90, 91, 92, 94, 95, 96, 98, 102, 104, 105, 106, 108, 109, 114, 115, 116, 119, 121, 122, 123, 125, 126, 129, 131, 132, 136, 141, 142
"fur desert" 94
fur trade 89, 90, 93, 97, 137

Garcés, Fray Thomás 71, 72
Garrard, Louis H. 115
geographical regions of North America 5
Gila River Trail 43
Gilman, Carolyn 11

183

Grand Portage 72, 80, 81
"grease trail" (overland trade route) 74, 76
Great Diamond Hoax 132, 134
Great Surveys (King, Powell, Hayden, and Wheeler Surveys) 131-137, 143
Gregg, Josiah 44
Groselliers, Médard Chouart 7, 39, 50

Hanna, James 75
Harpe, Jean-Baptiste de la 38, 57, 65
Harpending, Ashbury 134
Hayden, Ferdinand Vandeveer Hayden 131, 132, 136, 139, 140
Hearne, Samuel 6, 69, 70
Henday, Anthony 68
Hudson Bay 9, 39, 40, 51, 53, 54, 55, 56, 57, 63, 69, 73, 78, 81, 137
Hudson's Bay Company 9, 11, 12, 39, 40, 51, 55, 56, 63, 68, 69, 78, 94, 96, 97, 102, 111, 126
Hunt, Wilson Price 90

Iberville, Pierre Le Moyne 56, 57, 59
Indians 3, 5, 7, 8, 9, 10, 11, 12, 13, 14, 15, 17, 18, 19, 21, 22, 23, 25, 26, 28, 29, 30, 31, 32, 34, 35, 36, 37, 38, 39, 40, 41, 42, 43, 44, 45, 46, 48, 49, 50, 51, 52, 53, 54, 55, 56, 57, 58, 59, 61, 62, 63, 64, 65, 66, 68, 69, 70, 71, 72, 75, 76, 77, 78, 81, 82, 83, 84, 85, 86, 87, 89, 91, 95, 98, 100, 101, 102, 103, 104, 105, 106, 107, 110, 111, 113, 114, 115, 116, 121, 122, 126, 127, 128, 131, 136, 137, 138, 142
Inter Caetera (papal document) 1, 6

James, Thomas 86
Janin, Henry 133, 134
Jefferson, Pres. Thomas 77, 82, 83
Johnson, George 111
Jolliet, Louis 52, 53, 54

Kane, Paul 126
Kearny, Col. Stephen W. 43, 117
Kelsey, Henry 55, 56
King, Clarence 132, 133
Kino, Eusebio 51

Legardeur, Jacques (de Saint-Pierre) 66, 67
Le Moyne, Jean-Baptiste (Sieur de Bienville; known to history as "Bienville") 57, 58, 65
Lewis, Capt. Meriwether 8, 16, 21, 28, 77, 80, 82, 83, 84, 85, 86, 87, 89, 143
Lewis and Clark expedition 8, 16, 21, 28, 80, 82, 83, 85, 87, 89
Lisa, Manuel 87, 89
Long, Maj. Stephen H. 91, 92

Mackay, James 77, 78
Mackenzie, Alexander 73, 74, 75, 76, 77, 80
Magofflin, Susan 116, 117
Mallet brothers (Pierre Antoine and Paul) 64, 65

Manifest Destiny (doctrine of) 21, 109, 110
Marcos de Niza 29, 30, 31
Marcy, Capt. Randolph B. 91, 121
maritime explorations 22, 25-27
Marquette, Jacques 52
Maximilian of Wied-Neuweid (German Prince) 101
Mendoza, Antonio de 29, 30, 31, 32
mercantilism 20

Nelson, George 80, 81, 82
New France (French colonial holdings in North America) 7, 10, 12, 13, 14, 19, 20, 48, 50, 55, 56, 58, 62, 63, 66
New Spain (Spanish q holdings in North America) 6, 7, 9, 18, 20, 29, 32, 35, 36, 45, 54, 60
Nicolet (or Nicollet), Jean 49, 112
Nordhoff, Walter 42
North American Boundary Commission Survey 137
Noyon, Jacques de 55

Ogden, Peter Skene 94, 95, 96
Old Spanish Trail 47, 71, 97, 98
Oñate, Juan de 7, 34, 35, 36, 37, 38, 39

Palliser-Gladman expeditions 124
Parkman, Francis 114, 115
Passage (mythical trans–Mississippi waterway) 2, 4, 8, 14, 18, 19, 20, 22, 26, 27, 40, 41, 50, 51, 55, 62, 63, 64, 66, 67, 69, 73, 77, 84, 97
Pattie, James O. 98, 99
Perrot, Nicholas 10
Pond, Peter 72, 73
Portolá, Gaspar de 6, 24, 25, 70, 71
Powell, John Wesley 131, 135, 136, 139, 140
Pueblo Indians 18, 29, 34, 35, 36, 41, 122

Radisson, Pierre-Esprit 7, 39, 50, 51
railroad surveys 125, 160-162; *see also* Appendix 2
Rodríguez, Fray Agustín 34
Rupert's Land 39, 68, 69, 137
Russian American Fur Company 20
Ruxton, George Frederick 117, 118

Sacagawea (Shoshone wife of French fur trapper Toussaint Charbonneau) 16, 85
St. Denis, Louis Juchereau 59, 60
San Francisco 2, 20, 22, 23, 24, 25, 42, 70, 94, 96, 111, 121, 153
Serra, Fray Junípero 34, 70
Simpson, Lt. James H. 121, 122
Smith, Jedediah 21, 91
Stansbury, Capt. Howard 121, 122
Stuart, Robert 90, 91

Talon, Jean 14
Tanaghrisson (Indian leader) 15

Index

Thompson, David 78, 79
Treaty of Paris 19
Truckee (Paiute Indian leader) 109
El Turco ("The Turk") 31, 32
Twain, Mark 129, 130, 138

U.S. Geological Survey 1, 3, 8, 131, 133, 135, 139, 140, 143

Vallejo, Gen. Mariano Guadalupe 109, 110
Varrenes, Pierre Gautier de (Sieur de La Vérendrye, known as La Vérendrye) 63
Veniard, Étienne (Sieur de Bourgmont; known as Bourgmont) 61
Vial, Pedro 41, 44, 75
Vizcaíno, Sebastián 23, 24, 70

Voyageur(s) (French fur trader-explorer) 16, 50, 64, 76, 157

Walker, Joseph 102, 103, 104
Warren, Lt. Gouveurneur Kemble 123
Western Canada 9, 20, 39, 55, 56, 63, 79
Wheeler, George Montague 131, 135, 139, 140
Wilkes Expedition 110, 111
Wilson, Nick 127, 128
Wislizenus, Dr. F.A. 104, 105, 106
Wright, William (used the penname "Dan de Quille") 138
writers 1, 2, 5, 51, 69, 72, 98, 100, 101, 115, 116, 117, 118, 121, 126, 129, 143

York Factory 55, 56, 68, 81